BAD NEWS AT BLACK ROCK: THE SELL-OUT OF CBS NEWS

By Peter McCabe
Apple to the Core

BAD NEWS
AT
BLACK ROCK

THE SELL-OUT
OF CBS NEWS

Peter McCabe

ARBOR HOUSE   NEW YORK

10 9 8 7 6 5 4 3 2 1

Library of Congress Cataloging-in-Publication Data

McCabe, Peter, 1945-
Bad news at Black Rock.

1. Television broadcasting of news—United States.
2. CBS News.   3. CBS morning news (Television program)
I. Title.
PN4888.T4M28   1987   070.1′9   86-28896
ISBN: 0-87795-907-2

To my wife, Kathy,
and my son, Jason.

CONTENTS

PREFACE

Shortly after I went to work at CBS News in 1985, I rented the movie *Network*, which I had not seen since it was released in 1976. Paddy Chayefsky, the screenwriter, deserves full marks for prescience. A decade after he wrote it, the gist of his movie was enacted in real life.

The philosophies of the management of his fictional UBS and the management of CBS were remarkably similar. In the movie, Frank Hackett, the executive who takes over at UBS, declares: "I know that historically news divisions are expected to lose money, but to our minds this philosophy is a wanton fiscal affront, to be resolutely resisted." A decade later, money-losing news programs were a wanton fiscal affront to the management of CBS.

At CBS, I worked at the "Morning News," the news division's biggest money-loser. It was also a good news show, or at least it was until the decision was made to change it, and integrity was sacrificed for the sake of ratings. In 1985 a rating point was worth 850,000 households, and in May of that year the ratings of the "CBS Morning News" stood at 3.3, with a viewer share of 16. This meant that roughly 2.8 million households were tuned to CBS each morning, 16 percent of the nation's television sets. The ratings of the rival shows, ABC's "Good Morning America" and NBC's "Today," were much higher. While these shows were making money, the "CBS Morning News" was losing roughly $10 million a year. To boost its ratings to 4.0, the "Morning

News" needed another 600,000 viewers. With a 4.0 rating, the "Morning News" could raise its advertising rates from the $7,500 it was then charging for a thirty-second spot, and if the program could charge more, it might begin earning money for the network rather than losing it. Higher ratings would also help the profits of the network affiliates that carried the show and received time on the program to sell their own spots. And of course, if the "Morning News" were a higher-rated program, it would provide a stronger lead-in to the entire CBS schedule.

The question was, how to get those ratings. The answer, clearly, was *not* the way CBS went about it.

ACKNOWLEDGMENTS

I wish to thank the many people who agreed to be interviewed for this book. Given the political climate at CBS News and CBS Inc. during the past several years, it is understandable why many of those still employed there requested that their conversations with me be off the record or not for attribution. Others, with less to lose, did not mind talking on the record, and for the most part are quoted in this book. In both cases, I thank them for their time and patience, and for sharing their insights and information.

I especially wish to thank my friend David Black, who urged me to keep a diary as soon as I began to regale him with stories about life at the "CBS Morning News." And I wish to thank my friend Pete Bonventre for his many insights and for keeping me amused during the final months. I am grateful to my agent Al Lowman, to my editor, Allan Mayer, and to my publisher, Eden Collinsworth, for their receptivity to this project and their encouragement, and to my wife, Kathy, who had to live through the writing of it.

THE PLAYERS

CBS MORNING NEWS

THE ANCHORS

Bill Kurtis/Diane Sawyer	January 1982–December 1984
Bill Kurtis/Phyllis George	January 1985–June 1985
Phyllis George/Forrest Sawyer	July 1985–August 1985
Forrest Sawyer/Maria Shriver	September 1985–August 1986

THE EXECUTIVE PRODUCERS

George Merlis	January 1982–March 1983
Bob Ferrante	April 1983–March 1984
Jon Katz	March 1984–October 1985
Johnathan Rodgers	November 1985–March 1986
Susan Winston	May 1986–July 1986

THE STAFF

Bob Arnot	Medical correspondent
Pete Bonventre	Senior producer
Peter Boyer	Media correspondent
Pat Collins	Entertainment correspondent
David Corvo	Executive editor

Roberta Dougherty	Senior producer
Jude Dratt	Producer (booker)
Bob Epstein	Senior producer
Vicki Gordon	Associate producer (booker)
Jane Kaplan	Producer (booker)
Robert Krulwich	Economics correspondent
Shari Lampert	Associate producer (booker)
Peter McCabe	Senior producer
Rand Morrison	Coordinating producer
Ann Northrop	Coordinating producer
John O'Regan	Senior producer
Janice Platt	Associate producer (booker)
Milbrey (Missie) Rennie	Senior broadcast producer
Amy Rosenblum	Associate producer (booker)
Pat Shevlin	Coordinating producer
Margaret Shumaker	Associate producer (booker)
Terence Smith	Political correspondent
Shirley Wershba	Producer (booker)
Mike Whitney	Senior broadcast producer

CBS NEWS

THE OLD GUARD

Walter Cronkite	Director, CBS Inc.; special correspondent, CBS News; former anchor, "CBS Evening News with Walter Cronkite"

Don Hewitt	Executive producer, "60 Minutes"
Charles Kuralt	Anchor, "Sunday Morning"
Bill Moyers	Special correspondent, CBS News
Andy Rooney	Essayist, "60 Minutes"
Morley Safer	Correspondent, "60 Minutes"
Sandy Socolow	Producer, "60 Minutes"; former executive producer, "CBS Evening News"
Mike Wallace	Correspondent, "60 Minutes"

THE EXECUTIVES

Van Gordon Sauter	Executive vice-president, CBS Broadcast Group, 1983–86; president, CBS News, 1982–83, 1985–86
Edward M. Joyce	President, CBS News, 1983–85; executive vice president, CBS News, 1981–83
Howard Stringer	Executive vice president, CBS News, 1984–86; former executive producer, "CBS Evening News"
David Buksbaum	Vice president, news and operations, CBS News
David Fuchs	Vice president, news, CBS News
Mark Harrington	Vice president, news broadcasts and administration, CBS News

Eric Ober — Vice president, public affairs, CBS News

BLACK ROCK

William Paley — Founder and chairman of CBS Inc.

Laurence Tisch — Chief executive officer of CBS Inc., and Loews Corp.; largest single stockholder of CBS Inc.

Thomas Wyman — Chairman and chief executive officer of CBS Inc., 1983–86; president and chief executive officer, 1980–83

Gene Jankowski — President, CBS Broadcast Group

BAD NEWS AT BLACK ROCK: THE SELL-OUT OF CBS NEWS

I.
GREAT EXPECTATIONS

"All I want out of life is a 30 share and a 20 rating."
> —Faye Dunaway as Diana Christensen, vice-president of programming for UBS, in the movie *Network*.

"I'll do anything, *anything,* to get ratings."
> —Susan Winston, executive director of the "CBS Morning News," at her first meeting with the broadcast's senior staff, May 5, 1986.

Every Thursday at the "CBS Morning News," someone from the public-relations department would come by the newsroom and attach to the bulletin board a single sheet of paper containing the latest weekly ratings from A. C. Nielsen. Some producers would get up from their desks to read them; others wouldn't bother. By the spring of 1985, shortly after I came to work at CBS News, the ratings of the "Morning News" had been mired in the low threes for nearly a year, and it was depressing for the staff to receive this report card each week, a reminder that all its efforts had been unsuccessful. Fortunately for everyone's morale, the ratings sheet would be gone by the end of the day. Postcards from abroad, softball game results, the torrid love notes from a viewer in Missouri who adored newsreader Faith Daniels—these items would stay on the board for months at a stretch. But the ratings sheet was always the first choice of weapons in the newsclerks' ongoing paper-ball war, which erupted whenever the senior staff went into closed-door sessions.

On Tuesday, May 14, 1985, the ratings of the "CBS Morning News" stood at 3.3, dismal by any standard. But you would not have known this from the mood that morning in the basement cafeteria of the CBS Broadcast Center on West Fifty-seventh Street, where a champagne breakfast was under way.

Two hundred people packed the room. The gray formica tables had been covered with white tablecloths and draped with bunting. The flat, overhead lights had been turned off to enhance the party mood. The "Morning News" anchors, Bill Kurtis and Phyllis George, mingled with contributors, producers, and technicians, everyone juggling plates of scrambled eggs and drinking champagne out of plastic cups. In one corner, talking baseball, sat the newsclerks. If their opinion of the condition of the "Morning News" was less than sanguine, it was not shared evidently by the CBS News executives, who were out in force, and beaming. It was the executives who were throwing the party, and their smiles conferred upon their subordinates unrestrained encouragement.

I got to the party late that morning, having been held up in the control room, where I had been overseeing an after-air taping of an interview with Albert Brooks, the comedian turned film director. There was invariably a technical glitch at these post-tapings that would allow the director and his union colleagues to make a five-minute interview, due to start at 9:15, run past 9:30, thus entitling them to a full hour's overtime. This morning their excuse was a troublesome microphone. By the time it was fixed and the interview finally started, it was already 9:27. When the interview ended at 9:32, the crew bolted en masse to the champagne breakfast. If I'd had an alarm, I would have sounded it throughout the building. In all of television there is nothing so terrifying as an army of technicians in pursuit of free food.

I went back to the studio to see Kurtis, who had done the interview. He liked Albert Brooks, and assured me the interview had gone well. Then I went off to track down our finance manager, John O'Regan, who preserved his sanity by finding himself a new retreat within the Broadcast Center every few months. O'Regan was a man of infinite patience, who had been on the show for years, and he insisted on being informed about all studio overruns. When I told him about this one he made a note to himself, muttering: "I'm going to put a stop to this bullshit once and for all."

I listened to his familiar speech about how important it was to keep him abreast of all such infringements. I knew nothing would be done.

"Come on, John," I said finally, my ears closing up with indifference, "let's go get some champagne."

He brightened at the prospect, and we went downstairs to the cafeteria, where he quickly knocked back a couple of glasses of Korbel Brut. I was sure I would hear no more about the studio overrun. I joined the buffet line, opting for a bran muffin and some coffee—all my stomach could handle after a morning in the control room.

Morale boosters at CBS were generally worth avoiding. This, however, was a big one—attendance was almost obligatory. We were celebrating the broadcast's triumphant return from Europe, where it had spent the previous week marking the fortieth anniversary of V-E Day. Kurtis had reminisced with war veterans in Paris and Berlin. Phyllis had shown us around stately homes and English country gardens. We had met a lot of lords, duchesses, and rock stars. None of it really amounted to a hill of beans, but for the moment the TV critics, who rarely had anything nice to say about the "Morning News," had sheathed their swords. A few had even written words of faint praise: "The shows didn't break any new ground, but they were certainly colorful and entertaining"—that sort of thing. Yet something of the victorious mood of Europe from those dear, dead days appeared to have infected CBS News management. The verdict was in; in management's unanimous opinion the programs had been a huge success.

I was trying to glean some information about the next day's broadcast when the thumping of a hard object on a buffet table signaled silence. The president of CBS News, Edward M. Joyce, rose to speak.

Joyce was a dapper man of fifty-three with wavy gray hair. His background was in radio, and in his early career at CBS he had won several awards as news director at local stations. He had never been known for collegial warmth, and as he rose through the executive ranks he had gained a reputation as a man of few words. As president of the news division, he was a distant and slightly ominous figure, as reserved as the dark suits he wore. Even on this festive occasion he was true to form.

"I want to offer my congratulations," he told the room. "But I'm going to let Howard do the talking this morning. He feels the same way I do."

With that, Joyce handed over the proceedings to his deputy, Howard Stringer. Then he sat down, took off his glasses and began to polish them. Stringer, whose official title was executive vice-president of CBS News, drew himself up to his full six feet three inches.

Curly-haired, jacketless, and unabashed, Stringer could be counted on for something more florid. A producer of many

CBS News documentaries, he had enhanced his reputation at CBS as executive producer of the "Evening News with Dan Rather." It was his success at this last job that had earned him his place in management.

"I just want to say this," Stringer began in an accent that, despite his many years in the U.S., was still distinctly English. "I know you've heard me make speeches before, and you're probably sick of hearing them, and rightly so, because I always seem to be bringing you bad news. But for once I can say without hesitation I have something good to report. This is undoubtedly the best thing the 'Morning News' has ever done." In the hushed silence I half-expected someone to faint. Stringer pressed on: "And you should all be proud, all of you, for the efforts you've made and for the recognition you've brought to this broadcast this past week. I watched all the shows, and they were all superb, and frankly I think neither of the other shows could hold a candle to what we did this past week!"

Stringer was interrupted by applause and cheers.

"And so . . ." Stringer raised his voice above the noise. "And so . . . I want to thank especially Bill and Phyllis and Steve"—he meant Steve Baskerville, the weatherman —"for the splendid job they all did, and I want to say a special thank you to Jon Katz." Stringer draped an arm around the chubby, balding executive producer of the "Morning News." "Jon here talked me into letting you do these shows, and I'm glad he did. He said you could do it, and he was right, and I want to thank Ed for letting us do them." Turning to Ed Joyce, and away from the rest of the room, Stringer grinned. "I think the eight hundred thousand dollars we spent was well worth it, and I'm sure it will pay off down the road.

"So you've all proved you can do it," he went on, addressing the throng again. "And this should serve as an inspiration to you because you've proved something to yourselves. I know you've taken some knocks, and I see this as your response to all the nay-sayers, and to all the press who circulate rumors about the future of the 'Morning News.' And let me reiterate once again: we are one hundred percent committed to this broadcast, and if the press had any doubts about that, well, I think we answered them this week. So now I think you have something to build on, and it's important that you do this and carry forward the momentum you've built up. So I urge you to do the best shows possible—and with Jon here, and with anchors like Bill and Phyllis, you have a real shot. And if we can get the ratings up, then we'll really have a party, and next time we won't have it in the cafeteria. We'll have it in a restaurant and we'll make Jon pay for it out of his next raise."

Katz raised his eyebrows.

"Gee, thanks, Howard," he said.

"So you can all be proud!" Stringer concluded, raising his glass. "My compliments to all of you!"

As the cheers subsided and the party hubbub resumed, I made my way through the crowded room and wound up standing next to Kurtis. As we turned in circles to avoid plates and paper cups, he asked me what I thought of Stringer's speech.

"Stirring words," I said.

"Exactly," Kurtis replied. "That's exactly what they were —stirring words."

Phyllis was making her way across the room toward us. She was wearing a perfectly tailored lilac suit, and as usual she was being trailed by her assistant and her hairdresser, Vincent. The assistant was carrying a box, from which Phyllis was handing out blue coffee mugs inscribed with the legend "CBS Morning News." She had had them made up to thank the staff for its hard work during the week in Europe.

"And if anybody deserves one," Phyllis said as she approached us, "it's Bill." She handed Kurtis a mug.

"Well, Phyllis, thank you," Kurtis said. "That's a charming gesture, very nice indeed."

Phyllis continued on her round of the room, eventually winding up at the center of a clutch of CBS News executives. They had been pleased with her performance in Europe, and wanted everyone to know it. The previous week Ed Joyce had told an interviewer that Phyllis was a "generous, bubbling, enthusiastic personality" who "could handle a wide range of material" and was beginning to win over her strongest critics. This morning the executives were treating her like the belle of the ball, and they were virtually ignoring Kurtis. I had detected an edge in his voice earlier, and there had been a number of stories about him in the newspapers recently. One said he might be returning to his old job as a local anchorman at WBBM in Chicago. Another quoted unnamed sources at CBS News as expressing disillusionment with him.

"What am I supposed to do with this?"

The voice over my shoulder was Amy Rosenblum's. She was one of the show's bookers, and she was swinging one of Phyllis's coffee mugs around her finger.

"Bill thought it was a charming gesture," I said.

"Really?" Amy replied. "I'm surprised. He doesn't look too happy."

She was observant, but she had a louder voice than she realized. I ushered her toward a tight huddle of producers. They were all trying to decide on the correct level of emotional response to Stringer's compliments. Finally, Bob Epstein, a senior producer, said: "Maybe they'll start promoting the show." Everyone agreed this would be the best possible benefit.

The conversation broke up into self-congratulatory reviews of the previous week's shows. A few producers drifted across the room to get more champagne. I was left alone with Epstein.

"What's going on?" I asked him.

He looked at me cautiously, then he said:

"There's going to be a change in the show. At least that's what I'm hearing."

"What kind of change?"

"From what I'm hearing, we're going to be restructuring the show around Phyllis."

I looked across to where Phyllis and the CBS News executives were enjoying several big laughs. Kurtis was at the other end of the room talking with one of his piece producers. I knew right away Epstein's rumor was true.

II.

THE SUCCESSION

"I want to program it, develop it. I wouldn't interfere with the actual news itself, but TV is show biz."
> —Faye Dunaway as Diana Christensen, in *Network*.

"This is an institution that struggles to resist change."
> —Howard Stringer, executive vice-president of CBS News

In 1985, when Ed Joyce, Howard Stringer, and their boss, Van Gordon Sauter, decided to rebuild the "Morning News" around Phyllis George, they had been running the news division for more than three years. All of them had come to power in a rapid-fire series of events that began when the president of another network's news division started wooing one of CBS News's brightest stars. In 1979, Roone Arledge, president of ABC News, had been eager (some would say desperate) to hire Dan Rather away from CBS. From the moment Arledge first received a hint from Rather's agent, Richard Leibner, that Rather might be interested in talking to him, the ABC executive pursued the CBS newsman with the tenacity and patience with which Tristan pursued Isolde. In this case, though, the romance was conducted in such unlikely locales as rented hotel rooms and the dark corners of Chinese restaurants on the Upper West Side of Manhattan. Both parties were anxious to keep their liaison a secret.

Rather was a sexy prize, and he wasn't about to be won easily. Indeed, he made it clear to Arledge that he intended that the courtship be a long one—after all, he'd invested twenty years in his relationship with CBS. But each time Arledge and Rather met, Arledge would bring along a new bouquet. Arledge had taken the time to learn a great deal about his paramour, and each bouquet was carefully designed to impress Rather and to persuade him to yield. Arledge wasn't simply offering Rather security and wealth, he was proposing a thoroughly modern marriage of equals. Rather would not only anchor ABC's "World News Tonight," he would also have a big say in the running of the entire ABC news division. He would be free to script the marriage as he saw fit, and in such a marriage it was only right of course that he be free to decide which servants to hire and fire. Rather flirted, toying with the proposal for months. Then, when the intrigue had run its course, he sent Leibner back to his main squeeze, CBS, with instructions to talk freely about the new affair and what was being offered.

Bill Leonard, the president of CBS News, blanched when Leibner outlined Arledge's proposals. Arledge was offering Rather an enormous package, worth as much as $3 million a year, far beyond what any news anchor had ever been paid before. Leonard took the news of the offer to his corporate bosses at CBS Inc., knowing that a number of vague plans CBS News already had drawn up would have to be scrapped, and that they could no longer put off deciding who would succeed Walter Cronkite when the veteran CBS anchor retired.

Throughout the late 1970s, CBS News executives had av-

oided coming to grips with the question of who should succeed Cronkite. "The Star," as he was known around the
news division, had taken over as "Evening News" anchor in
the early sixties. Surviving some early trials, he had endured
to become a symbol, not just for the network, but for TV
news as a whole. Under his aegis, CBS News had become an
institution, a culture within the larger culture of CBS Inc.
Although CBS News had been founded on the reputations
of a group of correspondents led by Edward R. Murrow, and
was proud of this heritage, bonded by a sense of tradition
and a high-minded approach to news, it was during Cronkite's era that it grew into the top news organization in
broadcasting, the undisputed leader among the networks in
almost every aspect of broadcast journalism. Given all this,
it was hard to blame Dick Salant, who was president of CBS
News from 1960 to 1978,* for ducking the issue of the replacement for his avuncular star. Even if Cronkite had only
limited appeal to the younger audience, the one most prized
by advertisers, two decades of his nightly soothings had
made him a public institution, and the "CBS Evening News
with Walter Cronkite" still held a lock on first place in the
networks' evening news race.

Arledge's offer to Rather forced the management of CBS
to act sooner than it had intended. In January 1980, as ABC
stepped up its pressure on Rather, CBS executives met in
committee to consider their options. Before Arledge made
his offer, they had hoped that an anchor team of Dan Rather
and Roger Mudd would be the eventual solution to the succession. But those hopes, already dampened by a recent
newsroom spat between Rather and Mudd, were dashed
entirely by the price Arledge placed on Rather's head. So
the choice was now Mudd *or* Rather, and surveys clearly

_____

*He was replaced as CBS News president in 1964 by Fred Friendly, then
reinstated in 1966.

showed that as a ratings draw Rather was more valuable than Mudd. In the end CBS decided that it had no choice but to match the ABC offer—it simply could not afford to let Rather jump to ABC. After several meetings at the highest levels of the corporation, an offer to Rather was formulated.

Leibner was delighted when Bill Leonard and Gene Jankowski, president of the CBS Broadcast Group, laid it out. CBS management had asked Cronkite to fix a definite date for his departure, and Cronkite, who himself favored Rather over Mudd, had agreed. He would step down thirteen months hence, in March 1981. Rather would then take over as sole anchor, with a salary and benefits that were nearly equal to ABC's offer—or, as Leibner says, "were at least in the ballpark." Rather's agent had not imagined that CBS, traditional CBS, would go this far. "The deal was a long time in the making," he says. "And I was pleased when they came through. I felt I had educated them to the realities of the modern world."

Rather now had a choice to make, a choice between succeeding to Cronkite's throne at CBS News or taking Arledge up on his offer of slightly more money and shared control over a new dominion where Cronkite's ghost would not be around to haunt him. He agonized over the decision for several weeks. Finally, after several meetings with the company brass, he accepted the CBS offer.

So began the tumult that often follows the end of a long reign. To Bill Leonard fell the task of presiding over the succession. It was not a task he would enjoy. As soon as the announcement was made that Dan Rather would take over as "Evening News" anchor once Cronkite stepped down, the news division split into factions.

Mudd had covered Congress for the network since the early sixties and he was considered far more intellectual and erudite than Rather. He was also admired for the way he stood up to management, and for the fact that he was not afraid to speak his mind on controversial issues. Besides, he had been the regular substitute for Cronkite for many years. As for Rather, Mudd's supporters considered him an opportunist, a man who was always trying to curry favor. They recognized that Rather had equally good credentials as a journalist—Rather had risen to prominence at CBS after his coverage of the Kennedy assassination and had later distinguished himself as White House correspondent during the Nixon presidency—but they felt Rather was the sort who put career before principle. And they could cite one specific instance from the past to support this. In 1973, when CBS chairman William Paley had placed a ban on so-called instant analysis of news, Rather had been the only top CBS correspondent not to sign a letter of protest.

To add insult to injury, Rather's detractors were appalled at the network's cavalier treatment of Mudd, who was told that he had been passed over only two hours before the choice of Rather was announced. Even after the announcement was made and Mudd departed for NBC, some CBS staffers continued to hope that management would change its mind and offer Charles Kuralt the job. That summer, when Rather and Kuralt took turns substituting for the vacationing Cronkite, many staffers were openly rooting for Kuralt. Kuralt, after all, had gained considerable recognition for his "On the Road" series. At forty-seven, he was avuncular, reassuring, and trustworthy—in the eyes of many, a natural successor to Cronkite.

But management stayed with Rather, and they stayed with him despite his problems during the thirteen months he had to wait before his coronation. During those months Rather made the mistake of telling one reporter that as a young man he had once tried heroin, an announcement that got a lot of press. He was also roundly mocked for wearing native garb while on assignment in Afghanistan for "60 Minutes," an episode that inspired Tom Shales of the *Washing-*

ton Post to nickname him "Gunga Dan." Throughout those thirteen months, Rather's on-camera abilities—along with almost every facet of his character—were questioned in countless magazine and newspaper articles. The scrutiny was intense, more intense than anyone at CBS had foreseen, and Leonard found himself wishing that the date for the succession could be brought forward. But there was nothing anyone could do about that. There would be no pushing Cronkite aside any sooner than planned. Even if he was being offered a seat on the CBS board of directors, a salary of $1 million a year for seven years, and participation in special events and documentaries, Cronkite had never been one to relinquish any microphone or camera willingly. Throughout his long career at CBS, he had come to be considered by many of his colleagues the consummate air hog, and during his final days he began confiding to friends that he had been forced out. He seemed more and more determined to demonstrate his authority, and one day he burst into the newsroom, objecting furiously to changes that were being planned for the program—*his* program. The proposed changes were quickly quashed, and to assuage Cronkite it was decided that no changes would be made, either to the set or to the way the news was presented. Furthermore, for the sake of continuity, it was decided that Sandy Socolow, Cronkite's executive producer, would continue in the same capacity for Rather. Bill Leonard, who was due to retire in June 1981, was also persuaded to stay on an additional year. As a result of all this, Rather found himself forced to talk about continuing the great Cronkite tradition, and obliged to keep quiet about the innovations he had hoped to implement.

"I wanted there to be as little change as possible," Leonard says. "I may have been too slow in my moves, but it seemed to me that we were already making a radical move, and it would be enough of a shock for viewers to turn on their sets and not see Walter."

Within a few months of Rather's debut in March 1981, the ratings of the "CBS Evening News" fell by a full point. The audience share also dropped, from 27 to 24. The viewers were "sampling," as the Nielsen analysts say, looking elsewhere for the assurance that Leonard predicted they would feel they had lost. But even though an initial decline in ratings was inevitable—a decline invariably accompanies an anchor change, and after all this was Walter Cronkite who was being replaced—there was still a feeling of pressure within the news division.

With Cronkite finally on the sidelines, Rather was eager for change, and he detected resistance to his suggestions on the part of the news division's management. His requests for additional producers or particular correspondents were not being granted, and he found himself increasingly at odds with other areas of the news division. On the "Evening News" staff itself there were problems, too—in part because of a new hierarchical system that Rather himself had instituted. As one of his first innovations, Rather had created an "A" list and a "B" list of correspondents, which set forth his preference for how regularly a correspondent would appear on the "Evening News." The system not only smacked of blatant favoritism, but it deepened the divisions that already existed. Before long much of the anger that had been directed at Rather the previous year surfaced again.

But Rather kept to his system. By the summer of 1981 he began pushing for a change of executive producer. Bill Leonard was unwilling to accede. After all, Sandy Socolow was a valued employee of considerable standing. Meanwhile, Rather's on-air performance appeared strained. He seemed tense and theatrical, lacking the poise and assurance of the man he had replaced. It was not, as one CBS producer said, "the problems of the world that were getting him down, it was the problems within the news division."

By the fall of 1981, the broadcast's problems had become evident even to the casual viewer. In the last week of October, the unthinkable happened: the "Evening News'" ratings nosedived, and ABC's "World News Tonight" came in first. The next week, ABC came in first again, but this time NBC came in second. Never in the history of CBS had its "Evening News" been third in the ratings. Not only was this an enormous blow to the network's pride, but it meant that the "CBS Evening News" was forced to lower the price of its commercials, from roughly $40,000 for a thirty-second spot to about $30,000. In addition, it damaged the prime-time schedule, which no longer had a strong lead-in.

At Black Rock, the CBS corporate headquarters on Sixth Avenue, network executives decided they had seen enough. Third place for the "Evening News" was the last straw. It was time to act. Before they wrote off Dan Rather as a multimillion-dollar mistake, they intended to make changes, and make them fast. For starters, Bill Leonard would have to go.

In November 1981, CBS chairman William Paley had not yet surrendered full control to Thomas Wyman, the former Pillsbury executive he had appointed president of CBS Inc. and designated his heir apparent the year before. (Even when Paley did relinquish the chairmanship in 1983, taking his place on the CBS board of directors as founding chairman, he would continue to make his presence felt.) In any case, says Bill Leonard, it was Paley, along with Wyman and Gene Jankowski, who made the 1981 decision to stir things up at CBS News.

Throughout his career at CBS, Bill Paley had never been reticent about dabbling in the affairs of the news division, even to the point of selecting "talent." After CBS was trounced in the ratings by NBC's Huntley–Brinkley team at the 1964 Republican convention, it was Paley who made the decision to take Walter Cronkite out of the anchor chair and replace him with the team of Robert Trout and Roger Mudd. In 1973, during a visit to China, Paley had essentially hand-picked the next "Morning News" anchor with a casual inquiry to his escort, CBS vice-president Gordon Manning, about his "old friend, Hughes Rudd." Manning took the hint, and Rudd was given the job. (As CBS News's Moscow correspondent, Rudd had made a favorable impression showing the visiting Paley around the Soviet capital.) And in 1980, Paley had interrupted a European vacation to return to New York to participate in the discussions about Cronkite's successor.

With Rather now in trouble, says one CBS source, Paley had no compunctions about removing Bill Leonard. Certainly, he did not consider the fact that Wyman had just asked Leonard to stay on as president of news until June 1982 to be a problem. Paley had made no promises to Leonard, nor to anyone else for that matter.

There were four candidates for Leonard's job: Van Gordon Sauter, then head of CBS Sports; Roger Colloff, a vice-president for public affairs; Ed Fouhy, a former executive producer of the "Evening News"; and Ed Joyce, then head of CBS's New York station, WCBS. Leonard maintains that Paley, Wyman, and Jankowski "would all have had to be involved in the decision" about who was to replace him. But according to one source, "the final choice of a replacement for Leonard was left to Jankowski."

"It was Gene's call," the source says. "And he envisioned Sauter as the man with the flair, the straw to stir the drink, whereas Ed [Joyce] was the ideal mechanic." The decision, then, was to go with Sauter as the new president of CBS News, with Joyce as his deputy.

Whoever was responsible, it was certainly Jankowski who called Leonard to give him the bad news. The request that he stay on until June 1982 was being rescinded. Jankowski did not exactly want Leonard to vacate his office on the spot, but as of that moment Van Gordon Sauter was to be de facto head of CBS News—even if his interim title was only deputy president. "I guess keeping us both there for a while was Gene's way of working," Leonard says. Leonard did not learn that there was a second string to the new team until one of his own vice-presidents called to inquire about office space for Ed Joyce. Leonard had to assume that Jankowski had simply forgotten to tell him.

So Dan Rather had what he wanted—a president of news who would work with him to accommodate his every wish. And Van Gordon Sauter set to work right away removing Rather's thorns. His first move was to get rid of Sandy Socolow, the "Evening News" executive producer. Socolow was dispatched to the London bureau, while other Cronkite loyalists in positions of authority were transferred to more peripheral outposts. In their place entered a new team, who like Sauter owed their first loyalty to Rather. Among them was Howard Stringer, who had worked with Rather at "CBS Reports." Stringer had been under consideration to replace Socolow for some time, Leonard says, but Rather still put him through his paces in several interviews that December before agreeing with Sauter and Joyce that Stringer was the right man.

To Stringer, the move represented a major career leap. It may have been because he was marshaling his thoughts about the "Evening News," while still senior executive producer of "CBS Reports," that he was less inclined, or less able, to pay close attention to a documentary about General

William Westmoreland that was to air in January 1982. "It would be fair to say his plate was full," Leonard says.

The documentary, entitled "The Uncounted Enemy: A Vietnam Deception," claimed to have uncovered a conspiracy at the highest levels of American military intelligence under Westmoreland's command—a conspiracy, according to CBS, to deceive the American public, the President, and Congress about enemy troop strength in Vietnam. In the end, it provoked General Westmoreland into suing the network for libel.

According to Don Kowet, who co-wrote a May 1982 *TV Guide* cover story that called attention to distortions and misrepresentations in the documentary, it was the distractions of Stringer's new assignment that kept him from giving "The Uncounted Enemy" the critical attention it demanded. "If Stringer had paid attention to the thing," he says, "it would never have gotten on the air. It was a very large charge they were making, but these guys were riding high, and they were joking in the halls of CBS that maybe Westmoreland would sue."

None of this would catch up with Stringer for another year. (Westmoreland did not file his libel suit until September 1982, and the trial did not begin until October 1984.) Indeed, when Sauter, Joyce, and Stringer turned their attentions to the "CBS Evening News" in January 1982, there was little to distract them from the job at hand. They were intent, as Sauter has said frequently, on making Dan Rather happy, and make him happy they did. "I'm married to Dan Rather," Sauter proclaimed, and he proceeded to stamp out any lingering speculation that the Rather succession was in doubt. He let it be known that he was going to make the Rather broadcast work. Whether staffers approved of the changes or not, they began to recognize that a new era had dawned at CBS News.

WBBM, the CBS-owned-and-operated affiliate in Chicago, has traditionally been a training ground for CBS management—so much so that when I worked at CBS News, the management was known as the Chicago mafia. Sauter had once been the station's news director; Ed Joyce had been its general manager. Another former WBBM general manager was Robert Wussler, who had an important influence on Van Gordon Sauter's career.

When Bob Wussler first came to CBS News he was recognized as a young man in a hurry. He started in 1957 as a mail-room boy and quickly rose to head CBS News's Special Events unit—the operation that covers space shots, conventions, and elections. Eventually, Wussler was made president of the CBS Television Network, in charge of all prime-time programming, an appointment, according to one CBS executive, that reflected Paley's judgment of Wussler as a "superb showman." Others who didn't share Paley's enthusiasm for Wussler called him Mr. Flash, and critics said he rarely brought a project in on budget. Eventually, Wussler was demoted to president of CBS Sports, and was ultimately forced to leave the network after a minor scandal involving payments to players in CBS's "Winner Take All" tennis tournament. At the time Wussler denied that his resignation was linked to the scandal. Wussler now says: "Jankowski wanted to get rid of me. He was looking for a scapegoat, and I was ready to leave CBS anyway."

In 1972, all this was a long way in the future. Bob Wussler was about to be appointed general manager of WBBM, and he was looking for a news director. The man he hired was Van Gordon Sauter.

Sauter had begun his journalism career in print, working as a reporter for the *Detroit Free Press.* He also wrote for the *National Enquirer.* After the *Free Press,* he went to work for the *Chicago Daily News,* where he is remembered by one colleague as an "unaffected, hard-working reporter who would often have two or three by-lines in the paper on the same day." That led to his first job in broadcasting—as chief correspondent and later news director of WBBM Radio. From there he went to New York to become executive producer in charge of special events for the CBS Radio Network. It was here that he first met Wussler. A producer who knew them both says that Wussler, a graduate of Seton Hall in New Jersey, was impressed by the way Sauter, a graduate of Ohio State University, sprinkled his conversation with quotations from literature.

"I thought he was an interesting guy," Wussler says. "He was a person who obviously had a good handle on communications, even if, as he told me himself, he didn't own a TV set. But he got things done. He was a communicator and he could lead."

According to Gary Deeb, then a TV columnist at the *Chicago Sun Times,* "Wussler spent money like a drunken sailor when he was in charge at WBBM." And it was from Wussler, says one CBS correspondent, that Sauter absorbed two important lessons: first, how to be a splashy network executive; second, how not to be an "on-budget failure." But at the beginning in Chicago, vanity got the better of Sauter's judgment. He decided to put himself on the air as anchor of the early evening news. "He thought of himself as a bearded Charles Kuralt," says one correspondent, "and the truth was he wasn't very good as an on-air personality."

"He obviously wanted to do it," Wussler says, "and if I'd stayed on there, he might have been produced right." But Sauter was not a ratings success, and the experiment proved to be a temporary career setback.

With Wussler's help, however, Sauter managed to get himself appointed CBS News Paris bureau chief in March 1975. Several CBS staffers who knew him in Paris say his tenure was marked by a refusal to learn French, and by a devotion to the pinball machine in the coffee shop near the bureau. It was also in Paris that Sauter first met Bill Paley, whom he showed round the city much as Hughes Rudd had showed Paley round Moscow. In fact, as one reporter said, "there were times when it seemed as if Van was a one-man private travel bureau for Bill." When Wussler, with Paley's blessing, was appointed president of the CBS Television Network, he brought Sauter back from Paris and made him head of Program Practices, otherwise known as network censor, a high-profile job that made him visible to the senior management at Black Rock. But while the job as network censor enhanced Sauter's profile, it did nothing for his credibility as a manager. For that, he would need to gain hands-on control of a CBS profit center, and this he did in his next step. In 1977 he became general manager of KNXT, the CBS affiliate in Los Angeles. In California he adopted a new style, living the single life on a houseboat, coming to work in shorts and keeping a suit hanging in a closet in case anyone from New York dropped in. "What was remarkable about Sauter in those days," says one veteran CBS News producer, "was that he appeared to change personality completely, and accompanied it with a change of costume."

When he took over the news division in 1981, Van Gordon Sauter was a burly man of forty-six, with a light-gray full beard, darkening in the area of his moustache. He smoked a pipe, and favored tweeds and bow ties. He lived on Park Avenue and in Connecticut, and was married to the sister of former California Governor Jerry Brown. Almost everyone who ever worked with Sauter described him as astute. His style was to be personable, even friendly, and he called a lot of people who worked with him "big guy."

But the Falstaffian appearance and disarming manner belied a toughness that in 1981 was becoming all too apparent to the staff of CBS News. Sauter had not been appointed president to be charming and politic, and he took it as his mandate to make sweeping changes, to bring about a total overhaul. In doing so, as one reporter writing in *Esquire* said at the time, "he tossed some depth charges into the corporate fishbowl at CBS News, and some big fish began turning belly up." Bill Leonard had a long history with Sandy Socolow and knew what a valued employee he was, but Sauter's only loyalty was to Rather, and he acceded immediately to Rather's wish to replace him. Within days Sauter put an end to the difficulties Rather had been experiencing with the CBS News management. Soon the entire resources of CBS News were marshaled to the task of stabilizing the "Evening News" and trying to restore its ratings. Money and producers poured in, inevitably leaving less for other broadcasts. Correspondents Rather wanted were told to make themselves available to the "Evening News" instead of doing time-consuming pieces for programs such as "Sunday Morning." The correspondents Rather didn't want remained on his "B" list.

Then Sauter turned his attention to the style and content of the broadcast itself. Attention to detail was all-important here because viewers were still "sampling," and the competition between the network evening news programs was intensifying. Every weeknight, the executives of the news division would gather in Sauter's office to watch all three evening news broadcasts, conduct a postgame analysis, and make recommendations for improvements to the program. There they would sit throughout the two feeds,* pondering the finer points—was the lead right, or if not, what should have been the lead—trying to decide if the broadcast was well-paced, and of course keeping a close eye on Rather's

---

*All three evening network news programs go on the air at 6:30 P.M. eastern time. Some stations carry it live, while others broadcast a second, taped feed a half hour later. This second feed can be updated, if necessary, to include late-breaking news.

performance. And performance was the only word for it. Rather required close watching because of his intensity, and a great deal was being done to present him in a way that would make him appear less strained. One of Stringer's suggestions was that Rather be shot closer up, instead of with the standard three-quarter shot used, for example, for Tom Brokaw on the "NBC Nightly News." Stringer's argument was that Rather would then relax and not appear too emphatic. Other major stylistic changes were made. "Coming-up bumpers" were installed—those whirling chroma-key teasers before commercial breaks, which Socolow had resisted because he thought they were a blatant copy of ABC—and an insistent melodramatic jingle was superimposed over them. The familiar opening animation disappeared. And correspondents were told that whenever possible their pieces should be supplemented with graphics.

That winter, while the correspondents reluctantly went about dressing up their pieces, Dan Rather took to wearing a sweater vest. He began to relax. He began to smile in the right places. The broadcast's correspondents were then instructed that they, too, should relax. Be natural, they were told, don't be afraid to move about, be a bit more like local TV newsmen. Both Sauter and Joyce were well-schooled in the mechanics and philosophies of local television. Among the veteran correspondents and producers there were grumbles. The "CBS Evening News" was still a long way from your friendly hometown anchor team, and nobody was bouncing around on the set yet, but the program was moving toward sensationalism. Stories about drugs, murders, and singles habits began to show up in increasing numbers. What was occurring went beyond a shift in style; it amounted to a reorientation of the whole philosophy and approach to the "Evening News" broadcast. Sauter later told an interviewer: "We moved the broadcast out of Washington. We emphasized stories from across the country where we could tell national stories through human experience and human perceptions more than through statements of bureaucrats and politicians. We tried to find the theme stories that responded to what the aspirations and apprehensions of the American people were. We emphasized story telling, both verbally and visibly."

What this amounted to was a complete break with the headline-oriented news service, with its emphasis on news emanating from Washington, that had been the trademark of the Cronkite broadcast. The number of stories was reduced in favor of longer pieces that attempted to present the news in a broader context. Another innovation at the time became known as "moment theory," a moment being the visual image in a story that let the viewer know what it felt like to be affected directly by the story. News being news, the person affected in the story was often a victim of some sort; according to moment theory, the best TV news reports captured this person's distress on tape, and built it into a context that made it poignant.

The theory was Sauter's, and it flew with Rather, who began handing out "moment" buttons around the newsroom. From then on, CBS News correspondents scrambled to embellish their stories with "moments." If they couldn't find any, if their stories were dry and crusty, they often did not make it on the air. "You could call the official 'Evening News' philosophy the persistence of hope in the presence of despair," one writer stated. Certainly, it was fair to say that the broadcast had gone from "that's the way it is" to "this is the way it feels." The broadcast was not complete unless it took a good tug at your heartstrings several times within its twenty-two minutes. Throughout 1982, as the country tried to pull itself out of recession, there were a lot of unhappy farmers and laid-off workers on the "CBS Evening

News," people who would never know that their personal misfortunes were helping to build CBS's theory of moments into a coordinated ratings triumph.

Moment theory's moment finally passed in October 1982 when George Will wrote a syndicated column about the practice, attacking it as emotional manipulation. After that, it was decided that it would be wiser not to draw attention to the new orientation of the broadcast with gimmicky names. So talk about moment theory subsided.

But the team of Sauter, Joyce, and Stringer had already made an impact on the "Evening News" ratings. So had the "very" school of journalism, as one CBS correspondent called it. Stories that made the viewer feel very sad, or very happy, or very emotional in any way—along with the cosmetic changes that had been made, and the careful supervision of the anchor—were credited with causing the ratings to rise. The "CBS Evening News" moved back out in front of the other evening news broadcasts, and even if ABC's "World News Tonight" continued to lead in the largest urban markets, Rather was mopping up the heartland. In the upper echelons of CBS Inc., Sauter, Joyce, and Stringer were heroes. As corporate management saw it, they had done a tremendous job. They had brought the "CBS Evening News" back from the brink of disaster, at a time when network executives had come to regard evening news broadcasts as the backbone of their programming. Their power at CBS News was secure.

III.

MORNING MAKE-OVER

"If you call yourself the 'CBS Morning News,'
deliver news. But don't have Diane Sawyer
cooking hamburgers with James Beard on the
day KAL 007 is shot down."
—Steve Friedman, executive producer
of NBC's "Today"

It was with similar decisiveness that the newly appointed CBS News executives soon turned their attention to other broadcasts and departments in the news division. Their domain was a huge organization that provided the CBS Television and Radio networks with regularly scheduled news and public-affairs programs and special reports. With a budget at the time of nearly $225 million, CBS News employed between 1,300 and 1,400 people throughout the world. The programs that fell under its jurisdiction included the "CBS Evening News," the "CBS Morning News," "Face the Nation," "Sunday Morning," as well as "CBS Reports" and other programs produced by Documentaries and Public Affairs—including the highly successful weekly news magazine, "60 Minutes."

According to one CBS News vice-president at the time, "one of the biggest changes Sauter made was to have the 'Evening' and 'Morning News' programs report directly to him." He also significantly reduced the number of documentaries being made under the auspices of "CBS Reports." These were money-losers, and a lot of them had to go. At the same time, as the new management pushed through its changes at the "Evening News," it began to address itself to the ratings problems of the "Morning News," or "Morning," as the broadcast was then called.

Attending to the "Evening News" was a matter of trying to restore ratings. At the CBS morning program something else entirely was needed. The "CBS Morning News" had been a troubled child, and it had taken more than a few whippings during its infancy. Since then, efforts to rehabilitate it had never been sustained. Over the years, however, it had won its share of devotees. Many correspondents and producers within the news division had a soft spot for it. For some it had been their training ground—for Andy Rooney, Mike Wallace, Hughes Rudd, even Walter Cronkite. So what if it couldn't win the big one, many of them felt. So what if it choked when things got down to the wire. So did the Boston Red Sox and the Chicago Cubs. Like the Sox and Cubs, the "Morning News" had the kind of personality that attracts afficionadoes. Having never had much of a chance in life, it was difficult and curmudgeonly, like many of the people who had been associated with it.

In its first incarnation as the "Morning Show," which debuted in 1954, Walter Cronkite had been its host. In those "great early days of television," Cronkite, supported by a gag writer and teamed with a lion puppet named Charlemane, was pitted against NBC's "Today." "Today" had been launched in 1952, with Dave Garroway as its host. Since then it had been making a big splash with a chimpanzee called J. Fred Muggs. But compared to Muggs, Charlemane seemed a bit stiff and awkward, and when compared to Garroway, so did Cronkite. After five months he was replaced, and so began a procession of hosts and anchors on the CBS morning program that would eventually number several dozen.

Cronkite's replacement was Jack Paar, who in turn was replaced by Dick Van Dyke, who in turn was replaced by Will Rogers, Jr.—all within eighteen months. None of them could make a dent in "Today's" ratings. The name of the show was even changed, to "Good Morning," but polite solicitation didn't win viewers either. The Rogers era was memorable only for one incident, which occurred during the coverage of the Democratic convention in Chicago in 1956. Since Will Rogers, Jr., was the son of a cowboy, it was decided he should open the convention coverage by riding a horse up Michigan Avenue. He would then dismount in the lobby of the Hilton Hotel and go to work. The horse, however, seemed to understand that Murphy's law was written with morning television in mind, and on-camera it proceeded to leave its mark on the hotel doorstep. Correspondent Ned Calmer, waiting in the studio to read the news headlines, saw what was happening on his monitor and said to his writer, Sandy Socolow, "Good God, what a fuckup!" Unfortunately, the show's director had already cut away from the horse to the studio, and Calmer's comment went out over the air.

Not long after the horse incident, "Good Morning" folded its tents, and for five years CBS gave up trying to compete with "Today." A children's program, "Captain Kangaroo," was brought in to spare the network further humiliation. "Today" meanwhile had begun to demonstrate its staying power. The NBC management left Garroway in place for nine years, and in doing so made its broadcast an institution.

Then in 1961 CBS started a new morning program, "Calendar." Its hosts were Harry Reasoner and a Broadway actress named Mary Fickett, and one of the writers on the broadcast was Andy Rooney. "Calendar" was a quality show, more upscale than "Today," and it achieved a measure of acclaim, at least with the critics if not in the ratings. It had the advantage of being broadcast at 10:00 A.M., eastern time, an hour after "Today" went off. After its initial experiences with a morning program, CBS was not about to go head to head again with "Today" at 7:00 A.M.—at least it wasn't until 1965, when the CBS executives discovered they could make money in mid-morning with "I Love Lucy" reruns. But by then "Calendar" had been off for two years, and the "CBS Morning News" was being anchored by Mike Wallace.

The "Morning News" afforded Mike Wallace his big break. Until then he had introduced dance bands, hosted game shows, and hustled Parliament cigarettes. According to former CBS News president Dick Salant, Paley's attitude toward the broadcast was "do a hard news program and never mind the ratings."

"Paley cared a lot about the 'Morning News,'" Salant says, "because it was the only thing he was ever home to watch. Of course he watched it in a way ordinary people didn't watch it—lying in bed, being served breakfast by his valet, while ordinary people were getting their kids off to school."

Mike Wallace lasted until 1966, when he got tired of the hours and departed to cover Richard Nixon's comeback. Joseph Benti then anchored the program for four years, followed by John Hart. Salant says Paley still didn't care if the "Morning News" was a dirt patch in the ratings because everything else at the network was a bed of roses. In fact, for several years, the producers on the show joked that they were putting it on for an audience of one.

Then in 1973 the network hired Sally Quinn, pairing her with Paley's personal choice, Hughes Rudd. Quinn, the daughter of a three-star general, had worked for CBS News at the political conventions in 1968. She had since become a feature writer for the *Washington Post,* where she earned a reputation as a sharp-witted interviewer with a knack for eliciting embarrassing quotes from political figures. She was hired as Rudd's co-anchor partly in answer to the demands of women at CBS News, who wanted an anchor opening to be filled by a woman, and partly to compete with Barbara Walters, who was growing increasingly popular on "Today."

Adding to CBS's enthusiasm for Quinn was the fact that she was an attractive, willowy blond. Sally the beauty and Rudd the likable grouch—CBS believed they would make a scintillating duo. The company brought out its big guns for a publicity barrage on behalf of Quinn and Rudd, only to have it backfire. Three weeks before Quinn made her debut, a devastating profile of her in *New York* magazine dissected both her morals and her integrity, and from her first to last day on the air it was evident that she was entirely untrained and wholly unsuited to the job. With every television critic in the country taking shots at her, her career as an anchor ended after only four months.

After Quinn left, Hughes Rudd was paired with veteran Washington correspondent Bruce Morton, a gifted writer whose trademark was the finely crafted piece delivered in a low-key, earnest way. These two set a serious tone for the broadcast that would last for the next six years. The program continued to gain recognition if not ratings. Anchors came and went—by then the revolving door had become a tradition at the "CBS Morning News"—but the broadcast itself remained consistent. It had come to be regarded as an intelligent program for those interested primarily in news.

By 1981 the one-hour program had been retitled "Morning," and was hosted by Charles Kuralt. Later that year, when it was expanded to an hour and half, Kuralt was joined by Diane Sawyer. Sawyer had been a staffer in the Nixon White House before she was hired by CBS in 1978 as a Washington correspondent. The Kuralt–Sawyer "Morning" was a classy, low-key, serious broadcast, made up of hard news and long pieces from the bureaus, and featured an excellent sportscaster, Ray Gandolf. The critics loved the show's writing and its highbrow orientation, and Kuralt stated at the time that he felt no pressure to get ratings. Poor Kuralt. He was the proud proprietor of a vintage vehicle, apparently oblivious to the changes that were taking place both at CBS News and in television in general, changes that would soon run his classic car right off the road.

Until the late seventies, the networks never regarded network news as a profit center. Although two of the three evening news broadcasts had been generating huge revenues for years,* network news divisions as a whole still lost money because of the cost of special events and documentaries. There were sound political reasons for leaving things this way. Broadcasting is licensed by the Federal Communications Commission, and what better way for the networks to demonstrate their commitment to public service than by demonstrating a willingness to lose money on their news operations? But by the late seventies there was less heat from the FCC; as a result, the networks felt comfortable allowing their news divisions to show a profit.

In the meantime, at the local level, the profits being made in news were fast becoming obscene. An entire industry of consultants and experts had grown up to advise stations how to boost news ratings. Stations had gone from last to first place, thanks to the services of "news doctors," and the doctors' recommendations didn't merely involve fancier sets or better graphics. They recommended who should de-

*ABC did not go to a half-hour newscast until 1967, and it was several years before the program made money.

liver the news and what kind of news should be delivered. In the chase for ratings, local television news began to emphasize emotional content, human-interest stories, more blood and guts, self-help from tipping to toilet training, and of course news personalities—anchors and reporters who stood knee-deep in floods and impressed viewers with their activism.

When profitability began to matter to network news executives, it was inevitable that network news would be redefined in terms of the local style. ABC led the way in 1975 when it introduced a new program called "Good Morning America." Its host was David Hartman, a former actor, and he immediately struck a chord with the public. His genius lay in convincing viewers that he was a "little guy," just like them. "Tell us, the Average Americans," he would say to Cabinet secretaries, "what such and such a policy means for us." But even more important was the new ABC program's orientation. It paid lip service to news with its headlines and news-related "segments," but for the most part it filled its two hours with jazzy feature stories, celebrity interviews, diet doctors, self-help tips, and advice on how to manage everything from money to pets. The ratings rose quickly, putting pressure on "Today" to soften its content.

At first the impact of this kind of "localization" was felt mainly at ABC and NBC. CBS News was still prospering, and the news division was largely in the hands of people raised in the tradition of Murrow and Cronkite. "60 Minutes," the network's critically acclaimed and hugely popular news magazine, generated huge revenues, which more than made up for any losses incurred by the "Morning News." But in 1981, when Sauter and Joyce took over, the "CBS Evening News" ratings were down. Encouraged by their corporate bosses, Sauter and Joyce felt that a broadcast such as "Morning" could no longer be allowed to be a drag on profits. There were millions of dollars at stake in the morning time slot, and each network wanted a highly rated morning program. "Today" and "Good Morning America" were squaring off for a major ratings battle, while the CBS show, with its 2.8 rating, lagged far behind. Sauter and Joyce wanted into the fray.

"In 1982, the 'Morning News' had every opportunity," says Steve Friedman, the executive producer of "Today." "You could tell that 'Good Morning America' was going stale, and at 'Today' we were in chaos, experimenting with three anchors. People were turning the dials, they were looking for something."

Sauter and Joyce concluded that a mixed diet of news, information, and entertainment would do the trick. As a result, "Morning" and Charles Kuralt would have to go. The "Morning News" was to be revamped. It would be a different program entirely, if not an original one—Sauter and Joyce had already decided that to a large extent the new show would emulate the other networks' proven formula. Beyond this, they were not sure what they wanted. Sauter had the vague notion that the show ought to be "serendipitous." But if Sauter was still unclear about what the new show was to be, he was certain about who he wanted to anchor it. His choice was Bill Kurtis, a correspondent he and Bob Wussler had brought to WBBM in Chicago in 1973. Since then Kurtis had become a big success as WBBM's anchor, and late in 1981 he and Sauter met secretly at a hotel and worked out a deal for Kurtis to take over the "Morning News." Kuralt was out; Kurtis was coming. Unfortunately, the news that Kurtis was coming became known before it was announced that Kuralt was leaving. Kuralt, who was much loved at CBS News, heard about the decision only a few hours before it became a fait accompli.

"It was," says one producer of the show, "the only time

that I realized that Charlie had normal human foibles like the rest of us. He was thoroughly pissed off at the way things were handled. All along he and his executive producer, Shad Northshield, had been told there was no problem with their program." The single bottle of champagne Sauter sent to Kuralt's farewell luncheon did little to dispel ill feeling.

But of greater concern to the new CBS management was the question of who would produce the new show. As they saw it, there was nobody at CBS News who had the experience to produce the kind of show they had in mind. And so, a few weeks after the anchor change was announced, the other shoe dropped: the next executive producer of the "CBS Morning News" would be George Merlis, former executive producer of "Good Morning America." CBS News staffers were stunned. "Good Morning America," after all, was produced by ABC's entertainment division.

When Merlis got the call from Ed Joyce, he had been out of morning television for a year. During his four-year tenure at "Good Morning America," he had made the broadcast the top-rated morning show, putting an end, at least temporarily, to "Today's" invincibility. "It was not an act of genius on my part," he says. "It was a team effort."

George Merlis is a tense, thin man, fastidious about what he eats and the way he dresses. He is described by almost all producers who have worked with him as imaginative and creative. Joyce brought him to the Broadcast Center and introduced him to Sauter, and discussions about the new "Morning News" began. A source who was present at those meetings says that when Merlis pressed Sauter for a definition of the new program, Sauter hit on an analogy from his background in radio. "I want it to be like drive-time radio," he said, "a little bit of everything for everyone." Beyond this, Sauter was willing to go along with Merlis's suggestions. As Merlis himself says: "I gave them my ideas, and they accepted them."

So Merlis proceeded to reconceptualize the show. Since interviews were to be central to the new format, he began to hire "bookers"—the people who would book interview guests. He gave them the title of associate producer, a title other qualified CBS journalists had worked long and hard to earn. There were resentments and confusion. One day a new employee hired from "Good Morning America" showed up, and was asked by a "Morning" producer what it was she'd been hired to do. "I produce segments," the young woman said. It was the first time many people on the old CBS "Morning" staff had heard the term.

No less confused were the CBS news bureaus, who were being asked to shoot ninety seconds of Billy Joel or Joan Collins or whomever to set up an upcoming interview. Like their colleagues in New York, the bureau people were convinced that Merlis was out to create a replica of "GMA." And, indeed, when Merlis's show was ready, it was clear that he had divided the show into "GMA"-like segments. For its first hour the broadcast still reported on serious news topics, but added to the mix were an entertainment reporter (Pat Collins), a business reporter (Ken Prewitt), a new local-style sportscaster (Jim Kelly), a chatty weatherman (Steve Deshler), and news of interest to consumers. There were more chatty soft features in the second hour. The biggest change of all, of course, was the predominance of interviews. "When it debuted," said Bill Kurtis, "we were blasted by virtually everyone for taking a step down the road to entertainment."

Over the next few months, Merlis began to overcome the initial derision. The bureaus began to cooperate with him, providing the material he wanted. And whether he made a conscious compromise between "GMA" and what he imagined CBS News stood for, the new "CBS Morning News" at least contained a lot more hard news than its rivals. The traditionalists at CBS still hated it, but the program began to get better press. "It's the show that opinion-makers watch," wrote one critic, and after a few months its ratings began to rise. Then Merlis, having brought the broadcast closer to the other two shows, began looking for ways to distinguish it. "I spoke to the Broadcast Group's research people," he says, "and it was clear that they had no idea what their target audience was. At 'GMA' I had made a conscious attempt to go after women aged eighteen to forty-nine, so it made sense that at CBS I should have something for men, at least in the first hour. So I had Jim Kelly [the sportscaster] on twice, and lots of business reports with Ken Prewitt and Jane Bryant Quinn."

The show's ratings continued to rise. The new 1982 model "CBS Morning News" was off and running. "It was clear," says one senior producer, "that Merlis knew what he was doing." During Merlis's first few months as executive producer, meetings were held every week to discuss the show, first in Sauter's office, then in Ed Joyce's. "They were tough, and rigorous, and hands-on," said one producer, "and I was scared to death at the time, but in retrospect the meetings were good."

But after a few months Sauter appeared to lose interest in the show, and the meetings that were held to discuss it were chaired by Joyce. Merlis says: "My encounters with Sauter from then on consisted largely of him clapping me on the back, and saying 'capital broadcast this morning, George' or 'let's not have a repeat of that'." Furthermore, after those first few months, Sauter seemed less inclined to provide his new broadcast with the funds it needed. In his days as station manager, Sauter, in the tradition of his mentor Wussler, had been known for spending CBS's money freely, but he had since become known in every department except the "Evening News" as "Dr. No." And so for the "Morning News" it was "no" to expenses of various sorts, including staff, though some of these "no's" had to be rescinded when it was clear that the new "Morning News" could not be produced on the old show's budget. The set (and sets are expensive) was one area where Sauter intended to economize. He was steering all possible resources to Rather at the time, and so he was determined to save money by using the set of the sports studio. Before long, Merlis was having serious problems with the budget people. They were camped at his door, nitpicking over costs. They had not been able to make an accurate projection of what this kind of show would cost because they had nothing to base a budget on, and they began to make it difficult for Merlis, who had to produce and plan ahead while simultaneously spending his time fighting for every dollar.

Then in December 1982, an event occurred that "Morning News" producers remember vividly to this day—a two-day meeting at the Essex House hotel in New York to discuss the broadcast. Sauter, who had become enamored of people from print, had hired Jon Katz, a former newspaper editor, as manager of "Morning News" planning. It was at Katz's instigation that the Essex House meeting was held. The meeting was attended by Sauter, Joyce, Merlis, Merlis's deputy Marjorie Baker, Katz, a few other CBS News vice-presidents, and the morning program's senior staff. "It was clear from the start," said one producer, "that Sauter and Katz were holding a public forum to trash the show's executive producer. Van asked him to present the show's organization chart, and Merlis said, 'Well, there is no organization chart. I do this, Marjorie does this,' and so on. They told him to have an organization chart ready by tomorrow. So Katz and Van had it in for George, and once this was clear, Diane Sawyer sniffed blood."

Producers who worked with Merlis at the "Morning News" say he had no stomach for this kind of political infighting. Aware of the hostility his presence had aroused at the company, he was never outgoing to begin with, and as time went by he became less and less communicative. Editorially, too, he was losing support, though he maintains that there was never much editorial input from the management to begin with. To many staffers, Merlis appeared to be going through a mid-life crisis. Since he rarely set foot in the studio, he also seemed to be losing touch with his anchors, especially with Diane Sawyer, who was becoming increasingly critical of him.

"Diane tended to tire of people quickly," said one "Morning News" producer. "Merlis had always been in awe of her, and she sensed weakness. She felt he didn't measure up to her standards, and of course she was making a grab for power."

Even if the ratings were up—and the "Morning News" was regularly tying "Today" for the first time in thirty years —there were as many reasons to account for the broadcast's success as there were people ready to take credit for it: the new anchor team, the change in format. The opinion around CBS News was that anyone could have done it—an opinion that many "CBS Morning News" producers now acknowledge was a big mistake. But as Merlis was falling out of favor, Diane Sawyer was beginning to flex her muscles, and although anchor power in television in general was in the ascendant, Sawyer's ascendancy constituted a special case.

Not everyone who worked with Diane Sawyer at the "Morning News" thought highly of her. One senior producer called her a "real piece of work, who thought she was a better judge than anyone else of what the show should be." But she impressed many of the staff's associate producers with her intelligence, and since she had arrived at the

"Morning News" she had also impressed the TV critics, who had only nice things to say about her. She impressed Bill Paley too, enough to become his regular dinner date. "I knew that I wanted to be close to the power," she had once told a magazine reporter.

If ever there was any tendency at CBS News to treat Diane Sawyer lightly, it ended one morning at a meeting with the CBS News executives. A secretary came in to announce that Mr. Paley was on the phone for Diane.

"Tell him I'll call him back," Sawyer said coolly.

The executives were aghast. Nobody, but nobody, declined to accept a call from Bill Paley. From then on the management had to pay serious attention to her, so close was she to the real center of power.

And so when Sawyer went to see Van Gordon Sauter in March 1983 with the aim of getting rid of Merlis, Merlis's only lingering support was from the man who had brought him to CBS, Sauter's deputy, Ed Joyce. Sauter wasn't high on Merlis, and he had been hearing about Merlis's "failings" for months from his principal detractor, Jon Katz. "The problem," said one senior producer, "was that Sauter had no idea that Katz didn't know what he was talking about." And according to one CBS executive, "Sauter wasn't about to go against Diane Sawyer when he knew she was sitting down to dinner with Paley."

Sawyer told Sauter that her executive producer wasn't communicating with her. A few days later, Merlis was summoned to Sauter's office and told he was no longer the executive producer of the "Morning News." Joyce, who had supported Merlis as long as he could, had yielded under pressure. At the meeting he looked awkward and left the room.

And so the CBS News management fired an executive producer who had taken the "Morning News" from a 2.8 rating to a 4.0 in little more than a year.

"Given the opposition he had faced at the company," said one senior producer, "you have to admit that what he did was an achievement. Why they got rid of him in the face of the evidence of his competence, I will never understand."

Merlis, who claims he is still mystified by some of the circumstances surrounding his removal, says wistfully: "Maybe I made it seem too easy. Maybe they were embarrassed by success." He went off to Hollywood, and the pot that he had left gently simmering slowly began to boil.

IV.

THE EXECUTIVE PRODUCER

"You take a job like this to enhance existing programs, to develop new ones, and to bring out the best in your people."
—Howard Stringer, in an interview with the *Washington Journalism Review*

Only a few details about the internal machinations of CBS News were familiar to me when I went to work there in 1985—the year that CBS and CBS News themselves became the news. Little of what I have so far described was known to me then. When I applied for a job at CBS, I had given no thought to working at a particular news broadcast, nor did I object to working at any particular one. In early 1985 the "CBS Morning News," where I wound up, had not been recognized as a potential rival to "Guiding Light" or "As the World Turns." At that time it had shown only flashes of promise for providing its audience with the unforeseen twists and turns that every good soap opera should have. But the potential was there —a host of possibilities locked within the problem child.

What it needed was more twists and turns, and at a faster clip.

Nor can I say that I was totally naive about what to expect from television. I had worked as a reporter and an editor —or as people in television say, "in print"—and I had friends from print who had sojourned in TV, and some of them had run screaming into the night. So I made a solemn vow before I went into TV to keep a close watch on my mental balance, and I promised myself if it ever got too crazy I would get out. What I probably was naive about was CBS, but then again probably nothing could have prepared me for what life at CBS turned out to be.

The fact was, I was ready for a change of job. The monthly magazine deadlines had come to seem routine. I needed to learn something new. When I first approached CBS News I knew very little about the technical side of television, but I knew other print journalists who had picked it up as they went along, and I figured I could do the same. I knew very little about Van Gordon Sauter and Ed Joyce beyond what I'd read in the papers, but I knew of Howard Stringer's reputation as a documentary producer, and it was Stringer I wrote to. A week later his secretary called to arrange an interview. We set a date for what turned out to be an auspicious day at CBS News: the day that General William Westmoreland fought—and lost—his last legal battle with CBS, the day his $120 million lawsuit against the network was jointly terminated. My interview with Stringer was rescheduled for the next day.

I had followed the Westmoreland case closely, and it was clear to me as I took a cab to the CBS Broadcast Center that morning that even if the monkey had fallen from the network's back, the news division's reputation had been permanently sullied by the questionable methods of interviewing and editing used in the Westmoreland documentary. But such equivocations seemed far from the mind of Howard

Stringer when I presented myself at his office. As I waited in his anteroom, I could hear gales of laughter emanating from behind his door. When the door opened I discovered that the other party to the merriment was Dan Rather. I experienced a moment of empathy for Westmoreland, whom I pictured sitting alone somewhere, staring at the rings in his coffee cup.

Howard Stringer is a tall man with reddish-blond curly hair and cherubic features. I knew that the Westmoreland broadcast had carried his credit as senior executive producer, and I wondered whether he regarded this as a blot on an otherwise fine record. But as we began to talk, it became clear that his mood that morning was exuberant, and the exuberance carried over to the early part of our conversation. Unburdened, he talked freely about the lawsuit.

"All along I've maintained Westmoreland was ill-advised in bringing suit," he said. "To this day I still believe he was conned into bringing it."

We talked about the costs of defending the suit, and Stringer kept shaking his head. Then we got down to business. Stringer wanted to know a bit more about my print background. I filled him in.

"So why on earth do you want to work in television?" he asked eventually. "It's a bloody awful business."

I told him I was hankering for a career change, and that I thought I could make the switch to TV. "Stories are stories," I said. "I've been writing for magazines for fifteen years, and I always write with pictures in mind."

"Are you interested in management?" Stringer asked.

"Eventually, maybe. Most of the editing jobs I've held involved managing."

The enigmatic smile invited elaboration.

"It might help if I learned the business first," I said.

"Well, there are levels and levels of management,"

Stringer insisted, as if declining to acknowledge that I had a point. "Some people come here and only want to produce pieces, and they wouldn't be interested in managing at all. Frankly, I don't blame them. My job isn't exactly one of the fun jobs around here."

He told me that his job tended to be a thankless one, and that he spent most of his time resolving crises, though not always on the scale of the Westmoreland case. He said he never wanted to hear the word *deposition* again. Then he leaned back in his chair and changed the subject.

"You know I can't hire you myself," he said. "It has to be one of the broadcast producers."

I told him I wasn't aware of that.

"The question is who do I send you to see. . . ."

Stringer tapped a pencil on his enormous desk.

"The problem is . . ." he began.

He drifted off into thought and left the sentence unfinished. I finished it for him. "The problem is that I have no television experience."

"Well, it does make it that much harder for me to sell you around here," he declared, tilting his chair back. "I mean I'm not sure you'd want to work on the 'Evening News,' and frankly, great résumé or not, I can't really see how they could use you."

"I might contribute a few original ideas," I volunteered.

Stringer laughed. "But that's the point. The 'Evening News' would have only limited use for someone with original ideas." He picked up his phone and dialed a four-digit number. "I think the person you should talk to is Andy Lack."

Lack, I was to learn, was Stringer's closest friend at the network. Ten minutes later I was across the street in the building CBS News shares with the Ford Motor Company. After a short wait I was shown in to meet Andrew Lack, the executive producer of "West 57th Street," a jazzy spin-off of

"60 Minutes" then still in development. Lack seemed an intelligent, if cautious, man. I learned later that he had been executive producer of two other recent shows for CBS News, "Our Times" and "Crossroads," neither of which had stayed on the air long. Lack wanted ideas and I trotted them out. Then he asked me what experience I'd had in production. I told him I'd had no experience of any kind in television, let alone in production.

"That's really a problem," he said. "I need people with production experience."

I was beginning to feel caught in a chicken and egg situation.

"Why is it," I said evenly, "that production experience is so important when there must be three hundred people in this building with production experience, and judging from what I see on television, about three people with ideas?"

Lack allowed himself a hearty laugh.

"I take your point," he said. "But it's a matter of budgets. I can't budget for an ideas person. It's that simple."

I could tell that he was not persuaded. I didn't feel like suggesting to him that I use CBS's time and money to pick up a basic knowledge of how to edit tape, which, as they say in television, "isn't brain surgery." I wished him luck with the new show.

We stood up together and he escorted me to the reception area. As I was leaving I asked him the name of the new show —Stringer had told me that "West 57th Street" was merely the working title.

"Or is it a trade secret?" I asked.

"No secret," Lack said. "We don't have a title yet. But we'll come up with something."

I called Stringer to report there'd been no progress, and we set up another appointment for the following week. Stringer seemed mildly amused as I told him about the conversation with Lack. When I finished he said: "Hmmm, pity. Maybe you should meet Jon Katz."

"Who is Jon Katz?" I asked, feeling a little insecure that I didn't know.

"Jon Katz is the executive producer of the 'Morning News,' Stringer informed me. "He's from print too, and he's doing an excellent job with the 'Morning News.' I think maybe you two would get along."

And so a few days later, at 8:00 A.M., I was seated once again in the glittering chrome lobby of the CBS Broadcast Center, hoping this time I would be hired. Katz's assistant, a young woman named Elizabeth Citrin, eventually turned up to escort me to meet her boss. It was my first venture into the interior of the building, a low, oblong, brick structure that occupies an entire city block on Manhattan's West Fifty-seventh Street, one block from the Hudson River. The place, I discovered, was a maze of corridors leading on the ground floor to a rabbit warren of newsrooms, dead ends, and offices, and on the second floor to studios where most of the network's news broadcasts and some of its soap operas are aired or taped.

When we reached the "Morning News" newsroom, it was deserted, save for one newsclerk answering the phones. The show was on the air, and the staff was upstairs in the control room. Aside from the lack of people, it was like every other newsroom I had ever known, utterly lacking in creature comforts. The walls were discolored, the floors were stained, newspapers were strewn everywhere. I was shown into an office off the newsroom. Inside was the man Stringer had described as "another renegade from print, like yourself."

Katz was talking on the phone. Or rather, he was listening on the phone. The receiver was crooked between his shoulder and his ear, and he was slapping a softball into a large mitt. He was a big man, close to two hundred and fifty pounds, too much of which was concentrated in his gut. He wore baggy tan pants, a checked shirt with the sleeves rolled up, no tie. I guessed he was about forty, even though he was balding on top and was well on his way to a second chin. His eyes had a boyish twinkle.

He motioned for me to sit on a maroon couch under three large TV sets. As I sat down, the softball rolled out of his mitt and trickled across the desk onto the floor. I picked it up and put it back in his glove. Katz barely noticed. He had one eye on the monitors flickering at low volume above my head, and he was chuckling at something the other party on the phone had said.

"So write something nice about us, asshole!" he demanded suddenly.

The asshole's response was clearly inadequate because after a brief pause Katz added: "Piece of shit."

I fished in my jacket for a cigarette, and Katz, suddenly attentive, gestured for me to give him one.

I glanced around the office. It was windowless and had the feel of a bunker.

"Did you see the Higgins review?" Katz asked.

He wasn't talking to me, but I knew what he was talking about. A few days earlier George Higgins had written a complimentary two-column piece about the "Morning News" in the *Wall Street Journal,* proclaiming it the "best of the crop" of the morning shows for devoting more of its running time to hard news.

"You're surprised?" Katz was saying. "Why the hell should you be surprised? I mean, in a country of two hundred fifty million people, somebody ought to like us. Actually I think Howard said that, but don't quote me."

In the ensuing pause, I could hear Bill Kurtis on the monitor above my head talking about the controversy over the President's upcoming visit to Bitburg. Then he was drowned out by Katz: "Don't talk to me about the 'Today' show!" the executive producer of the "Morning News" exclaimed. "The 'Today' show's a fucking parade of Cabinet secretaries if ever I saw one . . ."

Another pause was followed by a few low chuckles, as the conversation wound down. "I know you will, you cocksucker . . . fuck you, too."

The conversation ended. Jon Katz, executive producer of the "Morning News," ex-managing editor of the *Dallas Times Herald,* a former reporter and editor at several East Coast dailies, swung his loafers off the desk, took off his baseball mitt, and shook hands.

"Hi! Jon Katz." He smoothed a few strands of wavy hair across a balding pate. "You want some coffee or something?"

"Coffee would be fine," I said.

"Open that door, will you?"

I opened it.

"Liza-beth!"

His voice carried down the corridor to the empty newsroom. After a few seconds, his assistant appeared in the doorway.

"Coffee. For him. How do you take it?"

"Black will be fine," I said.

"Hey—we got cream here. This is CBS, you want cream?"

"No, black's fine."

"Oh . . . *Liza-beth!"*

Elizabeth reappeared.

"Can we get some Cokes in here?" He swung around to open his refrigerator. "Look at this, two Cokes and one ginger ale. The place is falling apart. Has Epstein been in here again?"

"No, Jon. The door's been locked."

"If I catch Epstein . . ." He stopped mid-sentence, took off his glasses, rubbed them, replaced them, and focused on her sweater. "Elizabeth, is that a smile button you're wearing?"

"No, Jon. It's an antique pin."

"Oh, a pin, is it? Gee, that's very preppy, Elizabeth. Is that why we have no Cokes in here? Because you're out buying preppy clothes or mooning over some preppy boyfriend?"

His assistant closed the door.

"I really thought it was a smile button," Katz said sheepishly.

He leaned back in his chair and folded his hands behind his head. "So," he said, with a boyish grin, "Stringer's sent us a fellow Brit."

As Katz kept one eye on the monitors above my head, I started to tell him what I had told Stringer—why it was I wanted to work in television—but Katz got the point quickly and cut me off.

"I know what you mean," he said. "I don't know if I could go back to print either. I mean, don't get me wrong, print is far and away superior to this business. I mean, you can go crazy in this business if you have ideas, because the resistance to new ideas is unbelievable. I'll give you an example. Six months ago, I thought: 'Let's get an interview with Kim Philby'."

"That's a good idea," I said.

" 'Course it's a good idea. Well, I guess you'd know about Philby, being a Brit. So I sent a telex to Moscow. 'Suggest we make a pitch to Kim Philby for an interview for "Morning News"—signed, Jon Katz.' I mean Philby's getting old."

"Don't tell me he talked," I interrupted, fairly confident that if Philby had, I'd have read about it.

"No, but that's beside the point," Katz said, brushing this aside. "Guess what the return telex said?"

"What?"

" 'Who is Philby, and who is Katz?' "

"Unbelievable," I said.

"So you see what you're up against. At the same time you can have a lot of fun here. Open that door again, will you?"

Again I opened it.

"Liza-beth!"

"Yes, Jon," his secretary said calmly, as she poured my coffee in an editing room directly across the hall.

"Where's Corvo? Where is the vicious little guinea?"

"He's upstairs, Jon."

"Oh, right. Somebody's got to run the show, I guess."

Katz reached for his phone.

"I was going to ask," I said cautiously, as he dialed a number, "how come you don't have to be in the control room when the show's on the air?"

"Corvo's my deputy," he said, as he waited for the call to be answered. "He's running it right now." The phone wasn't being answered. "Least I hope he is. If not, I hope someone is." He tried another number, and added: "On a slow day after eight o'clock, I sometimes come down here and try to catch up on the paperwork."

Katz dialed another number. "What's going on up there, is everyone asleep?"

His call to the control room was finally answered.

"You all jerking off up there? This is Jon Katz, executive producer of the 'Morning News,' you heard of me? Oh, good. Let me talk to Corvo . . ." Then, in more collegial tones: "Hey—if there's a good beauty shot, let Baskerville go long next time up. The show feels like it's running into a wall. I mean the pictures aren't bad, and they're better than these goo-goos."

He hung up, and excused himself to make another call. While he was talking on the phone, I pulled out a notebook containing the ideas I'd jotted down while I'd watched the show the previous week. Then as I waited for him to finish his call, the door flew open, and a burly man of about forty-five charged in carrying two styrofoam cups, which I had seen hanging on the outside of Katz's door as I was shown in. They were held together by a piece of string, and on one of them was scrawled "Katz's Hot Line to Moscow."

"Oh, shit," Katz said to whomever he was talking to. "I'll have to call you back."

The new arrival took one of the paper cups, placed it on Katz's head and held the other to his ear. "I'm hearing nothing," he said to me, "not a brain wave." The newcomer wore a yellow shirt and a startling orange tie. I thought at first he was a senior technician on especially good terms with the executive producer until Katz introduced him as Eric Ober, vice-president in charge of public affairs. Katz said: "Stringer's sent us another fucking Brit."

"Let me tell you about this guy," Ober said to me. "This guy needs all the help he can get."

"There may be some truth to that," Katz said slyly.

"You want to look at a tape?" Without waiting for an answer, Ober shoved a three-quarter-inch cassette into a machine behind Katz's desk, and the screen came up with a piece by a consumer reporter talking about car detailing.

When it ended, Ober turned to me.

"What do you think?" he said.

"Of the reporter?"

"He doesn't talk like a Brit," Ober said. "He doesn't talk like Stringer."

Ober dived across Katz's desk and grabbed him in a head-lock. Pointing to a photograph of the two of them on Katz's wall, he said: "Do you know I'm the only friend Katz has at this network?"

"Why don't you fuck off, Eric, and let people do some work around here?" Katz said, smoothing his hair.

"His only friend," Ober said emphatically, opening the door to leave. "His only true friend."

The door closed, and between gulps of his Coke Katz started to tell me what a good guy Eric was. Then the door flew open again, and Ober said: "Howard wants to see us at nine."

Katz threw up his hands.

"This day's already shot," he told me. "I can see the kind of day it's going to be." With a look of serious reassurance, he added: "I don't want you to have to stick around here all morning. Let's get together later in the week. Watch the show, tell me what you think. Come up with some ideas, and before we talk you should come by the control room."

"Okay," I said.

"I mean it's important that you get a sense of this place. I'm sure you've got lots of ideas, but you can end up climbing the walls here. Okay?"

I nodded.

"Come on. I'll walk you out."

The show had just ended, and the narrow corridor outside Katz's office was filling up with technical staff and producers, the latter eager for Katz's opinions about their segments of that morning. Others were clamoring for his approval of whatever they were responsible for the next day. He fought his way through them. "Down! Off! Later! Later!" He steered me out of the newsroom and through the labyrinth of corridors.

As we walked along one corridor barely wide enough for two people, Katz was telling me that the CBS Broadcast Center used to be a milk packing plant. We were passing the "Evening News" newsroom, and he stopped to poke his head inside.

"Look at this place." He spoke quietly. "You wouldn't want to work here. They're all trying to get close to the throne in here. Look at these hound-dog looks."

In the "Evening News" newsroom I watched a few busy people stripping wire copy off printers. They didn't look too happy, so I took Katz at his word.

"This place is a glass house," Katz declared, as we walked on. "The walls have ears. Something's going on here today. I can feel it. I can smell it."

I had no idea then what he was talking about. All I could

smell was coffee and printer's ink. Katz steered me to the lobby, then headed off in the direction of Stringer's office. I walked out into the bright spring morning, thinking I should offer the experience of the past half hour to a job placement program. They could use it as an exercise in preparedness.

By the time I turned up at the "Morning News" control room the following week I had done my homework, learning a bit about its recent history. I knew it was a troubled show, that its ratings had fallen off since Diane Sawyer had left to join "60 Minutes," and that the hiring of Phyllis George had not restored them. Phyllis, from what I understood, was supposed to provide the shot of glamour it was felt the "Morning News" needed. From what I had seen of her she was glamorous all right, but she seemed to be struggling to gain confidence. Perhaps I was being kind. Friends who had been watching the show longer than I thought she was awful.

I had done some homework on Katz, too. I'd learned that he'd been hired by Sauter, who wanted an ideas man, an innovator, someone to enrich the mix. Other people had told me Katz was shrewd and that he played the buffoon to keep people off balance. I gathered he had come up through the ranks at a series of East Coast dailies, with stints at the *Boston Globe,* the *Philadelphia Inquirer,* and the *Washington Post.* A recent article about him in the *Washington Journalism Review* suggested he'd made a real mess of things at the *Dallas Times Herald* before coming to CBS News. In the same article, several of his former print colleagues described him as "disruptive," "divisive," and untrustworthy, though others considered him a brilliant creative force. I decided to bear in mind that these opinions weren't necessarily mutually exclusive.

When I reached the control room that morning, I could

see that Katz was in his element. He strode about the place, rubbing his hands, slapping people on the back, exhorting everyone who could make a difference to "speed this baby up." When he finally noticed me, he said: "Sit here," parking me in his executive producer's chair, while he went off to the studio to give the anchors a pep talk. Seated in his chair, I felt a bit like an imposter who was about to be unmasked at any minute. The entire scene was slightly overwhelming. In front of me was a vast bank of monitors, some with tape fast-forwarding, some in reverse, others stationary. The monitors were labeled with codes—M-I, V-3, L-SAT— codes that were beyond my grasp. "It's coming over the London feed now!" someone called out. A newsclerk burst through the room on his way to the studio with an update for the newsblock (the half-hourly five-minute news summary), while a few steps below me the soundmen argued among themselves about levels. A director called out camera cues. To my left sat a group of operators whose job I gathered was to superimpose printed words on the screen. Behind me a woman in a tight-fitting dress, whom I took to be a producer, was complaining to another man that she couldn't hear what was being said on the main screen. Hers was the only conversation I could understand. Given the decibel level in the room, I wondered how anyone could hear anything. Not that it mattered much to me because most of the conversations around me were being conducted in tongues I found incomprehensible. To my right an insistent voice shouted over a headset: "Kill one, one two! Kill one, one three! Go to one, one four!" I looked at the main monitor and realized that the clock above it commanded obedience to the second. Then the show went into commercial, and I felt slightly relieved to see Katz coming back from the studio.

"Figured it out yet?"

"I could use a little help," I said, trying to be cool.

"Those three monitors on the left. The top one is 'GMA,' the one below is 'Today.' The third one's us."

"That's great," I said. "That's the one part I understood."

A short man with a trim beard next to Katz laughed.

Katz said: "That's all you really need to know around here. Our stuff has to be better than theirs."

"Not always easy," said the man with the trim beard. "I'm David Corvo, by the way."

"You two haven't met?" Katz acted surprised.

"No, Jon, you didn't introduce us," Corvo said dryly. With a glance at the left bank of monitors, he added: "Fuck. 'GMA' has Victoria Principal. That's a nice hit."

Katz whirled around in his chair. "Jane!" he yelled to the far end of the control room. "Jane! Get over here!"

A tall, attractive woman with a mass of dark hair, broke off her conversation and hurried toward him.

"What's the matter, Jon?"

"See who 'GMA' has?"

"I know."

"Well, how come we don't have her?"

"She wouldn't do us, Jon," the woman said sweetly. "We tried and tried, but her agent said she would only be doing 'GMA' as a favor to Hartman. She wasn't even going to do the 'Today' show."

Corvo uttered a short laugh. "What Jane means," he said, "is that not being second is better than not being third."

"Sounds like bullshit to me, Jane," Katz said.

As the woman walked away, he said: "See what I have to put up with."

"Who's Jane?" I asked him.

"Jane Kaplan. One of the bookers. She's been with the show about eight years."

"Bookers book guests?"

"Hey—we're catching on. Next thing you'll be running the place."

"Camera two!" the director called out.

We were watching a discussion about the merits of Reagan's Star Wars program when Corvo suddenly leaped out of his seat.

"That name's misspelled!"

He dashed over to the chyron crew, the people responsible for our fancy computer-generated graphics, and the misspelled name was quickly wiped off the screen.

"No, don't correct it now!" Corvo shouted to the chyron crew as he returned to his seat. "It's too late now. Jeezus Christ!"

"David's in a particularly vicious mood this morning," Katz observed.

A producer came by and needed to talk to Katz. While they conferred I glanced over the legal-size sheet of paper in front of me. In the left-hand column was a list of numbers from 101 to 193. I made the connection between these numbers and the numbers I had heard being called out earlier. Next to this column were various notes such as "Bill, Boston Pops, NAT SOT VO."

"What does this mean?" I asked Corvo.

"It means Kurtis does a news item about the Boston Pops, and when the tape rolls, he'll voice-over (VO) natural sound (NAT). SOT stands for sound-on-tape. See that top monitor —that's for the prompter. That way we can see what Bill's reading."

"Newsblocks and intros."

"Right."

"And are the interviews scripted in any way?" I asked, hoping the question was pertinent.

"They have the questions on cards in their hands."

Corvo gave me a rundown on the bank of monitors. "That one, L-SAT, that's the London satellite. They're feeding on it right now. Those screens are tapes and graphics ready to roll. That one is the monitor for the studio."

He was interrupted. On the studio monitor, twenty feet from where Phyllis George was doing an interview, I could see Kurtis having his makeup touched up.

Katz leaned toward me.

"See the big screen in the middle," he said. "That's going out over the air. If that's black at seven o'clock we're in trouble." The show broke for commercial, and Katz said, "Come on. Let's go down to my office and we can talk."

We walked out past the greenroom to the elevators. As we rode downstairs, I asked him if the screen had ever been black. He told me that during the 1984 Republican convention in San Francisco he had been sitting in a truck shortly before air time when he noticed that there was nothing on his monitor.

"This thing supposed to be like this?" he had asked Corvo, who was a twelve-year veteran of television news.

Corvo leaped three feet into the air.

"So, what happened?" I asked.

"They filled the time in New York with something. I can't remember what it was. Those minutes of dead air are like a free fall. Kind of dreamlike and unreal."

Over the next year, I would come to know what he meant. The screen was never black while I worked at the "Morning News," but there were some close calls. The closest came one night when nearly every airport in the East was fogged in, and the next day's show had counted on about a dozen guests from out of town. By ten that night the bookers were ready to book their mothers.

On the way to his office Katz gave me a tour of the building. He showed me the tape room, the "Evening News" flash studio, installed after Kennedy was shot so that the "Evening News" anchor could go on the air at a moment's notice. Then he showed me the studio where WCBS-TV (the network's New York station) did its local news. It bore a striking resemblance to the "Morning News" set. When I mentioned this, Katz said, "Don't tell Kurtis that. He's been bitching about it for two years."

We reached his office and flicked on the TVs. As we watched the show, we went through my ideas.

"Carl Icahn is trying to take over TWA," I said. "You should interview him."

"Good idea," Katz said. "If we can get him."

"Malcolm Forbes is going to bid for a Fabergé egg at one of the auction houses. If he gets it, he'll own more than the Russians."

"Two for two so far," Katz said.

I started to talk about a piece on towns that were composed entirely of mobile homes when Katz interrupted me, gesturing to economics correspondent Robert Krulwich on the monitor.

"Maybe we should have Krulwich interview Icahn," he said. "Kurtis would toss him softballs, but Krulwich would go after him."

He asked me what I thought of Krulwich. "I think he's the best contributor on the show," I said.

"So do I."

After I'd pitched ideas for another five minutes, Katz cut me off.

"Listen, I think you could work here, but I want to be sure you understand what this place is like. I mean, there's a terror here about taking risks, doing anything new, and I want you to be happy here. I don't want you going back to your office and putting little pins into effigies of Katz."

I couldn't say I wasn't warned.

"Is there a job offer forthcoming?" I asked.

"Yeah, but first I've got to deal with the front office. That's a whole other story."

He reached into his refrigerator for another Coke.

"Remember, don't try to change this business," he said. "You can't change this business, and the people who try don't last."

He gulped his Coke and asked me how much money I wanted.

I named an astronomical figure, and he said, "You greedy fuck, that's more than I make."

We arrived at a ballpark figure, and a week later I met with the contracts lawyer and discovered that in the CBS scheme of things, I was being referred to as talent. I signed a four-year deal to go to work as a producer for the "Morning News."

V.

ASSAULT AT DAWN

"I realize that from the staff's point of view
what was going on at the 'Morning News' must
have seemed like absolute fucking madness."
—Ed Joyce, president of CBS News

On my first morning in the
control room, Katz introduced me to the staff with a sten-
torian announcement. He added, sotto voce, "I don't know
half these people myself." He was then summoned to the
studio, and Roberta Dougherty took charge of me. We went
downstairs to her office, to the booking area known as the
"firetrap," which was home to half a dozen of the show's
bookers, a few tape editors, and Roberta.

Roberta was to explain "packets" to me. She was one of
the show's senior staff, a woman of forty with many of the
mannerisms of a schoolmarm. She had been a teacher before
she had gone to work at "Good Morning America," where
she had risen to head booker. Three years ago she had left
ABC for CBS and had been working at the "Morning News"
ever since.

On the desk in Roberta's minuscule office were two sample "packets." These contained the information that was given to the anchors the night before the show, or if the story was late-breaking, early the next morning.

"What you're trying to achieve," Roberta explained, "is a nice, smooth segment."

"One in which nothing goes wrong," I suggested.

"Hmmmm, well, yes, that too, ideally," Roberta said.

She showed me the first packet, titled "Tornado Aftermath." It consisted of a "super sheet" containing the information for the chyron crew and the graphics people, a second sheet that detailed the transportation arrangements for guests (where they would be picked up, what time they would be on the air), a third sheet that gave all the pertinent background to the segment (this one began with an apology to Kurtis for having to start his day with death and destruction), and a fourth one that contained a list of suggested questions. Attached to these pages were a number of newspaper clippings about the recent tornadoes and their impact.

Roberta scanned the packet critically. She did not seem too pleased with the questions. She looked at the second packet, which dealt with friendship between men.

"Ah, this is more typical," she said. "And it's better. This is a better example of what I mean."

I read the questions. They were not searching. Were men capable of close relationships? Did men need the same things from friendships as women? And so on.

"The only problem with some of these," Roberta said, "is that they elicit one-word answers. It's important to avoid those. When you've seen a few 'yes-no' interviews, you'll know what I mean."

Roberta laughed and I asked her to explain the "Morning News" "system," something Katz had not found time to do. He insisted I'd pick it up soon enough.

"System?" an incredulous voice said from outside Roberta's office. "There is no system."

A younger woman, five feet one and button-cute, stuck her head round the door. "Hi," she said, "I'm Amy Rosenblum. You look like a nice normal person. Why would you want to work here?"

Again I'd been warned.

"I suppose Amy is right," Roberta conceded. "Things are a little chaotic around here since the last reorganization."

"There was a reorganization?" Amy said. "Nobody told me."

She wandered off down the corridor to her office, and David Corvo came by to offer to introduce me to the anchors.

We walked back to the newsroom. The glassed-in area of the room known as the fishbowl was jammed with producers, but the anchors weren't there. We went back again through the confused maze of corridors to the anchors' quarters, and I met Phyllis George in her office.

She was charming and cordial. I had seen her briefly earlier in the newsroom, where she stood in fascinating incongruity to everything that surrounded her. She had a firm handshake and a radiant smile, and she was interested in what I'd done before I came to CBS News. I started to tell her, then she said: "Oh, you'd know. The Hyde Park Hotel in London, is that a good hotel?"

"One of the best," I said, knowing I'd never been able to afford to stay there.

"We're taking the show to London in May," Corvo said. "Phyllis isn't sure they have plumbing in England."

"Oh, David, don't be silly."

Phyllis's secretary appeared to say Phyllis had a phone call.

"Nice meeting you," she said. We left her office, with its

tulips, teddy bears, and Kentucky Derby posters, and went next door to meet Bill Kurtis.

Kurtis was every bit as cordial. Off camera he talked in the same basso profundo that distinguished him on the air. He invited me to sit in the studio the next morning, and said he would explain how things worked between segments. At first meeting, each of the "Morning News" anchors seemed as pleasant a person as one would ever wish to meet, and I was disappointed when Corvo told me they didn't get along.

That day Katz had arranged for me to go out and see how a piece was shot. One of my initial suggestions to him had been a piece on Consumers Union, which was celebrating its fiftieth anniversary. Katz had liked the idea and assigned it, and in the control room earlier he had told me: "You might as well go see how good ideas get screwed up."

So that afternoon the producer and I picked up a car and a crew and drove out to Westchester. I was surprised how little equipment was needed; everything fit neatly in the car trunk. We spent an hour at the Consumers Union laboratory shooting luggage being bashed about on an enormous conveyor and exercise equipment being subjected to various tortures. Then Betsy Ashton, our consumer reporter, showed up and did two interviews. I watched, intrigued, as the cutaways were shot, those sections of interviews where the camera is on the reporter, who must keep still and look as if he or she is listening to the subject answer a question. These were necessary, the producer, Gail Freedman, told me, to disguise our editing of the interviews. Jump cuts, Gail said, weren't allowed on the "Morning News."

"Why not?" I asked.

"Don't ask me," Gail said. "The mucky-mucks decide those sort of things. I don't."

After shooting about an hour of tape for a three-minute piece, we stashed our gear in the trunk and drove back to the city. That evening I watched as the editor cut the stuff into a piece, following Gail's directions. It took several hours, but I soon realized that the process wasn't brain surgery. The rules were basically the same as putting together any other story, only in this case the pictures complemented the words. You didn't need words where pictures could tell the story. It was really quite simple.

So far my only difficulty was finding my way around the CBS Broadcast Center. I rarely went anywhere unescorted.

In the morning I sat in the studio, observing both anchors at work. It was obvious to me that Kurtis came prepared. He was clearly one of the most proficient newsreaders in the business, and whether he was reading the news or doing interviews he conducted himself with effortless grace. Phyllis, on the other hand, flitted between the studio and her dressing room in a state of near panic, often being briefed en route by equally panicky producers. She had no news background and was constantly concerned about her appearance, which seemed to me to be a case of misplaced priorities because if there was one thing Phyllis did not need to worry about, it was how she looked. She was every bit as glamorous as when she achieved celebrity on the beauty queen circuit in 1971, first as Miss Texas, then as Miss America. Since then she had hosted game shows, co-hosted "Candid Camera," squeezed in an eleven-month marriage to movie producer Bob Evans, divorced him, and had married John Y. Brown, Jr., the multi-millionaire former governor of Kentucky, by whom she had two children. I'd been told by a producer at CBS Sports, where Phyllis had previously worked doing sideline interviews during "The NFL Today," that she was fastidious beyond belief about her looks. As I watched her in the studio that morning, I could see nothing had changed. Between segments, there was always a touch of makeup necessary, or a sweep of the brush from Vincent, her hairdresser, who was forever in attendance, and enormous concern over whether her lipstick had smudged.

Toward the end of the show I walked back to the control room, which was separated from the studio by a storage area containing enormous banks of flats and great stacks of equipment that were used for the soaps. I watched the other side of the picture for a while—Mike Whitney, the senior broadcast producer from the overnight shift, talking to the anchors between segments (and sometimes during segments when there was something to be fed by earphone directly into the anchor's ear.) I was still slightly intimidated by the control room, even though it was beginning to make sense to me. It was, after all, a state-of-the-art facility, the same one used by CBS Sports to update the football scores. Katz had assured me, "there's a whole lot in this place you don't need to know," and dismissed about half the monitors with a wave of his hand. I sat next to him for a while, as he circled newspaper articles he thought might be interesting for the next day's show, then shortly before nine o'clock I went downstairs, where, with the aid of a rough map I had drawn up, I found my way to the office that had been assigned to me.

There were two kinds of offices for the "Morning News" staff: humble was one kind, humble and dreadful was the other. Mine belonged to the latter category. John O'Regan, the producer in charge of administration who had assigned it to me, began apologizing even before I saw it. When we reached it, he assured me that he could find worse if pushed to try. The room was windowless, of course, as were all but the management's offices at CBS News, even Rather's. And while the rest of the building might be slightly overheated, there was no danger of any such threat in my office. Cold air descended in an Arctic gust from a vent in the tile ceiling, powered by a fan that sounded as if it were directly behind one wall. With the office door closed I felt as if I'd been sealed inside the engine of a C-5A. The office, however, did have a monitor and a cassette deck, which was not quite the bonus it first seemed to be, because everybody came in to use it.

I was to share the office with one of the coordinating producers, Pat Shevlin. She had been out of the building the previous day, but she turned up that morning shortly after the show ended. She was an attractive, dark-haired woman in her mid-thirties, and someone had already told me that she was married to one of the producers of "Newsbreak."

I introduced myself, and as we talked, I had the feeling I was being inspected as if I were an unknown substance on a park bench. Like most of the staff at the "Morning News," she was apprehensive about me. Gossip ran rampant in the Broadcast Center, and I was rumored to be everything from a spy for Stringer to the next executive producer.

"So you never worked in TV?" Shevlin said.

"No," I said. "I've no basis for comparison."

Shevlin smiled.

"What a place to start," she said, as she went through her mail. "I guess you know what you're getting into."

"When did you start with the show?" I asked.

"Four years and three executive producers ago."

I was getting her drift. I asked her how the broadcast worked, and she explained that the staff was divided into a dayside and nightside shift, with a smaller contingent responsible for bridging the time period from late afternoon until midnight. A conference call took place between the senior members of the two larger shifts at 7:30 P.M.

She began stacking cassettes on a shelf as we talked. When she finished, she pointed up to the air-conditioning vent and said:

"I'm going to try to spend as little time in here as possible."

"Maybe I can block it," I said. "I might as well do something useful while I'm learning."

Shevlin grinned. "Come on," she said. "Lesson one begins in the fishbowl."

The fishbowl was the glassed-in area of the newsroom where the senior staff sat. Shevlin told me it was the best place to learn, and advised me to spend my time there. The other senior producers who sat in the fishbowl were Roberta, Bob Epstein, and Missie Rennie. Bob and Missie were responsible for the hour-by-hour assembling of the next day's broadcast, and I had met both of them the day before.

Missie had worked at CBS for twelve years, and for much of that time she had been assigned to the "Morning News." I gathered she was a wealthy woman, sufficiently wealthy that some producers questioned her sanity for holding a job in a newsroom. But clearly she was enthusiastic about her work and paid great attention to detail. It seemed to me she went everywhere with a yellow pad, on which she made interminable lists. With her fast stride, she scuttled about the "Morning News" area like Hattie Rabbit, reminding everyone of their derelictions.

When Shevlin and I arrived in the fishbowl, Missie was in the newsroom, chasing down a booker. At this time of the day, around 9:30 A.M., there was a general congregating in the newsroom and fishbowl, with a vast assortment of moods and tempers on display, depending upon how individual segments had fared. Epstein was in the fishbowl, rapping out the show's lineup on his computer terminal. Periodically he bounced around the room, tearing off wire copy and distributing it to bookers. He was an energetic man in his early thirties, with a full black beard. Efficient and authoritative, his aim was to get as many segments on the air as possible. To Bob, nothing was worth more than three minutes of air time. He was very much a child of TV, having started work at WBBM in Chicago right after college, and he spoke TV jargon almost as a second language.

I had noticed the day before that he had enormous lung power. It was all too evident this morning.

"Janice!" he yelled. *"Janice!"*

The full-throated summons could be heard in the "Evening News" area forty feet and two corridors away, but Janice, engaged in a conversation in the middle of the newsroom, seemed blissfully unconcerned. She was one of the bookers.

"Janice!" Epstein tried again.

"What?"

"Have you called Steinbrenner?"

The previous evening, only a few weeks into the baseball season, George Steinbrenner, the owner of the New York Yankees, had fired manager Yogi Berra.

Janice laughed.

"No, Bob, of course I haven't tried him," she said sarcastically. "I mean, do you honestly think I'd not call . . ."

"Never mind . . . just checking."

"He wouldn't do us anyway," Janice went on. "He only does us when he wants something. You know how it is with him."

Janice was the sports booker. She had great contacts in sports. She was also a very pretty woman, which certainly helped her cause.

"Okay, never mind."

Epstein didn't have time for explanations. He went on typing out his pre-lineup. The process of booking guests began long before the morning preceding the broadcast. It was the futures unit's task to line up interview guests for soft features and for news events that could be anticipated. A list of upcoming events was compiled by a researcher, then the senior staff would meet and decide what could and should be booked ahead of time. These assignments were then given to the bookers who would beg, cajole, and solicit guests either directly or through their press agents. The bookers' main equipment was their book or Rolodex, with its valuable home phone numbers and contacts. When a booking was firm, it was placed on a grid to which the senior staff could refer. On any morning we hoped to have seven of the next day's show's ten segments booked; the balance would be made up with news stories. Shevlin and I spent a half hour scanning the newspapers looking for these until the booming voice of Jon Katz announced from the corridor that it was time to meet.

We trooped down to his office. I had been to the morning meeting the day before and realized it was not a formal affair, certainly not with Katz running it. What with the general mingling in the newsroom and the fishbowl, a lot was decided almost inexplicably among the senior staff beforehand. The rough-hewn mass of a show was then submitted to either Katz or Corvo for his approval, and throughout the day, as the broadcast fluctuated, they would pay periodic visits to the fishbowl to deal with problems as they arose.

By now it was ten o'clock, but this morning Katz wanted to play. First we had to decide who would be the most neurotic booker on the upcoming London trip. There were many candidates. Then there was another time-out while Katz tried to figure out whether Missie Rennie's knee socks were the height of fashion or passé. Finally, after Katz had expressed his amazement at the number of Gucci bags associate producers' salaries seemed to be supporting at the "Morning News," we talked about tomorrow's broadcast.

"So what we got?" he asked Epstein.

Epstein ran down the lineup.

Katz threw out Charlton Heston immediately because he hated Charlton Heston. His decisions about what went into the show were often arbitrary, especially on light news days.

"What about a change of pace?" he suggested. "Can't we have a summer travel package? We've been doing so many Washington stories lately with all the Bitburg stuff. I think the country's getting tired of it."

"A summer travel package?" Shevlin said, with mild contempt.

Pat was very much in favor of hard news.

"Yeah, why not?"

"It's kind of early," Shevlin said.

"People are making plans."

Katz was dead set on a summer travel package, so we would be doing a summer travel package at 8:10. Pat Collins had a movie review, Phyllis would talk to college coach Jim Valvano about the NCAA basketball playoffs, and Krulwich had a funny piece he'd been working on about a minor scam he'd called "Bakergate."

"How weird is it?" Katz wanted to know.

"Pretty weird," Shevlin said.

Katz decided he'd better see it, though he generally had no problem with what Krulwich wanted to do.

"What about news?" Katz said. "What's the cover?"

Roberta said she felt we should definitely do something on the administration's reported plan to announce a trade embargo with Nicaragua.

"Maybe we should have a press panel," Katz said.

His suggestion was met with silence. I gathered Katz loved press panels, a group of newspaper editors debating an issue, but his senior staff hated them. Katz also loved what he called town meetings, two rows of citizens on bleachers, talking about the major issue of the day. The more argument the better.

"We-ell," Roberta began. "What about Lugar?"

Shevlin clapped her hand to her mouth. It was clear to me that Roberta, unlike the rest of the "Morning News" senior staff, did not know how Katz felt about Senator Richard Lugar.

Katz was picking his head up from his desk.

"Jeezus, Roberta, you want to put us all to sleep. You want to turn the broadcast into a total snore. That's the worse goo-goo suggestion I've heard in a week."

For the next five minutes Katz patiently explained to Roberta that he considered the head of the Senate Foreign Relations Committee dumb, a bore, untelegenic. Lugar was banned from the broadcast, as were all Katz's other "goo-goos," a list that included Ralph Nader and any ACLU types who might spout reformist ideas or protest on the side of righteousness.

"Can I make a suggestion?" Shevlin said, and she proceeded to offer an idea for a story. She had heard that a Pittsburgh hospital, in return for substantial endowments, was apparently giving wealthy foreigners in need of organ transplants preference over Americans.

"Gee," I said, "that sounds great."

I thought Katz would go for it, but for some reason he didn't.

Pat kept fighting. "It's a great story," she insisted.

"Why haven't I read about this?" someone said, which confirmed one of my suspicions about television news, namely that nobody listened to the word off the street.

Finally, another of the coordinating producers, Rand Morrison, said: "Well, I mean, it's not like foreigners aren't human too."

"Couldn't we send Arnot to do a piece?" Shevlin persisted. (Dr. Robert Arnot was the show's medical correspondent.)

"No," she was told, and so the next day Dr. Arnot demonstrated an exercise machine instead.

Katz looked over his lineup.

"We're weak in the seven-thirty half hour," he said. "Steinbrenner won't talk, eh?"

"No way," he was told.

In the end Katz opted for a story on stun guns, and the senior staff of the "Morning News" agreed it would try to come up with a politician who was neither dumb, nor a bore, nor untelegenic, who knew something about the administration's policy on Nicaragua, and, most importantly, was acceptable to Jon Katz. There was still one hole in the broadcast, but that would be filled with a news story.

Back in the fishbowl the senior staff went about setting up the broadcast. I read wire copy and tried to learn what everyone did. I could see why Missie kept lists. It was hard to keep track of who was doing what, which segments had tape setups, where each guest would originate from, how long each segment would be. All this information was gradually added to the lineup during the day, and would be turned over to another coordinating producer in the late afternoon or early evening.

The phones rang constantly throughout the day. Segments were discussed ad nauseam. Cassettes piled up in the fishbowl, got lost, and were recovered. Periodically piles of them fell to the floor, where everyone ignored them.

Around lunchtime Shevlin turned up a news story that necessitated broadcasting out of Cleveland.

"Cleveland's expensive," Epstein warned her. He was out of his seat, yelling across the newsroom.

"Kevin!"

"What?"

"Is there a cheap uplink anywhere near Cleveland?"

"No."

I had made it my goal to absorb a definition of every new term I heard him utter, even if it meant maximum exposure of my novice status.

"What's an uplink?" I asked.

"What's an uplink?" Epstein and Shevlin were in hysterics.

"An uplink gets you up to a bird," Epstein said. "You know what a bird is?"

"A satellite," I guessed.

"Right," they chorused.

Epstein even drew me a picture of an uplink. Three months later I still had not seen an uplink for real, but I knew what they did. And I knew there weren't any cheap ones in Cleveland, or Las Vegas, or half a dozen other cities where it was prohibitively expensive to originate from. But as Katz said: "There were certain things you needed to know, and certain things you didn't."

"I need a glossary," I told Shevlin. "I could use one for these bookers' names too."

I had slowly begun to match names to faces of the bookers. My immediate favorites were Amy, Jude, Janice, and Jane. Part of Epstein's job, which I was learning from him, was to match bookers with projects. You couldn't give Janice anything on politics because Janice didn't know much about politics, and if you stuck her with something she only half-understood, she would drive you crazy all day. You could give her sports, though, because Janice knew a lot about sports, but if Janice wasn't available and a sports story came up, you couldn't give it to Jude because Jude didn't know anything about sports, and she would then spend the next hour telling you that she didn't know anything about sports, by which time the story was probably old. You could give Jane anything related to entertainment because this was what she did best, but you had to be careful with Jane. When Jane said: "Do you want Robert Duvall?" you could not take it for granted that Jane could deliver Robert Duvall. Corvo made this mistake later that afternoon, and a half hour went by before he realized that the gaping hole that had opened up in the 7:30 half hour hadn't been filled with a Robert Duvall interview, the kind of segment Katz wanted.

"No, I meant, if I could *get* Robert Duvall, would you want him?" Jane explained patiently. "That's what I meant when I said, 'Do you *want* him?'"

"Well, of course we fucking would!" Corvo exploded, exasperated. "Jeezus Christ!"

When Jane had gone, Amy said, "Well, does she have him? Does she have Robert DeNiro?"

"Duvall," Epstein said.

"I know," Amy said with a giggle, waving him off.

"Put him on our wish list, too," Corvo said, and left the room.

"David's upset," Amy observed. She dropped a half-completed packet on my desk and asked me to help her with her questions. Her stratagems for securing guests were legendary, but she had a harder time putting together packets for the anchors. Most days around four o'clock she came to the fishbowl, gave one of the senior staff a quiet nudge, and asked for help with her questions.

"I'm good at getting guests," she said. "Questions I have a hard time with. You think it's easy getting guests. It isn't so easy."

I was to find out what she meant soon enough.

It was my second week and I had gone home around seven-thirty, pleased that I had booked Carl Icahn myself, a coup. After a thirteen-hour day I was stretched out on the couch when the phone rang. It was Rand Morrison, the four-to-midnight coordinating producer, and he had some bad news.

"Carl Icahn just canceled."

"He did *what?*"

Icahn was the cover story for the next day, and I'd been assured the booking was solid.

"His PR man called," Rand said gravely. "He said he can't do it. He didn't say why."

I had visions of the black screen Katz had painted for me.

"So what do we do now?" I said, feeling helpless and slightly guilty, though it was no fault of mine.

"See if you can get him back," Rand said resignedly. "In the meantime, we'll try and work up something else."

I went back to the Broadcast Center to find the fishbowl in a mad scramble. Rand was on the phone to London, talking to the booker there about trying to put together a South Africa cover story. This was about all the major news there was, and whatever we led with in the morning had to be of some importance. We had counted on Icahn. The trouble with trying to get a story from South Africa was that it was 3:00 A.M. in South Africa, and it would be another five hours at least before we could be certain of a guest.

While Morrison and another producer worked the phones, I called Icahn's PR man. He explained that Icahn's lawyer had advised him not to do any television interviews until after he had testified before Congress, which he was due to do at ten the next morning. It was a matter of form.

"Form!" I protested vehemently. "There's a lack of form in our broadcast tomorrow, an eight-minute hole, in fact!"

I insisted that the PR man give me Icahn's hotel phone number in Washington, and reluctantly he did. When I called Icahn, he was out to dinner.

Two hours later I succeeded in reaching him. I patiently explained the problems he was causing us, and the prominence we intended to give to the interview, his first ever on network television. He repeated what his PR man had said —that he had to follow his lawyer's advice. I told him that half a dozen people were going to be scrambling throughout the night to fill the gap he had created, but he wouldn't budge.

"I've got six hundred million dollars riding on this deal," he said. "I can't do it."

"Six hundred million!" I exclaimed. "What's that compared to my ass?"

Icahn laughed.

"I know you guys," he said. "You'll pull something out."

I left the broadcast center only after I extracted a promise from the overnight staff that they would call me at home when they had a segment. They did. At 4:00 A.M.

The next morning when I walked into the building, the first person I ran into was Amy. She asked me how the Icahn interview had gone.

"You should watch the show," I said.

"Well, how was it?"

"He canceled."

"He canceled?"

"Yes, at eight o'clock."

Amy thought this was highly amusing. Her laughter echoed down the corridors of the building, and she told everyone: "His first guest canceled. His first guest!"

"Now he's a booker," Janice agreed. "Now he knows what it feels like."

I took a lot of teasing that day about the cancellation. And even though Icahn had promised me that when he started giving interviews he would give his first one to the "Morning News," he did not do us the next day, nor even the next month. Six months later, at a time that suited him, he gave us his first network interview.

"I guess there is honor among greenmailers after all," Rand said at the time, recalling the crazed evening.

By then I was an old hand. We shot the interview at his office to make sure he wasn't going to bolt again.

———

In some fields of work the process of initiation is a slow one. Time spent on the perimeter makes the learning process all the more sublime, like college days with their easy inconsequence. Eventually, months or even years down the line, it comes almost as a surprise to discover that the apprenticeship is over, that one is a novice no longer.

I had no such introduction to the "Morning News." I took the crash course. "I want you to get dirty right away," Katz said, and I did.

My official title was planning editor. It was the title Katz had held when he first came to the "Morning News," and which he had bestowed on me like a mantle. Nobody took it literally. To be in charge of planning at the "Morning News" would be like being in charge of dust control at a rodeo. When I started at the show, the staff numbered 150. A year later, when it was down to 120, it was no less unwieldy. I don't mean to suggest that the show was overstaffed—far from it. A live, two-hour, five-day-a-week news broadcast is like a giant animal that must eat constantly to maintain its weight. The "Morning News" devoured people and stories and was always hungry for more. When I say it was unwieldy, I mean it was a difficult place to manage. Katz's solution was not to systematize at all, but to fly by the seat of his pants and try to carry the unruly mass along on a wave of enthusiasm.

I was being groomed to take charge of booking, and I did what was expected of me while my education went on. I came up with ideas, handed out assignments to the bookers, read their packets, and did my part in getting the show on the air every day. When I had a spare moment, I did a little planning. The pace was frantic. People had little time for extended cordiality, and it didn't take a big story for a crisis to occur. In fact crises occurred mainly when there wasn't a big story, and it was six o'clock in the evening, and there were still two holes to fill.

Working at the "Morning News" quickly developed several attributes I hadn't known I possessed. The first was an ability to compress a whole series of instructions into a declarative sentence or two, while at the same time conducting three separate and unrelated conversations on the phone. Second was a capacity for infinite hope because no matter how hard everybody worked, the ratings never budged. Third was being able to convince my body that the over-the-counter drug market and an ample supply of caffeine could sustain it over a fourteen-hour day for weeks at a stretch.

The hours were brutal. The day began at 6:00 A.M. and rarely ended before 8:00 P.M., and there were always phone calls at home in the evenings, and on weekends, and in the middle of the night. After my first few weeks I was given a beeper. My wife hated it, and I could never leave it lying around the apartment for fear she would test its durability with her heel.

But after a while I got used to the hours. The alarm would go off at six. By six-thirty I would have showered and read one newspaper. I would read another in the cab on the way to the broadcast center. I'd arrive just before seven and watch the show in the control room, which continued to hold its initial fascination for me. During those first few weeks I got to book and produce a few segments, and discovered that strange tension that every live producer experiences: praying the thing goes well, knowing you've done a good job but knowing also that you can't control what the guest says or does.

Rarely did a show begin without a premonition that something would go wrong, and usually something did. A line would go down, or we'd lose audio, or a guest would be a total bore or, worse, completely out of it. David Carradine was our biggest dud—he was in a hostile and obnoxious mood when Jane Kaplan picked him up in the lobby of the Parker Meridien—and we still, to our subsequent regret, put him on the air (because the show, as I learned to my disbelief, had no backup piece in its bank). Other times guests would go off on strange tangents, as TV actress Phylicia Ayers Rashad did, insisting she owed it all to God, and wanting to talk about little else. Meanwhile the anchor began to turn green, and the booker in the control room went white. Or worse still, one of the guests would be late. Then segments would have to switched, messing up Katz's nicely drawn plans for a well-paced broadcast. Instead of being able to pick up the show's pace at a crucial moment with an appearance, say, by rock star Phil Collins, we would get stuck with two doctors talking about strokes. Katz would drop his head in his hands and within seconds the phone in front of him would ring, and he would pick it up, knowing it was probably Joyce or Stringer.

By nine o'clock, when the show ended, most of us were emotionally drained. That's when preparations for the next day began. The staff would move from the control room down to the fishbowl, where the first order of business would be the second-guessing. When I first started at the "Morning News," I didn't take the second-guessing seriously because I didn't fully appreciate how seriously television people took themselves. To me, it seemed that the reticence of one celebrity on the "Morning News" was rather a minor matter in the total scheme of things. But in television news a mistake or an embarrassment on the air is the real-world equivalent of a nuclear accident. So by 9:30 A.M. at the "Morning News," when the twenty minutes of morning TV that most people had watched was a vague memory to most of them, producers' errors were being scrutinized and blame duly apportioned. Consequently, when the senior staff trooped into the fishbowl to read the papers and suggest story ideas, there were always a few bookers missing.

In one respect this was just as well because the fishbowl was, if not the nerve center of the "Morning News," at least the place where the hour-by-hour decisions were made, and it was always a mob scene. I took some notes on the fishbowl one morning, after an unexceptional broadcast, on what was a fairly typical day, if ever there was such a thing at the "Morning News." Epstein was on the phone, talking so loudly that another decibel would have rendered the instrument superfluous. Across the desk Missie Rennie was making some social plans and trying to get her pearls repaired. Two calls for her from the Washington bureau were on hold. Rand Morrison was hearing out a complicated explanation from Robert Krulwich about why the Saudis were screwing their OPEC partners. Pat Shevlin, with whom I was by then good friends, was looking up the sterling exchange rate in anticipation of the trip to London. Above Epstein's head three TVs were on. One carried Donahue, another Regis Philbin, the third the feed of the last hour of the "Morning News." Regis was cooking, Donahue was taking off his tie to cheers, and we had Phyllis talking to an Episcopal minister about euthanasia. In an hour or so two of these screens would carry the silent, flickering images of the soaps, while the third would be tuned to CNN News. But now the volume on all three was turned up.

Behind the three TVs was a large blown-up picture of a view of several empty lots, beyond which lay the Hudson River. In the chaos of the fishbowl, with its filthy couch, its spilled coffee cups, the constant emptying of trash baskets containing dumped wire copy, and the periodic crashes of piled cassettes, it had never occurred to me until then to inquire why the room, so short of space, contained this huge photo. I asked Shevlin. She said it was the legacy of a former executive producer, who, when he had taken over the

"Morning News" and was moved into the Broadcast Center, had missed his old view, and decided to bring it with him.

I understood. His notion made sense to me.

I went back to taking notes. At the time, the fishbowl, an area about twelve by fifteen feet, contained four desks, four chairs, three shelves of tapes, a seven-foot couch of indeterminate color on which were strewn roughly three dozen cassettes, five filing cabinets, and five banks of phones each containing twenty lines, about eight of which were lit, while another three were going unanswered by the clerks in the newsroom. The people in the room numbered fifteen —five members of the senior staff, six bookers, the show's director, one correspondent and his producer, and the man emptying the trash. There were *sixteen* people if you counted the poor anonymous clerk from the "Evening News," who had the unenviable task of trying to track down one particular cassette. He was standing in the doorway, trying to figure out which of the inmates he should talk to; while he hesitated he had been elbowed three times and heard one "sorry."

Immediately outside the fishbowl, in a non-glassed-in area roughly the same size, about a dozen of the show's technical staff—sound men, graphics people, and assistant directors —were raising another ruckus. I estimated that a good 30 percent of the noise inside the fishbowl was generated by the TVs, about 40 percent by the six bookers, who wanted praise or reassurance that their segments that day were fine, about 10 percent by leakage from outside, and the balance by Epstein himself. The loudest bookers were Janice, who had to tell you chapter and verse about her every segment, and Amy, who, as Katz said, had either received too little or too much attention as a child—he could never decide which.

Among the snatches of conversation recorded that morning were the following:

"So was it fun?"

"Where's the Style section?"

"Who gets the regular? No, mine's the black. I like my coffee like I like my women—hot and black."

"Nice shoes!"

"You're really disgusting, Eric."

"Did you see the story on virginity in last Sunday's *Times*?"

Then, over the heads of everyone in the room, Janice yelling and pointing frantically to the CBS monitor: "Oh, this is the part! Rand, turn up the TV, I want to hear this!"

"Don't you think it's loud enough?"

Phyllis, on the monitor: "Well, being from Denton, Texas, I really find that hard to believe . . ."

Epstein: *"Janice! Turn that fucking thing down!"* He stood up, a ruler in hand, and with practised aim knocked the volume control lower. He fell back into his chair, and yelled: "KEVIN!"

No answer.

"Kevin!"

From outside the room: "WHAT?"

"How much does it cost to come out of San Antonio?"

"I'll look it up."

Krulwich: "So if the Saudis were to pump all the oil they could pump, these other countries would be . . ."

"Fucked?"

"I guess so . . ."

Amy: "Our viewers care about Arabs . . ."

"Hey, don't take my Life section."

"You know Jude's still trying for Sheik Yamani—you know that, don't you?"

"No, I didn't know that. Nobody told me that. Well, do you still want this?"

"Well, we don't know about the Yamani thing. Ask Bob. Bob? Oh, he's still on the phone."

Janice: "By the way, are we covering the Masters golf tournament this year?"

Amy: "You think you're going to get an answer in here? You're crazy."

"Bob's getting mad."

Amy, ripping open her paycheck envelope, and announcing to all within the room: "I don't get paid enough to work here!" She tossed the deduction slip into the cassette bin.

Rand: "Amy, that's not trash."

Amy: "Now it is." Looking up at the ABC monitor: "Hey, that woman on Regis looks like my Aunt Betty."

"Where is Shirley, by the way? Shirley in yet?"

"Course not, it's only nine-thirty."

"Quiiieeetttt!"

"Shhhh, Bob's on the phone to London."

"No—Philadelphia. It's Philadelphia."

Shevlin: "I'm on with London. Who needs to talk to London?"

"No, I was saying, 'Bob's on the phone.' I only thought it was to London. He can't hear."

"Jeeeezus Christ! Can someone close that door?"

Amy: "Bob's getting his period."

Crash!!!!

"Pick 'em up."

"Oh leave 'em. They'll only fall again. I never understood why they stack cassettes in here anyway."

"Are we updating?"

"Course we are. Didn't you watch the show? You ought to watch the show."

"Jude's in a house in Fire Island?"

"So, if we're going to do the Saudi oil thing, I want to use piles of dollars . . . fake dollars, of course."

"Is that legal?"

"What the hell?"

"What's that smell?"

"No, I said, 'What the hell?' "

"It's my breakfast."

"Oh."

"Hey. Guess what? Appollonia's going to be on 'Dynasty'!"

Chorus: *"Book her!"*

I put away my notebook and went to find out what the "Evening News" clerk was looking for.

He was looking for a show cassette that contained a guest they wanted for a fifteen-second bite on the "Evening News." I knew all about the guest, and it was easier for me to walk over to the "Evening News" and give them the information from the packet than to try to find the cassette. The "Morning News" area was forty feet from the "CBS Evening News" newsroom, even closer to Rather's exalted throne.

I left the newsroom and walked across the hall. Here the mood was much more intense than at the "Morning News" —we were second-class citizens and they treated us as such. Off and on during the day, one of the show's staff, usually Epstein, would have to go over to the "Evening News" to confer with the foreign desk, which tended to keep little secrets from us. But although there was overlap between the broadcasts, most of the time we were not in the same business. The "Morning News" was about 30 percent news, 20 percent contributors, and 50 percent guests.

Along the corridor outside the "Evening News," I ran into Stringer.

"How's it going?" he inquired. When I told him everything was going fine, he asked: "Did Katz share the latest audience research with you yet?"

"Not yet."

"Well, it's interesting," Stringer went on. "Your audience is even more female than we realized."

We walked down the "Evening News" corridor, and Stringer outlined the new information. I already knew that within the first hour of the broadcast the number of men watching declined precipitously. So usually, after the middle of the second half hour, by which time we had done the serious stuff, the broadcast would be watered down. The 7:45 segment was considered a kind of pivot because at this point the men went out the door en masse. "But by eight-thirty," Stringer explained, "the number of men watching is even more minuscule than we thought. So it's important to persuade the ladies to stay tuned rather than switch to the others."

I wasn't sure what more we could do. After 7:45 we already supplied a steady diet of consumer tips and movie reviews, and in the 7:30 and 8:30 half hours, which were the rated ones, we usually featured a celebrity. The other shows did the same, of course. Nothing on morning TV shows happens by accident, except mistakes.

I left Stringer at the front corridor and made my way back to the "Morning News" fishbowl. The bookers had cleared out, and most of the overnight staff had left. With the door closed, the room was quieter. Roberta was on the phone to Washington, in search of a political guest to talk about the President's trip to Europe. As she was talking to the Washington booker, Missie said:

"What about Brzezinski?"

"We-ell." Roberta thought about this. "We-ell, you know the trouble with Brzezinski. He won't do it unless he has five minutes all to himself."

"We let Brzezinski dictate to CBS News?" I asked.

Roberta glared at me. She had good contacts with Brzezinski. I was still new to CBS, and didn't realize the force of such remarks.

"What about Kissinger?" Missie suggested.

I groaned. If there was one thing that galled me at the "Morning News," it was our habit of revalidating the people whom the American public had had the good sense to wheel off the political stage.

But Roberta had even closer contacts with Kissinger's office.

"Good idea," she said, and was on the phone immediately. She reached Kissinger's secretary, and said: "This is Roberta Dougherty from 'CBS Morning News.' In regard to the President's trip to Europe, we wandered if Dr. Kissinger would be prepared to join us on the broadcast tomorrow to talk about this."

I cringed.

"Yes," Roberta went on, "yes, the person we'd like to invite him to talk to is Bill Kurtis."

Everybody in the fishbowl grinned. Roberta was making the safe assumption that Katz would never allow Phyllis to interview Kissinger. In the past, Phyllis's interviews with politicians had bordered on disaster.

"Oh, dear," Roberta was saying now. "That's too bad. Well, thank you anyway."

Kissinger's schedule would not permit him to make himself available tomorrow morning to "join us."

"Thank God," I said.

"Well, I still like my Pittsburgh hospital story," Shevlin announced, folding the newspaper.

"I didn't hear," Roberta said as she hung up the phone. "Which story is this?"

"Never mind," Pat said.

It was already ten-fifteen. The senior staff's morning meeting with Katz was supposed to start at ten.

"Has anybody buzzed Katz?" Shevlin inquired.

"I did," Epstein said. "He's in his office with the door closed."

"Counting his ginger ales," I said.

Epstein didn't laugh. He seemed to have been in a funk all morning.

Through the fishbowl glass I watched Phyllis sweep through the newsroom, her two full-time assistants in tow —Phyllis rarely went anywhere alone. She looked stunning in a bright red dress, and when she reached the fishbowl she said she was just dropping by because she wanted to run some ideas by us. This statement made everybody nervous.

"I would have run them by Jon," Phyllis said sweetly, "but I can't find that boy."

"He's in his office, with the door closed." Epstein said.

"Well, let me run them by you anyway . . ."

Everyone dutifully listened. Phyllis had in mind another series of taped interviews like her Women of Influence series, only this time the subjects would be famous couples. The other women in the fishbowl, who often seemed uncomfortable in Phyllis's presence, groped for some degree of unison, and finally said it sounded like a good idea.

Phyllis beamed. "I mean everybody's interested in couples," she said. "So what do we have for tomorrow—oh, by the way, the Barbara Walters piece is ready."

"Oh, wonderful," Missie said, adding with a breathy laugh, "I don't really know what we have tomorrow because we haven't had our meeting yet."

"Katz will want to see the Walters tape," Epstein said. "If he ever comes out of there."

"I'll go rouse him," I volunteered. "He said he wanted to see me anyway."

I walked down the narrow corridor and knocked on Katz's door. When I was called in, he said: "Sit down. Gimme a cigarette."

I gave him one. He drew on it heavily and coughed.

"Give it up," I said.

He shook his head. "I just had a very strange experience," he said.

He had the look of a man who had just balanced his checkbook without quite knowing how he had done it.

"One of the production assistants, you know the one, big brown eyes, was just in here. She says: 'Jon, I'll do *anything* to be a producer.' "

Katz was looking perturbed.

"Well, I mean, that's never happened to me before. I mean, in newspapers it never happened. I'm telling you this is a weird business."

I stifled a laugh.

"And since you're so sensitive," Katz went on, "I may as well tell you I'm leaving you here when we go to London. You and Epstein. Somebody's got to be here."

"I don't mind," I said. "I lived five years in London. Does Bob know?"

"I told him last night."

"That accounts for his wonderful mood this morning. By the way, Phyllis wants to see you in the fishbowl."

"Phyllis is in the fishbowl? Well, why didn't you tell me? You know nothing's getting done in there."

He took down a big, club-like softball bat from his shelf and headed out of the room.

"Phyllis!"

Katz always greeted her with a roar, as if he could knock her off guard with sheer ebullience. She was sitting on the couch, still talking about Barbara Walters. The taped interview had been screened.

"Well, Jon, you're here finally, and too late," she said.

"Too late for what?"

"Jon," Phyllis said in her sweetest voice. "Don't you know it's rude to keep a lady waiting?"

"He's been doing that for the past hour," I said, unable to resist.

Katz took a swat at me with the bat.

"Gee, Phyllis," he said. "I've been telling the press how great you are."

"Took you this long? Was I that good?"

At some moments you had to love Phyllis.

Katz said: "So what have I missed?"

"Here." Phyllis handed him the tape. "I've got some work to do. Take a look at this. Bye, you all."

"Well, hi, kiddies," Katz said to the rest of the senior staff. "Are we all just brimming over with wonderful ideas this morning?"

"Oh, we were just saying," Pat Shevlin said, "how we could hardly wait for Katz to get here so we could unburden ourselves of these wonderful ideas."

"And are we all looking forward to London?"

"Some of us are," Epstein reminded him.

"Ah, Epstein! Trying to lay a guilt trip on me. Hey, Epstein, that kid of yours recovered yet?" Katz was convinced that Epstein, who had a two-year-old daughter, was the ultimate overprotective father.

"She's fine."

"Every time the kid sneezes," Katz told the rest of us, "Epstein pitches into *Gray's Anatomy* and comes up with a syndrome. What was it last week? Stomach blockage? How's the kid's stomach blockage, Epstein? She still suffering?"

"It went away," Epstein conceded. "It was gas."

"Gas!" Katz was being merciless. "How many man-hours did this broadcast lose, Epstein, because your kid had to burp?"

Epstein was saved by the urgent bell on his computer.

"So how is this?" Katz asked, waving Phyllis's Barbara Walters cassette.

Everyone said it was fine.

"So let's meet," Katz said, and the senior staff of the "Morning News" trooped down to his office.

VI.

THE HUG

"Did you hear there's a job opening for anchor of the CBS 'Morning News'? Applications can be picked up at the post office."
                                        —David Letterman

By the time the "Morning News" took its broadcast to London in May 1985, I knew a lot more about the history of the program than when I had first set foot in Howard Stringer's office. I also knew a lot more about Jon Katz. He did have a lot of ideas, and I could see how this would impress Sauter, who had the reputation of being receptive to new ideas. But Katz had not learned much about the technical side of television in his three years with the broadcast, and everyone who worked for him considered this a major drawback. He claimed he had never had the time, but he had had plenty of time for politics, and they weren't the kind we were covering in the broadcasts.

A year after Sauter had hired Katz as news planner, Sauter had told the *Washington Journalism Review*: "Any time you hire an outsider in a fairly visible way, it's a gamble." By 1983 Katz was managing editor of the broadcast, and for him it seemed the gamble of going from print to TV was about to pay off. Katz had begun undermining George Merlis almost as soon as he came to the "Morning News." He had

Sauter's ear, and Merlis was allowing himself to be steamrollered. Before long Katz was drawing up lists of people he thought should be fired from the program and was showing these to Sauter. By the spring of 1983 George Merlis was gone, in part due to Katz. But Sauter did not pick Katz to replace Merlis—Katz would have to bide his time for a year. The man Sauter chose as Merlis's replacement was Bob Ferrante.

Ferrante had been running the CBS nighttime program "Nightwatch." He had known Sauter since 1968, when Ferrante was news director at WBBM and Sauter was just a pup. Ferrante had done a good job running "Nightwatch" with virtually no budget. Now, as his reward, he was being handed the "Morning News." He was a forceful, opinionated man, and it did not take him long to restore morale in the wake of George Merlis's departure. During his second week as executive producer, the "CBS Morning News" ratings rose to their highest ever—4.2, surpassing "Today." The champagne corks flew, and Ferrante claimed credit, even if it was Merlis who had laid the groundwork.

But whatever had worked for Merlis, it did not stop Ferrante from changing the program. Like any executive producer, he felt obliged to put his stamp on the broadcast. He increased the number of segments and speeded up the show. He intended to build it into what he called the "unauthorized news."

To this end he made use of Katz and a former editor from the *Minneapolis Star,* Steve Isaacs. Both were loud, abrasive, heavyset men with a taste for offbeat stories. They sat side by side in the newsroom and referred to themselves as five hundred pounds of bullshit. Ferrante, in effect, delegated the day-to-day running of the broadcast to them, while he continued to tinker with what he considered the finer points—for example, persuading entertainment reporter Pat Collins to be more critical. (Collins had a tendency to like everything.) For a while everything at the "Morning News" looked rosy for Ferrante. But then a change was made in the CBS News management structure that was to increase tension throughout the news division as a whole. In September 1983, Sauter fulfilled his cherished ambition of moving up the corporate ladder to Black Rock, where he was installed as executive vice-president of the CBS Broadcast Group. In his place, Ed Joyce was named president of CBS News, with Stringer as Joyce's deputy.

And so began an era within an era at CBS News, an era dominated by Joyce's rather grim personality. According to Robert Chandler, a former vice-president of CBS News, Jankowski, the head of the Broadcast Group, had designated Joyce to be the "tough guy" when Joyce and Sauter were appointed. "It was the height of the raiding season," Chandler says, "when the networks were going after each other's news talent. And Jankowski made it clear in a speech to us that Joyce's job would be to deal with contract escalation problems and to hold down costs in general."

By the time Joyce took over as news president he had already proved himself tough. Some network staffers thought he enjoyed the role. He was from local TV, and it was felt by many that he harbored a deep and abiding resentment toward network news people. But it would be another eighteen months before Joyce would take a swipe at the "Evening News." When he made his first cuts, it was not the "Evening News" that suffered. The blood lay on the floors of the other newsrooms, including the "Morning News." Ferrante was told to cut costs, and a round of firings ensued. If Ferrante was finding it painful to make sacrifices while the "Evening News" was spared, so were the staff. Most of them were already working fourteen-hour days, and now they were being told to work harder.

In fact, the "Evening News'" seemingly insatiable demand for resources and the feeding of Rather's ego were becoming an increasing source of bitterness at the "Morning News." Whenever Ferrante landed a major scoop, such as the exclusive interview he obtained with Margaret Thatcher, he was told by Joyce, "That goes to Dan." Joyce knew whom he had to please, and at that time he wasn't taking any chances. But the bitterness began to manifest itself. One day Steve Isaacs wound up going to lunch with Rather, and instead of conducting a courtship, he made the rash mistake of criticizing the "Evening News" to Rather's face. At CBS, people who make critical remarks to Rather do so at their peril. Within days Isaacs was gone from the "Morning News," assigned to the purgatory of "Sunday Morning," where he served out three years before being terminated in a later round of layoffs.

But budget cuts weren't the only problem confronting the CBS management in the fall of '83. A year earlier, General Westmoreland had filed his libel suit against CBS News, and by the fall of 1983 Joyce and Stringer were overwhelmed with the Westmoreland defense. "We never saw them," said a top producer, "and the show began to unravel."

The ratings were falling too, never to regain their peak of 4.2. As for Ferrante, it was well known by then that he, too, had several times criticized the favoring of the "Evening News." He had been quoted in one magazine as saying, "Our role is not to be the press release of the air. In a half-hour program that may be adequate, but on a longer news show we have the chance to transmit experiences of people involved in the news, not just the official version."

"Evening News" staffers who read that had a fairly good idea of the half-hour program to which Ferrante was referring. And that winter, in front of Joyce, Stringer, and Rather, Ferrante blew up about the lack of support the "Morning News" was getting. During the New Hampshire primary he also made the mistake of telling a group of "Evening News" correspondents that he didn't want them delivering to his program "the ritualistic horseshit" they served up for the "Evening News." The correspondents squawked to Rather.

Ferrante's timing could not have been worse. By then, like his predecessor Merlis, Ferrante too was falling out of favor with Diane Sawyer. She began to complain about him to Joyce. Her method of undermining him was the same she used on Merlis. She stopped talking to Ferrante, then complained to the management that he wasn't communicating with her.

"What were they [the management] going to do?" Ferrante says today. "They were afraid of her and her little dinners with Paley. Joyce wasn't going to stand in her way. Neither was Stringer. They were both putting their own careers above any form of management."

Sawyer was after Ferrante. Rather had no love for him. All it took to bring him down were some timely kicks in the shins, and in March 1984 the broadcast landed neatly in the lap of Jon Katz.

"**I**ntelligent, well-read, gracious, pretty, hard-working, and witty" was how Diane Sawyer was once described in an *Esquire* profile. The writer neglected to add "political." Sawyer had been a loyal staffer at the Nixon White House in the early seventies, and her hiring at CBS News as a Washington correspondent was not popular initially. But Sawyer brought all her poise and political skills to her work, and she and Katz soon formed an alliance. "They liked each other," one senior producer said. "He was cerebral enough for her, and she liked the fact that he was smart. They could spar with each other."

Sawyer says she paired well with Katz despite their arguments over content. But the minute she had an executive producer she could finally live with, she surprised him with a new agenda.

For some time she had been disappointed by the management's general lack of support for the broadcast. "I cared passionately about the show," she says, "and it was disspiriting that Bill [Kurtis] and I had not received the support for the show we wanted to do, an intelligent show. And was I tired of the hours? Yes."

She had known for months that Don Hewitt, the executive producer of "60 Minutes," wanted to hire her. The management knew she wanted to leave the "Morning News," but it was several months before the CBS executives did anything about it. According to a good friend of Sawyer's, this annoyed her. Sawyer says the CBS News executives were divided on whether she should move to "60 Minutes." "Ed Joyce was opposed to me leaving," she says. "Stringer was for it." But finally, after several months of rumors in the press that Diane Sawyer would be leaving the "Morning News" for "60 Minutes"—rumors which, Sawyer says, Joyce blamed on her—the president of CBS News finally agreed to announce the move.

Sauter, Joyce, and Stringer had dallied and delayed three months. Precious time had been wasted that could have been devoted to finding a successor. No tryouts had even been scheduled. So for the next six months, as the "Morning News" ratings eroded, CBS News put on an anchor merry-go-round in the morning, trying out various women for co-anchor, in stints that lasted up to several weeks.

They tried out Maria Shriver for a few days, she of the lovely cheekbones and mass of dark hair, but Shriver, then the show's West Coast correspondent, was considered too inexperienced. "Besides," says Art Kaminsky, Shriver's agent at the time, "we had already decided not to campaign for it." They tried out Meredith Vieira, who had better on-air presence, but Vieira, they felt, wasn't right either. Among the staff, the favorite candidate by far was Jane Wallace, who along with Vieira was later to become one of the four correspondents on "West 57th Street." Wallace was Katz's choice too, and she paired well with Kurtis, who also voted for her. And she was Ed Joyce's pick. On the first day of Wallace's tryout, Joyce called the control room to exult: "She's sexy, she's wonderful, she's terrific!"

Wallace, however, had some trouble reading from the prompter, and she went to Lilyan Wilder, a voice coach, for lessons. The voice coach, however, overstepped her area of expertise, advising Wallace to get her hair cut short, which she did. This was a big mistake in the eyes of CBS management, since Wallace did not inform them of her plans in advance. Then Wallace made an even bigger mistake —on the air. Not realizing that her mike was open one morning, she asked one of her producers: "Why are we doing this bullshit?" The comment went out over the air. It was well known around CBS News that Wallace had a tendency to swear like a truck driver, but her use of strong language on the air, although unintended, killed her candidacy with Sauter. And unlike the votes of Katz, Kurtis, and even Joyce, Sauter's vote, along with Gene Jankowski's, was one that counted.

The choice of news anchors is a prerogative reserved for the very highest levels of management at CBS. Executive producers rarely, if ever, have a say in these matters, and in this case neither did Ed Joyce, president of CBS News. The decision to hire Phyllis George was made above him.

"It is fair to say that it was not something I wanted to do," Joyce says. "It was a foolish decision and it certainly wasn't mine. I can't absolve myself completely because in the end I acquiesced, but it was Sauter and Jankowski who wanted her."

Joyce and others at CBS News maintain that Sauter had

Phyllis George in mind all along. He had been instrumental after all in bringing her to to CBS Sports when he was president of Sports, and it was his idea for her to make those twinkly sideline appearances during "The NFL Today." According to Ed Hookstratten, Phyllis's agent, "[Sauter's] endorsement of George was strongly supported by Gene Jankowski," Sauter's own boss, who also happened to be a long-time admirer and friend of Phyllis and her husband.

"How they could make the choice of Phyllis is beyond me," says Dick Salant, former president of CBS News. "They knew Phyllis was a hopeless case from the Sports division. But there again, Jankowski had no idea what news was about. He always used to say, 'If you don't have the steak, sell the sizzle'."

Jankowski's background was in sales. He had been with CBS since 1961, and had moved up through the ranks in a variety of administrative positions before being made head of the Broadcast Group in 1977. And it was with his enthusiastic endorsement that the decision finally was made.

In December 1984 Stringer, Katz, and his deputy, David Corvo, who were in Los Angeles talking to a company about new graphics for the "Morning News," got the word over the phone from Ed Joyce. They stared at each other in disbelief for a long time, then Katz finally said: "Maybe they know something we don't." Katz at least had received the courtesy of a call. Bill Kurtis wasn't to learn who his next co-anchor was until he read the announcement in the *New York Times.*

"It was a communications slip-up," Joyce said.

Phyllis George was Van Gordon Sauter's idea of "the woman of the eighties"—minus the few pounds she would have to lose before she started at CBS News. She was hardly your typical working wife, but what wattage! The management now intended to give the "Morning News" a $2 million overhaul, $600,000 of which was for the set where the former Miss America was going to sit.

And what a deal her agent, Ed Hookstratten, had struck with CBS News. "It was an entertainment-style contract," said one agent. The salary was roughly a million a year for three years, plus all sorts of perks, including a hairdresser, assistants, and a limousine constantly at her disposal. Katz heard these numbers and whistled. This was a lot of money for a broadcast that not long ago had been laying off $30,000-a-year assistant producers. Given this outlay, Katz knew who would be calling the shots. He had no doubt whose inclinations and intransigences would have to be considered at every stage of the process.

So up she came on the screen one morning in January 1985—"Bingo!" as Kurtis said—sparkling and chattering about how much she looked forward to the challenge of the work, and asking Kurtis if he wanted to hear about her problems in moving to New York. (Kurtis said no.) To accompany her arrival, CBS fired a publicity barrage from the same old long guns it had used to herald Sally Quinn. The critics settled in to watch, and for the next three months, while Phyllis's presence made barely a blip in the ratings, they took increasing joy in noting her predilection for embarrassing gaffes as well as a style that suggested she could have used another year or two of education. Before long most were sniping at her freely. The major exception was Tom Shales of the *Washington Post,* dean of all TV critics. He was lying in wait. He had gone to lunch with Phyllis at the Four Seasons, where he had been more impressed by her looks and her presence than he was with her abilities as an interviewer. In the story he wrote after the lunch, all he did was quote her, but that was enough to get the point across: "If I hadn't come from Denton, Texas," she told Shales, "I wouldn't be sitting here right now with this great job and my great husband and my two children. The values that mom and dad—who are still alive, and I love 'em, I love 'em to death—taught me then, are with me now. I mean, I still say 'please' and 'thank you.' I'm a nice person. I still go to church."

Katz groaned. He had been sent along by CBS management to protect Phyllis, but as she babbled on to Shales, all he could do was tell Shales that Phyllis had stopped the "Today" show cold—which was about as far from reality as it was possible to get. What Katz did not say was that in her three months at CBS News Phyllis had stopped a few producers cold, too. Stopped them and dumbfounded them. She had introduced Aretha Franklin as Aretha Jackson, and she told viewers that "Armand Hammer has an art collection so magnanimous you can hardly put a price in it." She had asked Jane Kaplan to book John Candy, and Jane had booked him, but when Candy turned up in the studio, Phyllis said, "Who is that fat guy?"

Jane stared at her.

"Phyllis, it's John Candy."

"Who?"

"John Candy. The one you asked me to book. The one in *Splash.*"

Phyllis had no idea who Jane was talking about.

But such moments of daily life at the "Morning News" were not seen by the management. They saw what they wanted to see. Star quality. Sizzle.

By the time I came to work at the "Morning News," it was clear that Phyllis was a major problem. In one of my first discussions with Missie Rennie, she had advised me how important it was to play to the strengths of our anchors.

"What are Phyllis's strengths?" I asked.

"We-ell," Missie said, struggling to be diplomatic, "let's just say it's important not to play to her weaknesses."

It quickly became apparent to me that it was not easy to

build a program around Phyllis George. Every day we performed all sorts of inverse somersaults, so that Phyllis would *think* she was doing substantive stories when in fact she was not. Almost all the substantive stories, certainly anything that concerned a major political or social issue, wound up with Kurtis. Phyllis got the human interest stuff and the entertainment, and even then there were problems. And when the problems arose, the critics pounced, as when Phyllis asked comedian Billy Crystal if Fernando Lamas (on whom Crystal had modeled his most popular character) had ever written or called him, and Billy said, "Er, well, I think he died a few years ago."

In our lineup meetings, Katz's head would sink forward to his desk top when a producer would propose something for Phyllis that he was sure she couldn't handle.

"What, are you nuts?" he told us one morning, when someone suggested that maybe Phyllis could interview Senator Bill Bradley. "Why don't you go all the way? Let's have her interview William F. Buckley or George Will. *What's wrong with you people?*"

Yet only a few months earlier, when Phyllis first joined the show, she had demanded to do interviews with politicians, and backed by Sauter and Jankowski she had gotten her way. And until she had proved to her champions in management, as well as to several million viewers, that she couldn't do them, Katz had been obliged to accede to her. Now he no longer did. But the problem still was how to divide up the show so that there was something resembling equal time between the anchors. The solution was to hire a political correspondent to handle some of the Washington stories, and so in came Terence Smith, a veteran print reporter who had covered Vietnam, the Middle East, and the White House for the *New York Times*.

But this took care of only part of the problem. Each day at the morning meeting when the rough lineup was presented to Katz, he would tear at his hair as he tried to figure out what to give Phyllis. Usually the issue was left unresolved. It then became the senior staff's burden, as Katz would disappear to the front office to pal around with Ober or Stringer. Throughout the day we would be jumping through hoops, excluding many good stories because Kurtis already had half the show and we had to find things for Phyllis to do. Consequently many good stories, stories off the news, important stories, bit the dust. Finally, after several rejiggerings of the lineup, Epstein would say: "Okay, let's try this, it just might fly." Or we'd make a decision we could live with because it was the lesser of two evils, or because after fourteen hours at the "Morning News," we were tired and wanted to go home—only to have Katz explode on the evening conference call.

"What! Are you nuts?"

And so within a few months of Phyllis's arrival on the show, many of her pieces were being shot outside the studio. If she did a bad job, the piece could be edited to look better. As a result, Phyllis did a number of good interviews, especially for her "women of influence" series with Gloria Steinem, Diane Feinstein, Sally Ride, and Jane Fonda, among others. And with people from her own social milieu like Malcolm Forbes or heart surgeon William DeVries she wasn't bad at all. She was disarming and unthreatening, and at times this worked for her—people would reveal things to her. But live, on camera, she was error-prone and nervous. As she glanced at her notes and flubbed her lines, she often communicated to the audience that she had no idea what she was talking about, and as Katz said: "It wasn't the fault of the camera." To make matters worse, she didn't do her homework. And when she was having her hair done in the mornings, a producer could not have gotten in to see her if the world had blown up. Still, while she was no journalist, she sure lit up the screen, and when she swept through the newsroom, wearing that smile that had lit the beauty contest runways, the grungy, windowless place never looked better.

Epstein and I enjoyed a rare, restful five days when the broadcasts originated from London the week of May 6, 1985. There were no world crises, and we had a bank of backup pieces ready in case L-SAT went down. All we really had to do was book the show as far ahead as possible, and enjoy the entertainment provided by Amy. Amy was feeling rejected because she hadn't been asked to go to London. She was especially mad at Roberta, whom she felt favored Jane Kaplan; she was sure that Roberta's favoritism was the reason Jane had gone to London instead of her. So we let her take long lunch hours because she insisted that shopping would be good therapy. One day when a story broke and we did need her, we had her paged at Bloomingdale's; to our amazement, we got her.

In the mornings we watched the broadcast in the control room. Again there was little to do; everything was being fed from London, except for newsblocks. We lounged in our chairs, viewing the shows almost as critics because we'd had little hand in putting them together. They looked good. The weather throughout Europe that week was perfect. Remote broadcasts were always a risk, and the CBS News management was not prepared to trust such a project to Katz alone, so they sent along Joan Richman, a vice-president and head of Special Events, to supervise. But nothing untoward occurred. The broadcasts were all polished and smooth. Kurtis gave viewers a feel for the mood of Europe at the time of the German surrender, interviewing members of the French resistance and correspondents from the Murrow era such as Charles Collingwood and William Shirer. On the light side, Phyllis's interviews had gone well too. She'd been carefully produced, and with the historic footage of people embracing in Piccadilly Circus to the singing of Vera Lynn, the shows had actually been moving at times.

On Thursday, Stringer came by the control room and plopped himself into one of the seats next to us. It was immediately clear that he was much enamored of the broadcasts. He told us that going to London was a far better choice than going to Vietnam, as "Today" had done, to record the tenth anniversary of the fall of Saigon.

"They keep getting better and better every day," he beamed, as he watched the show, "and I think Phyllis has been excellent, just excellent."

Epstein and I glanced at each other.

"You know she had some reservations about this trip," I said.

"No, I didn't," Stringer said. "What were they?"

"She was concerned that all the historical stuff happened before she was born."

Stringer laughed and waved it off.

"Oh, well," he said, "that's Phyllis. Sounds like something she'd be quoted on."

He gave me a cagey look, and departed for his office. Epstein and I went back to killing time.

So the London week was a big success, and the verdict of the management was communicated across the Atlantic. On Friday we heard reports of one very drunken windup party. And on Monday, May 13, when everyone was due back, I expected the mood in the control room among Katz, Corvo, Missie, Roberta, and the rest of the staff to be self-congratulatory, if somewhat anticlimactic after all the hoop-la of the previous week.

I arrived at the control room that Monday on the dot of 7:00 A.M. Over the weekend there had been a fire at a soccer stadium in England, and when I walked in, I thought for a moment that this was what I was seeing on the monitors. But within seconds it became clear that something else was going on. There were no greetings from the people I'd not seen in a week. The place was in a flap. Corvo gave me a quick briefing: as the overnight staff had started to move upstairs for the broadcast, word had come in that a pitched battle had broken out in Philadelphia between the police and a black radical group called MOVE. We'd been fortunate to have a network correspondent, a producer, and a camera crew in Philadelphia that morning, and by 7:00 A.M. they were sending us live pictures.

Breaking stories such as this, stories where we actually put the drama live on the air, were not that common at the "Morning News." The last major story that had broken on our time was the downing of Korean Airlines Flight 007, and there weren't any live pictures of that. But this morning we had all the visuals we wanted, and Katz had blown off everything else that had been scheduled for the first half-hour. We sat there watching the drama unfold, water pouring onto MOVE's building. Then shots rang out. Cops and camera crews dived for cover. It was heady, dangerous stuff. More to the point, the "CBS Morning News" had great pictures, and the other two broadcasts didn't.

Katz rubbed his hands with glee, relishing victory.

"See if you can get closer!" he yelled into his headset to producer Bev Jackson and correspondent Chris Kelley. "Jeez, this is great!"

Then a hail of bullets sent everyone diving for cover, with cameras and pictures spinning wildly.

"Keep your heads down!" Katz roared.

As soon as the pictures stabilized, Katz bounced around the studio, slapping the backs of everyone in sight.

While all this was going on, the guests who had been scheduled to appear that morning waited in the greenroom. In Washington, we had Senator Bill Bradley and Congressman Jack Kemp on hold. They had been moved into the studio and I could see them on the monitor reading the newspapers. We had checked with their staffs, and were told "they can wait, they're pros, they understand." So Bradley and Kemp went on reading the *Washington Post,* taking what seemed to me to be surprisingly little interest in the MOVE drama.

"A clue to the real nature of politicians?" I asked Corvo.

At 7:40, Bradley and Kemp finally got their five minutes to talk about tax reform, before departing to whatever breakfast appointments they had.

After eight o'clock, the MOVE confrontation turned into a standoff and we decided to limit our coverage of it mainly to the newsblocks. The regular show went on. Phyllis did an interview with Patty Hearst. Kurtis talked to mountaineer Dick Bass about climbing Everest. Pat Collins did her entertainment review, and Dr. Lawrence Balter, our resident child psychiatrist, gave viewers some theoretical advice on how to discipline their kids. When the show ended, and we were making our way down from the studio, Katz was still bubbling about the MOVE scoop. He disappeared into his office to field calls from the TV press and to laud it over "Today" and "GMA," a rare opportunity.

I went to the fishbowl where the producers who had not gone to London were reuniting with those who had. The mood among the latter group was ebullient. Mike Whitney, the senior broadcast producer, was telling everyone how good Phyllis had been.

"She was trying harder," Whitney said. "I was putting stuff in her ear, and what was coming out was different, but it was still good."

And Jane Kaplan had a story to tell.

"Yes," she was saying to a small group who stared at her in disbelief. "At the party they actually danced together."

Our anchors had danced together? *Our anchors?* Nobody could believe it. By now it was common knowledge that Kurtis, in most every respect a perfect gentleman, had nonetheless let it be known that he was less than enamored of working with Phyllis George and didn't like what her hiring represented.

As Jane was talking, our attention was drawn to the monitor in the fishbowl. From the "Morning News" update came more footage of water pouring over the MOVE headquarters.

"Look at this," someone said, "it's still going on?"

It was less dramatic than two hours ago. And it would stay that way until the police dropped their bomb later in the day. But for now the program was on standby. We were responsible for news until noon, and we were going to have to update the story for the Midwest and the Pacific Coast.

Epstein was on the phone trying to find out if CBS wanted to do a special report on the MOVE drama, which would have preempted us. While he listened, the rest of us performed the main morning chore of going through the papers.

"Did you read this story," Pat Shevlin asked, "about Scholastic Aptitude Tests being worthless? I think we ought to do something on that."

"It's a snore," Epstein said, still holding.

"Well, we often say that," Shevlin persisted. "But I think people are interested. I mean it's scandalous that all this attention is paid to SATs if they're really useless."

"Didn't we already do something on SATs?" Missie Rennie asked.

"No, we talked about doing it, but we never did."

"It's still a snore," Epstein said.

"Now, Bob, I'm surprised at you. You're a parent. If your daughter was older, you'd care about this story."

"You know Katz will hate it," Epstein said.

It was true, Katz would hate it. Maybe not at the meeting when he was in a good mood, but when its turn rolled around in the studio and three furry people out of an Ed

Koren cartoon stopped the show dead with a discussion of SATs, he'd hate it sure enough. Then he'd appear later in the fishbowl, reminding the producer that SATs were her brilliant idea, and that if she really wanted to run the show into a wall, maybe she should dream up something on foreign aid.

Nobody at the "Morning News" relished these lambastings, and people often made sure that anything risky was carried out in concert with others. Epstein's argument put Shevlin on the defensive.

"I'll see if I can find an interesting way to do this," she said, dropping the subject.

Epstein's intercom buzzed. Katz was finished regaling the press and he wanted to meet. We gathered up our notes and trooped down to his office.

"Kiddies!" Katz was sporting new loafers. "Well, are we all happy to be back again?"

Epstein took a deep breath, doing his best to ignore the remark. We listened to the stories. Shirley Wershba, an older booker who took no nonsense from anyone, had made Katz help her edit tape one day when she was busy, which everyone agreed was one of the high points of the trip.

"So who was the most neurotic booker?" Epstein asked. This led to a ten-minute discussion in which everyone had a different point of view.

The MOVE story was still playing on Katz's monitor.

"This is great to come back to," he said. "We were all over it. They all called—Shales, the *Times,* the *News.* We should get some good play on this."

He brought his softball bat down on his desk.

"Right, Epstein. Gloomy Gus. You'd think you'd been working the past week. Okay, what do we have for tomorrow—aside from this MOVE thing—we should do something more on that."

Epstein started to run down the lineup, but Katz interrupted him.

"Oh, before I forget—Pat, open that door, will you."

Shevlin opened it.

"Liza-beth!"

"Yes, Jon."

"Put out a memo. Party in the cafeteria. Nine-fifteen, tomorrow. Everyone to attend."

"Another party?" Shevlin said. "I don't know if I can take another party."

"Can you believe it?" Katz said. "They want to give us a party. We're really loosening the purse strings around here. Okay, what have we got for tomorrow?"

And so the meeting kicked off in good humor, and the day went by on a wave of self-congratulatory good feeling that carried over to the champagne breakfast the next morning. Everyone drank, and the producers felt they were being deservedly praised. I watched several of them light up as Stringer spoke his "stirring words."

Then Epstein told me the news about the program being restructured around Phyllis, and I decided right away to get the story direct from Katz.

As the party started to break up, I caught up with him on his way out of the cafeteria. For a big man he moved at a brisk pace, especially when he was on his way to establish his presence in the front office. High points at the "Morning News" were rare enough, and I assumed that if there was any more glory to be gained from the London trip, Katz would be willing to bottom-fish for it. I was right. He was on his way to talk to Joyce and Stringer. I reminded him that we hadn't yet discussed the next day's show.

"Walk along with me," he said, and we went over ideas as we proceeded along the corridors.

"So what have we got?" he asked me. Before I could

answer he went on: "Any dirt? Any affairs start while I was gone?" I had not talked to him alone since the London trip.

I told him I'd heard nothing, and he told me I was a useless Brit who claimed to have been a reporter. Then he said he wanted to send Bill Kurtis down to Philadelphia to take a walk through the rubble.

"Let's do it Friday," he said. "Got any other great ideas?"

"We ought to do something soon on the Von Bulow trial," I said. "The country's loving it."

"Fine."

"We should pitch Ueberroth about the drug tests, and Webster about the Sikh plot."

"Fine. Book 'em. Book those babies."

"And I still like my idea about the town in Florida with all the AIDS cases."

"I'll read about it in Gay Lifestyles," Katz said. "What else?"

"You're wrong," I said. "It's a good story. How about the drought? Maybe that's your kind of story?"

Katz told me we could do a drought story when there was mud coming out of his faucet.

"We're still after Dotson–Webb, of course," I said.

"Keep on 'em."

"And that's about it, other than the MOVE stuff," I said. "What this I hear about the show being restructured around Phyllis?"

Katz stopped in his tracks.

"Who told you that?"

"Little birdie. Come on, Jon. What's the story?"

"Well, it's true," Katz said. "I mean Kurtis's future is uncertain."

He looked awkward and trapped.

"Keep that to yourself," he added.

I said I would, and I asked him what time he wanted to have the meeting.

"I told Corvo to start it," he said. "I'll be back around eleven." He disappeared into Joyce's office.

I collected my papers from my over-air-conditioned cubicle and went to the meeting. The rest of the senior staff came in with their clips and notes. Corvo stroked his trim beard and listened as I ran through what I'd discussed with Katz. Unlike Katz, he ran an orderly, almost subdued, meeting, laced occasionally with his dry wit. He concentrated especially on the visual elements of a story and the pacing of the broadcast.

That morning, it was agreed, we would try to book FBI Director William Webster and baseball commissioner Peter Ueberroth. Shevlin said nobody connected with the Von Bulow trial wanted to talk—yet.

"This is the time we need a legal correspondent," I said. Corvo agreed.

He was handed a rough lineup. The show so far consisted of a Pat Collins entertainment review, a piece from Kurtis on the end of the B-17 bomber, and an interview with ballerina Cynthia Gregory. Someone said we might get an interview with Patrick Ewing, the basketball star.

"If we get Ewing, we don't need Ueberroth," Corvo said. "That's too much sports."

It had been made plain to us that Ed Joyce didn't like sports, so sports was kept to a minimum.

When Corvo toted up his lineup, there were still a couple of holes, but these would fill up with news.

"What's the story on Dotson–Webb?" he inquired.

"We're still going after them," I said. "But the 'Today' show will have them first."

Still, I added, we could probably count on them. I would be hearing within the hour from Janice, who was trying to book the segment. Dotson and Webb were listed on the lineup as possibles.

Then the meeting broke up, and the senior staff went to the fishbowl to hand out the assignments.

I had been watching the Cable News Network in the fishbowl the day convicted rapist Gary Dotson was brought out of an Illinois prison. With his wimpy moustache and downcast eyes, mumbling "no comment" as he was escorted away, he did not seem to fit the cloak of the wrongfully imprisoned. Nor did I care for his erstwhile victim, who was now recanting her rape charge, the unconvincing Cathleen Webb. As I listened each day to the live hearings, her account of her born-again experience seemed less pertinent than her studied pauses, her lack of memory for detail.

In the meantime, however, Dotson–Webb had escalated through those various phases—from story to carnival—that delight the publishers of tabloids and the producers of morning TV. America couldn't get enough of them and had relished every moment of the hearings as Illinois Governor James Thompson pressed Webb for more detail on the condition of her underpants. Over the previous weekend, Thompson had announced he was commuting Dotson's sentence to time served, even though he did not believe that Dotson had been wrongfully convicted at his first trial. Call it human interest if you will—as a couple, Dotson and Webb were the most prized morning show guests in the country at that moment, hotter even than the Mayflower Madam, Sydney Biddle Barrows, who had not yet talked to the press. It was now Tuesday, and neither Dotson nor Webb had spoken publicly since the hearing had ended on Sunday.

Over the previous several weeks, of course, we had booked and "done" everybody peripheral to the case. We'd interviewed the families, lawyers, friends—we'd even had Cathy Webb on the show when she first announced her recantation. Throughout the hearings our bookers had baby-sat, guarded homes and hotel rooms, phoned in questions, and fought off the enemy, making sure we were represented on the story. Now the action had moved from Chicago to New York. Webb had arrived on a United flight from Chicago the day before. Dotson was due to arrive today on a plane chartered by NBC. It was evident that "Today" would have the first live interview with the two of them. Our best chance was to be second. But now, as I was about to learn for the first time, we were about to hit a snag.

"There's a problem."

The sing-song voice was Janice Platt's. She was calling in from a Manhattan hotel where she was hoping, against all the odds, to talk to Gary Dotson when he arrived.

"What's the problem?" I asked.

"Cathy Webb doesn't want to do us."

"Why not, fer chrissakes?"

"She won't *do* it." Janice's voice rose to a plaintive wail. "She didn't like something Maria said to her the last time she was on the show."

I remembered Maria filling in, but I couldn't recall Maria saying anything that might have upset Webb.

Janice, as she always did, then had to explain every chapter and verse of the problem. Through it all, I gathered that Webb had taken some comment Maria had made about her religious conversion as derogatory.

"Who are you dealing with?" I said.

"The lawyer."

"Can't you get to her?" I said.

"Of course not!" Janice sounded indignant. "The 'Today' show's got her locked up."

"Well, get back to the lawyer," I said. "Tell him there must be some misunderstanding. Besides, Phyllis will do the interview, and Phyllis is very religious."

A few hours minutes later Janice called back.

"There's another prob-lem!"

"Shit," I said. "What now?"

"They're on 'GMA' second. They don't want to do us at all."

I was silent.

"You know what I think," Janice said. "I think we'd never have had this problem if they'd let us do what 'Today' did —charter a plane." After Janice's long, detailed estimate of what it would have cost to charter an aircraft, and her review of all the occasions when this had been done in the past, she said: "Well, do we want them third?"

"I'll find out," I said. "Call me back."

I went to find Katz, knowing he would not be pleased with the news. All morning television executive producers act as if the American public stands in front of its TV sets each morning comparing the shows, noting that ABC had Dolly Parton before CBS. There was great pressure to be first with a guest, and each day we would examine the log published by *Radio and TV Reports* to see what the competition had carried the day before. It was amazing at times to see a group of men and women with years of accumulated journalistic experience among them, fretting because "Today" had featured the girl scout who sold the most cookies, while we had not.

But that afternoon, I couldn't find Katz. O'Regan told me he had gone home early for some reason. Instead I found Corvo. He was on his way to the front office, and I said: "Since you're going there, you might as well tell them they may be seeing Dotson–Webb on the other two shows, and not on the 'Morning News'."

"Shit," Corvo said. "How come?"

I explained why, then went back to the fishbowl. A few minutes later Corvo buzzed and asked me to come to his office. When I walked in, his chair was tilted back and he was staring at the ceiling.

"Question?" Corvo said. "Do you think Joyce or Stringer

or anyone else in the front office knows we book guests into hotels on this show?"

"I guess," I said. "Why?"

"Buksbaum didn't."

David Buksbaum was vice-president in charge of news and operations. He paid only periodic visits to the "Morning News," usually during crises.

"I couldn't find Joyce or Stringer," Corvo said, "so I went to talk to Buks about this, and I got yelled at about how much we were spending on hotels. That was all he wanted to talk about. Never mind. I'll try and get Katz if he ever turns his beeper back on."

He went back to refining his lineup, and I went back to the fishbowl to await the next bulletin. A few minutes later Janice called again.

"You want me to still try and book them?"

"Yes," I said.

It was the philosophy we all lived by. When in doubt, book 'em. In the final analysis, you could always cancel, and we did. Often.

I left the newsroom that evening at eight o'clock. Before I left, Janice assured me that the issue of religious convictions had been resolved to Cathy Webb's satisfaction.

"That's a great relief," I said.

They had still not agreed to appear on the show, however, and I left it that two bookers were to show up at the "GMA" lobby at 8:00 A.M., and try at the last minute to persuade Dotson and Webb to appear on CBS. We would be third after the other two shows, but we'd known losses of pride before on the "Morning News."

I emerged into the summer twilight and waited for a cab. The air was cool and clear, one of those perfect New York days that occur only about ten times a year, and which I had missed entirely. I decided Gary Dotson and Cathleen Webb had occupied enough of my thoughts for one day. I was regaining that wonderful perspective that always returned as soon as I stepped outside the CBS Broadcast Center.

My alarm went off at 6:00 A.M. on Wednesday, May 15. I got up and turned on the TV. I had logged seven hours of sleep, a blessing. All too often the phone would ring at 3:00 A.M. Some problem had arisen, or worse, a celebrity had died, peacefully, presumably, in his or her bed, in which case the overnight staff would want me to think of someone who could say nice things about the dead person.

I listened to the headlines, and having established that the world had not changed substantially since my head hit the pillow, I got up and made some coffee. The only new story was that the state of Maryland was limiting withdrawals from some of its savings and loan associations.

I showered, shaved, and dressed, picked up the papers at the door of my apartment, and took the elevator downstairs. In the taxi I glanced over the *Times* and the Life section of *USA Today.* When I got to the Broadcast Center, the usual line of limos was outside the entrance. Guests were emerging, people who didn't know me, but for whose presence here I was partly responsible. An odd feeling. On the way to the control room I passed the greenroom, where the guests who'd already arrived were being served coffee and orange juice. It was always a bizarre mix—senators, actresses, children who owed their lives to a medical miracle, ordinary people caught up in some horrifying news event which they were now about to share with ten million others. They waited their turns to be escorted to the studio, being entertained in the meantime by one of the set decorators, Budd Gourmen, who took upon himself the role of jester, loosening up our guests so that our anchors could then freeze them.

I helped myself to some coffee and went into the control

room. The director and the technicians were in their final stages of preparation. Corvo was in his chair, surrounded by the usual chaos. I settled in next to him.

"Where's Katz?" I said.

"Out sick."

"Oh." For once I would not lose the Style section of my *Washington Post* or my copy of *USA Today*.

"Thirty seconds!" shouted the floor director.

On the enormous bank of monitors in front of us, I watched Bill and Phyllis attach their mikes and adjust their smiles. Some tape was coming over the London feed. Charts of mortgage rates covered several screens.

"Fifteen seconds!"

"Quiet!"

The noise level dropped a decibel or two as the clock ticked toward seven. We began with a "cold open," a piece of footage whose sudden appearance serves to heighten drama and dissuade viewers from going to the bathroom. This morning it was a replay of the police bombing of the MOVE headquarters in Philadelphia. "This morning," Kurtis read in his fine basso, "we will be talking to two people who lost their homes in this fire."

The police bomb went off yet again, then the show's fanfare music came up, and the gold opening animation floated across the screen.

Kurtis, sleek and smooth as usual, in pale gray suit and snappy tie, told us what was in store, then tossed to Phyllis, radiant as always in a pink dress. Her hair, which had been worked on for an hour, was perfect. So was her makeup. Her cheeks lit up the morning. She stumbled over one tease, and Kurtis smiled his on-camera forgiveness, then he read the newsblocks.

At 7:10 I strapped on a headset to hear what Dotson and Webb were saying on the "Today" show. Jane Pauley was doing the interview. The couple seemed nervous and reticent. Webb looked frumpy in a flower-patterned dress, and Dotson tugged at his tie. Their lawyers did most of the talking.

As it was winding up, I felt a nudge in my ribs.

"How was it?" Corvo wanted to know.

"Only okay," I said.

"Are we going to get 'em?"

"We'll know soon after eight."

"We'll blow off Pat Collins if we do," he said, looking over his lineup.

Kurtis was finishing his interview with our Philadelphia couple, who were saying less than kind things about Mayor Wilson Goode. We went to commercial, then Phyllis came on and tossed immediately to Terry Smith, who would interview a couple of congressmen. It had to be this way. Phyllis had done nothing of substance yet, but you had to establish her presence on the show.

"In our next half hour!" our announcer boomed. "A conversation with ballerina Cynthia Gregory!"

"Holy shit," Corvo said. "How come I get the feeling I can't wait?"

He slid off his chair, and went back to the studio to boost any flagging spirits.

During the local cutaway (during which affiliates insert local headlines and weather), the noise in the control room rose again. Two techs were arguing about the audio levels. The associate director, Eric Siegel, wanted to know where in his contract it said that he had to sit next to someone who put mayonnaise on a salami sandwich. A page sprinted by, headed for the studio with a minor newsblock update. A couple of bookers were complaining loudly about having a segment dumped. It was routine hubbub, although it occurred to me that an outsider would have thought something earth-shattering was taking place.

After the next newsblock, Phyllis interviewed Cynthia

Gregory. The general opinion was that Phyllis had gained confidence while in London—at least this was the view being propounded by the front office. I watched her closely. When she read from the prompter she still seemed to me to be reading without thinking, and despite the best efforts of the director, the camera caught her looking at her notes. I couldn't see any improvement.

"Call for you on 46!"

I picked up the phone. It was Shari, who in partnership with Janice was on the trail of Dotson–Webb. She was excited.

"They said they'll do it!"

"It'll be tight," I said, glancing at the clock, which showed 7:48. "They haven't been on 'GMA' yet."

"I know," Shari said breathlessly. "They're on at 8:10. Janice talked to them before they went in and they said they'll do it."

"Call for you on 82!"

"Hold on, Shari," I said.

I passed the word to Corvo, and punched 82.

"They're going to do it!" Janice shrieked.

"I know," I said. "Shari's on the other line."

"Can you believe we're chasing these two all over town and this schmeggegi driver wants to stop for coffee?" Janice said. "Now he's a booker and he thinks we're . . ."

Janice started to go on and on, but I cut her off.

"Listen up," I said. "As soon as you get them in the car, one of you call and let us know they're coming. Then take a cab."

I got back to Shari and repeated what I had told Janice. When I got off the phone, Corvo was calling Katz at home. I punched in on the same line.

"What's the matter with you?" I said.

"Little bronchial problem. Nothing serious. Listen, nice going. Let's go for it."

If he'd been here, he would have rubbed his hands, pummeled my back. He would have told an impertinent tech, "Get your ass out of my chair!"

I hung up and went out to the greenroom to get more coffee to bring my bloodstream up to cruising speed.

Joan Lunden did the "GMA" interview. It wasn't any more lively than "Today's." During the interview Corvo said, "By the way, does Phyllis know anything about this?"

Phyllis had received a background packet the night before, which gave her the history and outcome of the case, as well as a list of suggested questions.

"Has she read it?" Corvo asked.

"Shit, David, I guess," I said.

Corvo knew better than to take chances. At 8:15, between segments, he slid off his seat and went back to the studio to make sure she'd read it. She had. She'd been told there was a chance Dotson and Webb might be on the show. She was familiar with the case.

I looked at the clock as the Lunden interview ended. 8:17. Our entertainment reviewer Pat Collins poked Corvo in the back.

"You're bumping me for this?"

She was only half-joking.

"No Pat," he said, "you're still on. We're blowing off something else."

Two minutes later, the phone rang.

"They're on their way!" Janice yelled. "Shari's with them!"

She hung up, and I let Corvo know, so he could change the lineup if necessary.

Ten minutes later, a page ran in from the greenroom. Shari, flushed and breathless, was two paces behind him. It was 8:33.

"Take 'em right in," Corvo said.

Shari darted out to the greenroom, then found out that the message had been relayed ahead of her. Dotson and Webb were already being seated in the studio. We could see them on the monitor. Catching her breath, Shari began filling me in on the details of the chase. Corvo stroked his beard and listened, mildly amused.

Janice arrived in the control room, just as we were coming out of commercial.

"Ready camera one!" the director shouted. "And roll!"

The cheerful intro music started up, and the printed title, "Newsmaker," appeared on the screen. When the music subsided, Phyllis read:

"For the past two months we've been hearing about the strange case of convicted rapist, Gary Dotson, and of the woman who now says the rape never happened—Cathleen Webb. Today, three days after Dotson's sentence was commuted, he and Mrs. Webb are talking to each other in public for the first time, and they've joined us this morning with their lawyers."

The camera gave us a group shot as Phyllis, underscoring the fact that they'd been on other shows before the "Morning News," said brightly: "Do you all feel like you've been at a track meet this morning?"

Corvo groaned.

Addressing them like young lovers, Phyllis continued: "What were the first words you said to each other at your meeting last night?"

"I don't remember who spoke first," Webb said, "but I asked for Gary's forgiveness and it was given sincerely."

"I was nervous," Dotson said, "but I'm glad I met her."

"Did you have dinner together?" Phyllis asked, continuing the lover theme.

"No," they replied in unison.

"Didn't go that far, eh?" Phyllis remarked.

At this point Dotson's lawyer, Warren Lupel, interrupted with some legal pablum. Then Phyllis asked Webb if she could live with her burden. Webb said she no longer had a burden, and thanked her husband and the Lord for their support.

I glanced at Corvo, but he was being summoned to the phone.

"Is this a new beginning for you?" Phyllis asked Dotson.

"Oh, definitely."

The lawyer interrupted again to talk about the upcoming effort to reverse the previous conviction.

"Why did you go on the morning talk shows?" Phyllis asked.

"To show Gary's character," Webb said. "Gary doesn't have the character of a rapist."

Phyllis then asked Dotson about his movie offers. "I saw you signing autographs yesterday," she said, "and you were handling it like a real pro . . ." This brought out a brief smile, so Phyllis tried an abrupt transition. "How's your mother?"

Dotson assured Phyllis his mother was fine.

With Corvo on the phone, the director looked at me. There was no reason not to wrap it up.

"Thirty seconds!"

Then Phyllis said: "How about you two shaking hands at the end of a long day?"

They obliged.

Then with a breezy laugh. "How about a hug?"

Dotson and Webb smiled awkwardly, frozen.

"We'll be right back," Phyllis told the viewers, all the time smiling radiantly. Clearly she thought nothing was wrong.

The director spun round. His look demanded confirmation that something was definitely wrong here. I faced the screen in stunned silence. Corvo hung up the phone.

"Were we still on the air when she said that?" he snapped.

"We sure were," I said.

The director nodded.

"Oh, shit," Corvo said through gritted teeth. "Shit, shit, shit."

The phone in front of me rang. It was Stringer.

"Yes," I said, "that *was* what she said. Yes, I found it hard to believe too. No, nobody else here could believe it either."

He asked for Katz and I told him Katz was at home. I gave him Corvo.

Downstairs in the newsroom, phones were ringing. Viewers were calling to register their complaints. Minute by minute, hour by hour, the brouhaha built. When Tom Shales of the *Washington Post* called, Katz was not at the office to talk to him. Katz was said to be ill and unavailable for comment. Stringer didn't talk to Shales either, but Phyllis did. She said: "I knew I had to go a different route."

Next morning the *Washington Post*'s two-page-long story began: "Collectors of seemingly idiotic remarks made by Phyllis George on the 'CBS Morning News' hit a vein yesterday . . ."

Around noon that Wednesday I wandered through a rather bleak newsroom, and passed the bulletin board. A new set of ratings had been posted. They were for the much-heralded week of the broadcasts from Europe, and they were on the board a day earlier than when we usually received them. Although we were up one-tenth of a point to 3.4, we had made no gain on the other two shows, which were up also. After all that effort. I crumpled the ratings sheet into a ball and lobbed it at one of the newsclerks. Then I rounded up Shevlin and Epstein, and the three of us left the building to treat ourselves to a long liquid lunch.

VII.

TRIAL BY PRESS

"I feel like a juicy spare rib in a nest of starving wolves. I get ten calls a day from reporters asking about our show. That's more than some senators get, I bet."

—Jon Katz

When I arrived in the control room the next day, the mood was subdued. Corvo was in the executive producer's chair, Mike Whitney next to him. There was no sign of Katz. When I asked where he was, Corvo told me he was still sick and that his bronchial infection might keep him out for a while. Most of the staff, myself included, believed that Katz really was ill, largely because he had had the foresight to fall sick the day before Phyllis requested the fond embrace. Only later, when it became clear that there were other reasons why he might be feeling low, did his malaise begin to seem suspect.

There was very little news that morning, and for once the show went as planned. There were no glitches, and under scrutiny Phyllis held up. Over the course of the two-hour broadcast, her interviews with basketball star Michael Jordon and entertainer Peter Allen were seamless. But a good show that morning did little to relieve the general gloom that was evident when I went downstairs to the fishbowl. By then everyone had read Tom Shales's story in the *Washington Post.*

Shales had pounced. Phyllis had told him that her request was "kind of one of those quick little comments from me" that was "not intended to cause any uproar." But Shales thought there was uproar enough to devote three columns to a story called "Invitation to a Hug." All the CBS switchboards had received complaints, he noted. Several CBS correspondents had told him they considered Phyllis George an embarrassment. Steve Friedman, the executive producer of "Today," had said he hoped the people who ran the "Morning News" would continue to do exactly what they were doing. Phyllis had told Shales: "I wanted to get the personal side. I don't think it's such a big deal."

But it was a big deal. The press had paid a lot of attention to the Dotson–Webb case, and the couple's joint appearance on the morning television shows allowed an encore. Phyllis's request gave the papers their headline, and the columnists took advantage of the opportunity to review her other gaffes. Over the next few weeks the Hug became a joke on the Johnny Carson show, and even wound up as the subject of a *New Yorker* cartoon. If everyone who had heard about the Hug had actually seen it, our ratings would have topped "GMA" and "Today" combined. As we took stock of the full extent of the damage in the fishbowl, it was becoming obvious to most of us that Phyllis George was about to become 1985's Sally Quinn.

It wasn't easy to get the bookers motivated that morning. Their assignments took a low priority as they sat in the newsroom talking about the incident. Shari was feeling miserable.

"If we hadn't chased them so hard," she kept saying, "none of this would have happened."

"You didn't hug anyone," Amy told her.

"What if they had hugged?" Janice was saying. "Then it

wouldn't have been such a big deal. Everyone would have called it a coup."

Amy rolled her eyes.

Ira Sutow, the newsblock producer, was chewing gum and reading aloud quotes from the out-of-town papers. "Here's one," he said. " 'It could have been worse. She could have asked them to do it'—only kidding."

"I wish someone would hug me," Jude said.

Several people obliged.

"Where's Katz?" Janice asked.

"Out sick."

"He would be," Amy said, and went off to rehearse guests for a swimsuit fashion segment.

I went downstairs to the cafeteria and ran into Corvo.

"Let's meet right away," he said, "I have to go to the front office at ten."

I didn't need to ask why. When we got back upstairs, he quickly reviewed the show's lineup and approved most of it. The broadcast was fairly solidly booked. Terry Smith had a series of Washington reports which he had compiled into a notebook, and Pat Collins and Robert Krulwich both had segments. Maria Shriver would do a story about a man known as the Voice of Hollywood. Kurtis was going to take his walk through the rubble in Philadelphia. Phyllis would do two segments, an interview with three "beautiful older women" and the swimsuit fashions. It was all safe, harmless stuff. Corvo let it be known that it was important to get through the rest of the week without taking any more torpedoes.

When the meeting was over I walked back to Phyllis's office. A small knot of producers was already there trying to cheer her up. Everyone was trying to one-up each other with gallows humor.

"You all still love me?" Phyllis said finally, with a bright laugh. "Then how about a hug?"

She was doing her best to appear unperturbed, but I had heard that she had been in tears earlier. It was well known around the "Morning News" that Phyllis was sensitive to press criticism, and that the negative reviews bothered her a great deal. Before she came to the "Morning News" she had been warned that female anchors invariably got bludgeoned in their first year. But every day, it seemed, there was a hostile item in some paper about her, and while it was she who was feeding the critics the ammunition, she tended to think that they ought to see things her way. She thought they ought to bear in mind that she was new to the role, had a lot to learn, and was doing her best.

Finally, I went back to my office to read the mail and to pick up any stray messages that might actually have found their way to my desk. As I flipped through several magazines, I came across an issue of the *American Spectator* that contained a particularly rough diatribe about Walter Cronkite. It seemed to me the column might serve a purpose. I ripped it out, and went back to see Phyllis.

Her door was open. She was talking to Marjorie Baker, who had once been a vice-president of documentaries but now worked as anchor producer at the "Morning News." Her main duty was to look after Phyllis.

"Phyllis, I want you to read this," I said, handing her the article with the top folded down, so she could not see who the column was about.

Marjorie looked on, curious. As soon as Phyllis read the first few lines, she exclaimed: "God, this is awful. Who is this about?" She turned the page. "Walter Cronkite! Oh, poor Walter. I hope nobody shows this to him."

"I just wanted you to see you're in some pretty solid company in the flak zone," I said.

Marjorie was now reading the column over Phyllis's shoulder.

"This is amazing," she was saying, "this is one of the toughest attacks I've ever read."

"But how can people write things like this?" Phyllis asked. "I mean people shouldn't be allowed to write these things. What's Walter done to deserve this? He isn't even on the air."

"No, Phyllis, the point Peter is making," Marjorie said patiently, "is that even someone like Cronkite has to take attacks in the press. You can't let these things get to you."

Phyllis gave the column the back of her hand. Then she proceeded to tell me what she had told Shales, that she had been trying to draw Dotson out. Finally her intercom buzzed.

She had to take a call. Marjorie and I glanced at each other as we closed the door.

"She's pretty upset," Marjorie said. "She just takes it so personally."

We went back to the fishbowl, where a few members of the senior staff were sounding off with some strong expressions of ill feeling about Phyllis George.

"She's got to go," Ann Northrop, one of the coordinating producers, was saying. "If this show's ever going to have a prayer, she's got to go."

Nobody disagreed, but Shevlin warned Ann to keep her voice down.

In the fishbowl I went over the next week's grid with Missie. Then I went back to my office and looked through all the newspaper articles about the Hug request. It always seemed to me that events on the screen took on an inordinate importance within the CBS News building; from this standpoint, the whole world was watching all the time. But for once I had to admit that CBS was not overreacting. We were taking broadsides, and every critic in the industry seemed to have a negative opinion.

Then, as I flipped through the *Daily News*, I came across

an item in Liz Smith's column. It stated flatly that Bill Kurtis would soon be leaving the "Morning News." I had to assume that, with all the flap over Phyllis, it had escaped everyone's notice.

The bitter war between CBS management and Bill Kurtis had begun two months earlier, in March, when *Chicago Sun Times* television critic Gary Deeb wrote that Kurtis was unhappy working with Phyllis George at the "Morning News," and might soon be returning to WBBM.

Shortly after Phyllis was hired, Kurtis had talked to CBS management about his future. He had told Sauter, Joyce, and Stringer that he would buy into their Phyllis George plans, and would try to make a go of it with her. But he wanted them to realize that this wasn't his kind of journalism, and that he didn't want to continue doing it when his contract was up in a year. He was aware that WBBM, where he had worked before coming to the "Morning News," had a ratings problem, and he thought that he might be its solution. He still liked Chicago, and he remained immensely popular there.

Chicago was also the former stomping ground of CBS News president Ed Joyce, who had been general manager of WBBM when Kurtis was its anchor. Gary Deeb was well known to Ed Joyce, and vice versa. During Joyce's tenure at the station, Deeb had written a number of less than kind things about Joyce. After Joyce had made several cutbacks at the station, which in Deeb's opinion were designed to impress his corporate bosses in New York, Deeb had called him an "over-toilet-trained accountant." He had also labeled Joyce the "Velvet Shiv," for what he considered to be a friendly exterior that masked a willingness to stick knives into newsmen's backs. Around CBS News, the label Deeb had given Joyce had stuck.

But it was not these labels that were the source of Joyce's anger when he summoned Stringer and Jon Katz to his office to discuss Deeb's column about Kurtis's future. Joyce was convinced Kurtis had planted the news to speed up his agenda.

"It had to be Kurtis who planted this," he fumed. "Kurtis or his agent. They both talk to Deeb all the time."

Katz said: "We all know Bill talks to the press."

"Well, that does it," Joyce snapped. "From now on we're going to restructure the show around Phyllis, and we're going to strike back."

A few days later, on April 8, an item appeared in the *New York Daily News* under the by-line of George Maksian. It read: "Reports are surfacing that Bill Kurtis is about to jump ship as co-anchor of the 'Morning News' . . . a CBS management source acknowledged over the weekend a feeling of 'disillusionment' with Kurtis's performance on the 'Morning News' and 'his lack of team spirit'."

The "Velvet Shiv" had struck.

"It was intended to extract pain," Kurtis says today. "It was intended to intimidate me, and to make me shut up."

(Deeb, incidentally, insists he did not come by his information from either Kurtis or Kurtis's agent, Don Ephraim.)

Leaking to the press was a game CBS management knew only too well. It was one of the principal features of its management style. Cultivation of the news media, television and otherwise, had come to full flower during the Westmoreland case, but it had been characteristic of Sauter's and Stringer's and Joyce's styles even before. Sauter and Stringer in particular granted interviews freely, and made themselves available to reporters—Stringer even allowed *Variety* reporter Kevin Goldman to wander the halls of the Broadcast Center. Sauter's favorite trick, as one CBS correspondent said, was to go off the record. More than a few reporters came away charmed.

By the time I arrived at CBS, Stringer and Sauter seemed to be spending much of their day talking to the TV columnists. Stringer used them almost as a means of interoffice communication, "setting off his little land mines," as one CBS correspondent put it. Leaks to columnists were carefully orchestrated, and the CBS News management was not above leaking information about each other.

The press of course welcomed the leaks and ran with them. But it didn't just listen to management. Information was information, from wherever it came, and a number of people within CBS News who were antipathetic toward management began to hold off-the-record briefings of their own. When others played the game, however, CBS News management reacted badly. After all, its superiors at Black Rock read the papers; for some of them, this was their only means of knowing what was truly going on at the news division. So, in some respects, the CBS News executives did for the TV press what the moguls of Hollywood did for Hedda Hopper—they created them, then paid the price.

Hence the explosion in Ed Joyce's office and his expressed desire to "strike back." CBS News was starting to become a glass house and the management was spending more and more of its time dodging stones. Which was why everyone was warned not to talk to the press about Phyllis, and all inquiries about the Hug incident were to be fielded by the management.

Late in May, a week after the Hug, the anchors went to San Francisco for the affiliates' convention, the annual gathering of network and affiliated station executives. For the "Morning News" the event was a charade, a farce that could have played for high ratings in any prime-time sitcom slot. The conference was held at the Fairmont Hotel, the working sessions at the Masonic Hall, and both Kurtis and George were ordered to attend together and to smile. They were featured in a tight scripted, upbeat presentation that had been put together months earlier. It had been designed to raise hopes and expectations for the "Morning News," but by now of course it was widely known that Kurtis would be leaving. Not only was he in negotiations with WBBM, he was also talking to ABC's Chicago station WLS. CBS management was trapped: it could not announce that Kurtis was leaving because he hadn't yet signed with WBBM. So the farce was played out, to a disbelieving audience, and CBS News drove another stake into its diminishing core of credibility.

While Kurtis and George were in San Francisco, Bob Schieffer and Maria Shriver sat in for them. And for two days the show was better served than it had been in four months —with anchor chemistry. Schieffer seemed much looser on the "Morning News" than he ever had been when he substituted for anchors on other broadcasts, and his humor and intelligence quickly endeared him to the staff. So too did his reaction to Shriver, whom he clearly liked, even asking to be placed closer to her on the set. And if Maria at times succumbed to giggle attacks when Schieffer said something only mildly amusing, their relationship was a refreshing change from the almost icy restraint that prevailed between Kurtis and George.

"Can you believe this?" Pat Shevlin asked in the control room one morning. "These two actually like each other."

Even when Schieffer accidentally spilled coffee on Maria that morning, it seemed human and endearing. On another morning Shriver went outside to West Fifty-seventh Street for a demonstration on how to protect a car against thieves. With Murphy's law at work once again, the segment wound up being conducted against the background roar of a city garbage truck. On the monitor I could see Schieffer struggling to contain his laughter. When Maria finally gave up, he said: "Okay, Maria, let's see if you can make it back to the studio in two minutes in those heels."

Corvo roared.

"Did he really say that? Gee, that's great."

"Do you think," Pat Shevlin wondered, "there's any chance Bob would want to be the anchor of the 'Morning News'?"

Corvo shook his head. "Bob doesn't want the job," he said flatly. "He doesn't want to leave Washington, and he doesn't need the headache."

But Corvo's denial didn't prevent hopes from being nurtured at the "Morning News" that the management might decide to cut its losses and go with an entirely new anchor team. If the staff had had any say in the matter, Schieffer and Shriver would have been hired on the spot. Maria was conscientious. She did her homework. And unlike Phyllis, she had the same journalistic frame of reference as the staff.

I was sitting in the newsroom with her later that morning when Ann Northrop came by. Maria was to interview Jann Wenner, the publisher of *Rolling Stone*, who had just bought *Us* magazine, and I was going over questions with her because I knew Wenner. Ann was standing over us holding a newspaper clipping.

"What's up?" I said, when I realized she had something to show me.

"Read this," Ann said. "This will brighten your day."

The clipping reported that CBS News executives had been talking to Susan Winston, the former executive producer of "Good Morning America," about coming to the "Morning News" as its new executive producer.

Maria and I both read it, and I began to put two and two together.

"So," I said, "is Katz really sick?"

"Well, if he wasn't, I bet he is now," Northrop said sarcastically. "Wouldn't you be sick if you read this?"

"You used to work on 'GMA,'" I said. "What's the story on this woman?"

"She's tough, smart, and humorless," Ann replied.

"It's all too much for me," Maria said. "Too much going on around here. Thanks for your help with the questions."

Maria went back to her office.

"She's great," Ann said. "If only."

We went back to the fishbowl, where a copy of the clip about Winston was receiving a lot of attention. People were already distraught. If it was true, they were saying, Winston's hiring would only mean another step down the road to entertainment. Nobody had any doubt that the story had been planted deliberately, timed to coincide with the CBS affiliates' convention. With the ratings of the "Morning News" congealed in the low threes, it was essential that CBS News management generate some feeling of hope among the affiliates. The rumor that CBS was considering bringing in a new executive producer would show that they were paying attention to the program.

A few days later, the Winston rumor was confirmed by a story in the *New York Times.* Stringer had been interviewed by the paper, and had used the occasion to crush any "Morning News" staff hopes for a new anchor team. Despite the Hug, Phyllis George still had the full support of the management, and Stringer made it clear that nobody should have any doubts on that score.

"The overreacting to her conversation with [Gary] Dotson," Stringer was quoted as saying, "is symptomatic of the way we all try to destroy people who have too much of an advantage."

Was Stringer talking for himself, or was this a royal use of the word "we"?

"Phyllis George is . . . very effective, very bright," he went on. "She is under a particularly vicious spotlight. It is extraordinary and relentless. In the end, what will count will be audience reaction."

"He's damn right about that," Northrop said with disdain as she read the interview.

And Kurtis? Well, Stringer had a roundhouse punch for Kurtis—and for the staff as well.

"It's tough to get the staff to respond if you don't have two anchors who are excited and refreshed for the challenge," he said, adding "it is hard to see the circumstances under which he [Kurtis] would suddenly express enthusiasm."

Kurtis had no comment.

The *Times* story made it clear that Stringer had indeed discussed the executive producer job with Susan Winston. And sure enough in the same column, the paper quoted Winston on the future of morning news programs. "Good Morning America," she said, the show she had inherited from George Merlis when it was already number one, "reached out into the country" and "grabbed the hearts of folks . . ." And here was a tip. Winston was talking about the next big change that would come about in morning news programming. There was, she said, a whole new audience out there that wasn't yet watching: a lot of families in which both parents worked. The people in the fishbowl read this and groaned. They were sure of what was about to come down.

They needn't have worried. Stringer and Sauter had not been able to strike a deal with Winston—at least not yet. Oh, they wanted her. That was clear. But they were not about to agree to her demands. There was no problem with the salary. She wanted $350,000 a year? She could have it. She wanted a six-month escape clause? That was okay, too. But control over CBS's $3 million investment in Phyllis George? No way. CBS News was not about to hand Winston the power to fire Phyllis.

So one morning in early June, Shevlin and I arrived at the control room at the same time to be met by the familiar greeting of "Kiddies!" Katz was back, large as life and looking no worse for wear after a week in Cape May.

Dismissing the stories that he was about to be relieved of his command, he too began telling the press that Phyllis brought charm and energy and versatility to the program, even though he was telling his staff that Phyllis didn't know which end was up. And, like his bosses, he too would soon embark on a new agenda, intended to pay back the press for its mistreatment of the "Morning News."

As the Kurtis imbroglio, which had been fought in the press, drew to a close, the CBS News management and Katz made a decision to go on the offensive. The guns were to be primed by Katz, but the shells they hoped to land were to be delivered by Peter Boyer. Formerly the TV reporter for the *Los Angeles Times,* Boyer later moved on to become television columnist of the *New York Times.* In the first week of June 1985, he was the media critic for the "Morning News."

He had been hired earlier that year, and spent his first few months at the program learning his new trade. He wasn't at ease on camera, and he resisted being highly produced, believing that what he had to say was important enough not to need a lot of flashy graphics. For a while Katz took a hands-off approach, and Boyer was allowed to come up with his own ideas as he assimilated into television. This changed in June. Suddenly Boyer couldn't get his ideas approved by Katz. Around the office he appeared unconcerned, but behind his placid mask he was annoyed.

Boyer finally confronted Katz. According to Boyer, Katz told him: "They [Joyce and Stringer] want you to focus on print." They began to push him. To his credit, he resisted.

"They didn't exactly tell me to attack print," Boyer says. "It was a matter of leading me in this direction so that I would get the point."

Ed Joyce says "attack" is too strong a word. "It was Katz's suggestion originally," he says. "He thought Boyer should report aggressively about print, and yes, we wanted him to do this. But nobody told him exactly what to say."

Though Katz will not comment on the matter, he does not deny that he asked Boyer to attack print.

To the surprise of the management, Boyer proved stubborn. He wanted to do a week-long preview of the fall TV season, and after much persuasion Katz finally agreed to air it. As it turned out, Boyer had less than nice things to say about the upcoming CBS schedule—and some very complimentary things to say about NBC's. After the series ran, Boyer says, Katz called him to his office and lambasted him.

"Five affiliates have threatened to drop the 'Morning News' because of this!" Katz told him.

More meetings ensued, at which Katz kept pushing Boyer to focus on the press. Boyer kept refusing. In the meantime, perfectly fine stories of his were not getting on the air. Since Boyer would not go along, about all Katz could do was keep him off the air—and begin a campaign disparaging his on-camera performance.

For a while Boyer remained calm. Then his jaw began to tighten and his frustrations mounted. After a few months, as the full implications of what was going on became clear to him, he got mad.

There were more meetings, but still nothing was resolved. Finally, in November, Boyer marched in one morning and dropped a bombshell. He was resigning. He had been offered a job as TV columnist at the *New York Times.*

Boyer won't comment on his last few days at the network, but one CBS source said, "It would be hard to overestimate the panic that followed his announcement. They could hardly believe that he could go to his new job without carrying a grudge." For his part, Boyer admits that he got a number of frantic calls from Joyce and Stringer begging him to stay. But he remained firm. He had seen enough.

So too had Kurtis. Early in June 1985, his future was finally settled. He was going back to Chicago, to WBBM. Now everyone could be friends again. The management would say that Bill was a great fellow who had done a good job. After weeks of grousing about Kurtis around the office, Katz told the *Washington Post* that Bill was a true professional, and that he only wished Kurtis had not gone public with his grumbles about Phyllis.

With his future decided, Kurtis seemed to enjoy his last week on the "Morning News." It was a busy one. A lot of stories broke that week. The body of Josef Mengele turned up. Karen Ann Quinlan died. A Providence jury acquitted Claus von Bulow. Amy and Jude had been in Providence for the three days before the verdict, and they had done an excellent job contacting the judge, jurors, and the principals in the case, and extracting commitments for them to appear on the "Morning News." With Kurtis now a lame duck, Katz decided Phyllis should do the interviews with the children of Sunny von Bulow as well as with Claus von Bulow himself. There were some tense moments in the control room during the two days of their respective appearances, and a lot of speculation on whether Phyllis would ask them to hug. But this time there were no disasters, and the interviews went smoothly.

With Kurtis leaving, there was also a lot of speculation about who would replace him. It was well known by then that Bob Schieffer would be filling in, but only temporarily. Apparently nothing had been decided yet. I asked Kurtis if he knew anything. "No," he said. "But who they pick will give you some idea about their commitment to this program."

We were sitting in his office early in the morning, going over questions for a Tom Wolfe interview I had booked for him. It took no more than five minutes; it was always a cinch producing for Kurtis. "This is the kind of celebrity I don't mind doing," he said pointedly.

I had already decided I would miss Kurtis. It was hard enough in television news to get a good, original story past an executive producer, and if you succeeded you often had to sweet-talk an anchor or correspondent into doing it. All a producer's effort is worth nothing without access to the "talent" because in television news only the on-camera people are allowed to appear to have access to stories. There were, of course, capable correspondents at CBS News, but with some you practically had to feed the words into their mouths. After a few months as a producer at CBS News, I firmly believed I had a future as a ventriloquist.

Kurtis, however, made life easy, and after the show on Friday, June 14, there were a lot of sad faces among the producers at his good-bye party in the studio. After the months of open warfare, it was hard to believe some of the speeches. Katz said Bill was a great guy with the world's greatest collection of ties. Stringer made a florid speech, and I realized it was only two months since his post-London speech, with its high hopes for the future of the program. All the CBS News executives had turned out. So had Rather. After all, since Kurtis was going to WBBM, he was still part of the CBS "family." A five-piece band played, and singer Sandra Reaves sang a salute to Kurtis. There was a gag reel, too, featuring one female co-anchor after another—Meredith Vieira, Jane Wallace, Maria, and Phyllis—all saying their piece about Bill. It ended with Diane Sawyer, who declared: "I don't care what the other girls say, I did it with him first."

Then the people closest to Kurtis went down to his office and drank straight whiskey.

Later that morning two busloads of producers were ferried through the weekend traffic out to Kurtis's home in Westchester. It was a warm, humid afternoon, and a hundred people spent several hours in Kurtis's garden, easing a feeling of sadness with excellent champagne. When all the good-byes were said, and we headed back, I sat next to Jude on the bus, listening to her complain that she didn't want to do any more crash stories like the Von Bulow trial or the recent fires in Florida. She wanted to sink her teeth into some major political stories. I said I understood, and promised I would try to steer more her way, little knowing that, even as the bus made its way down the Bruckner Expressway, events were going on in another part of the world that would give us more than enough of a major political story —indeed, would turn the next three weeks into the busiest of our lives.

VIII.

A NETWORK HERO

"I don't know why everybody isn't more informed. I found myself looking at the television.
You pay attention to some things more than
others."

> —Ralf Traugott, while being held hos-
> tage in Beirut by the hijackers of
> TWA flight 847

On the afternoon of June 14,
1985, as we were being driven back to New York, a TWA
Boeing 727 was making an unscheduled trip across the Med-
iterranean. TWA's flight 847 had been hijacked shortly after
takeoff from Athens earlier that morning, and the plane had
already made one visit to Beirut. The pilot, Captain John
Testrake, had received permission to land there after the
hijackers had threatened to blow up the plane. Once the
aircraft was on the ground, nineteen women and children
were permitted to slide down emergency shutes to safety.

The hijackers then ordered the plane refueled. When
their demands were not met immediately, they began beat-
ing passengers. Captain Testrake again persuaded the Bei-

rut airport authorities to do what the hijackers wanted. After the plane had taken on fuel, the hijackers ordered him to fly to a second destination, Algiers, where twenty-one more passengers were allowed to disembark. Then, after five hours on the ground, the plane headed back to Beirut. It was during this leg of the journey that one of the hijackers ordered stewardess Uli Derickson to instruct the passengers to keep their heads down. The hijackers then shot and killed a twenty-three-year-old U.S. Navy frogman, Robert Stethem. A few minutes later, when the plane landed in Beirut, they dumped his body on the runway.

While the plane sat on the ground, a group of Shiite Moslems boarded it and systematically robbed the passengers of their valuables. They also herded off the plane all passengers bearing official identification, as well as those they thought had Jewish-sounding names. The following morning, Saturday, the plane left Beirut once again for Algiers, where another forty-nine passengers were released. Then the hijackers announced their demands. Unless Israel released 766 prisoners from its Atlit prison camp, they warned, a price would be paid. At 9:00 A.M. Sunday, the plane departed again for Beirut. When it landed this time, it remained on the ground, with thirty exhausted passengers and three crew on board.

I had intended to spend that weekend at the beach, but when I read the papers Saturday morning I knew there was very little point going anywhere. The way the drama was developing, I would certainly have to come back. Katz would want a full-dress show Monday, no matter what happened in the interim, and so I stayed in the city, listening to the hourly bulletins. As I expected, around four o'clock Saturday afternoon, I got a call.

It was Katz's secretary, Elizabeth.

"Jon wants you in Sunday," she said. "Before noon."

I said I'd be there. When I got off the phone, I called Amy and Jude and told them to start making contacts at TWA.

Sunday I was awakened by Epstein, who told me the plane was still on the ground with the passengers still on it. I told him I'd see him in a hour. I got up and made some coffee. I could picture the kind of day it was going to be in the frenetic fishbowl, and I felt a shared sense of identity with the passengers aboard TWA flight 847.

By the time I got to the Broadcast Center, half the senior staff had already arrived, and there were four or five bookers working the phones in the newsroom. Roberta had been there an hour and she was frantically getting things going. She had her book, her great booker's book, a book only a former head booker at "GMA" would have, and she was handing out assignments at random to everyone within earshot. I went downstairs to the cafeteria for more coffee, knowing it was pointless to do anything until Corvo or Katz arrived. When I came back, Missie had joined Roberta, and Epstein was shouting on the phone, so I went back to my office and called a couple of journalists who'd worked in the Middle East. I added their suggestions for guests to a list of my own.

When I returned to the fishbowl, Katz was there. Roberta was telling him: "Of the people who've been released, we've been in contact with . . ." and she began running down a list of names. Before he could interrupt, she continued: "Now, with the relatives of people who are still on board the plane, Amy's been in touch with . . ." and she ran down another list. Katz was practically ready to gag her.

Finally he jumped in: "I think we have to advance the story. A lot of people who were released will be on the local shows tonight. CNN's been running interviews with them all day."

"Yeah, but I think you'll want to hear from them again

tomorrow, Jon," Rand Morrison argued. "This is a summer weekend, and a lot of people won't have seen those interviews."

"We need one person who can tell us what it was like on that plane, and tell it well," Pat Shevlin said, trying to bring to the discussion enough authority to settle the matter.

"Shevlin? What is this?" Katz started giving her the impromptu backrub he often gave to whoever was sitting in the most accessible chair. "This sounds like conviction to me. Okay, but I think you need people who can talk about hostage negotiation—unless they're released of course."

"We have pitched Moorhead Kennedy," Roberta said. "He'll do us, but he's on 'GMA' first."

"Moorhead!" Katz exclaimed. "What would a hostage show be without Moorhead? Fine—book him. We wouldn't want him first anyway. We'll need him later in the program. What about the stewardess, Derickson?"

"No luck yet. We've pitched her through TWA, and Janice has gone to her house."

As Katz was making other suggestions, Shari and Amy burst into the fishbowl.

"We got one!" Amy said. "She'll do us. Her name's Susan Traugott and her brother-in-law is a hostage. She's great, a real talker! How many more of these schmeggegis do we want?"

Opinion was divided. Some people thought we should try to put two or more relatives in the same segment. Others, myself included, felt a one-on-one interview would be more compelling.

"There's no shortage of things to ask," I said.

Shari and Amy and a couple of other bookers appeared to have taken up permanent residence in the fishbowl, adding to the din. Katz gave up trying to compete with it. He moved the senior staff down to his office for the first of about a half-dozen meetings that day.

Aside from the MOVE drama, this was the first time since I had come to the "Morning News" that we were working on a major breaking story that had not already received the validation of print. Wires, newspapers, magazines, and press releases—these were what normally absorbed the attentions of the "Morning News" senior staff. The fact is, the basic source of information for television news is the print media. Unlike a newsroom at a newspaper, where the word off the street is taken seriously, because it may lead to a story nobody else has, and where a tip from a source is followed up for the same reason, the tendency in television news is to greet whatever has not already appeared in print with suspicion. But the hijacking was a big breaking story, with information popping up from every source, and all leads and ideas were fair game.

As we discussed the show, we watched the CNN interviews with the released passengers.

"Can you imagine what it must be like on that plane?" Katz said. "After three days."

"Disgusting!" Shevlin exclaimed.

"Missie, Judy Hole for you on 3701," I said.

Missie was keeping her usual mammoth lists of all the assignments made to bookers. All afternoon she had been issuing reminders about things long since taken care of, then checking off the items on her list, point by point.

"Judy Hole's in charge of the terrorism panel," she was saying now. "She needs to give people times."

"Well, if we have principals and hostage families in the first half hour," Corvo said, "we'd probably want the panel at seven-thirty."

"Who's Judy trying for?" Katz said. "Who do we want on this panel?"

"Well, there's Paul Wilkinson . . ."

"Yeah, he's good."

"I have his number," Roberta said.

"Shouldn't this panel be about negotiation, not terrorism?" Corvo asked. "I mean, the question you want to ask these guys is how do we get these people out."

"That's a good point," Katz said.

"We should have someone who can talk about military options," I suggested.

"Maybe we should mix it up." Katz took down his baseball mitt and started whapping the ball into it. "Have one terrorism expert—Wilkinson. One military guy. How about someone from a police department who negotiates for hostages? I guess it's not the same thing."

"Stansfield Turner could talk about the military option," someone said.

I groaned. I never felt Turner, the former CIA director, had anything interesting to say. But Katz said Joyce liked him and that settled that.

Katz turned up the television to listen to a network newsbreak. Corvo began to draft a rough lineup. When the newsbreak was over Pat Shevlin said, "There's that man up at Harvard, who heads the negotiation project. We've had him on before . . ."

"Roger Fisher!"

"We could go long with this panel if we get all these people," Katz was telling Corvo. "Okay, who can we get to talk about Shiites?"

"There's several people," I said. "There's a man called Clinton Bailey. Another guy named Peter Awn. There's a guy at West Point called Richard Norton, who's very good on the Middle East. But your best man is Fouad Ajami, and he's Shiite."

"How Shiite is he?" Katz wanted to know.

"He's director of Middle East studies at Johns Hopkins," I said.

Katz looked at me suspiciously. "He won't be wearing a jellaba, will he?"

"No, Jon, he won't," I said. "He'll probably be better dressed than you."

And so for the rest of the afternoon our "pitches" went out to the most desired guests, or if they were unavailable, to those one notch less desirable. The bookers would report back on who could appear, and from where. Our ideal was to have guests in the studio in New York, because face-to-face conversations with the anchors were preferred. But trips to New York, even with travel and hotel expenses paid, didn't necessarily fit into politicians' plans, nor into the plans of people caught up in their personal crises. Often they could only go to the nearest affiliate or bureau, where line costs of between $1,500 and $2,000 per remote would mount up. Fortunately, in June 1985 the "Morning News" had not yet hit the budget crunch, and Katz was still spending freely.

The program began to build—out of chaos, a semblance of order. Guests were booked and were waiting to hear what time they would be on the air. Other guests were trying to decide whether they should "do" us or the competition. The scene in the "Morning News" fishbowl, of course, was also being enacted across town in the newsrooms of the other two morning shows, and so every once in a while one of our bookers would barge into the fishbowl and announce: "They can't do it. They're booked on 'Today'." Or "Forget it. 'GMA' has him." Or "We can have them, but we have to go second." There was constant juggling with the lineup. Hours were devoted to achieving the right mix and balance for a well-paced broadcast. Bookers became exasperated with the frequent changes. Guests who did not fit into the latest plan for the show would be canceled, then they might be re-booked—that is if they were still speaking to us. Politicians were used to being jerked around by television news programs, and they would either play ball or jerk us around in turn, depending upon how badly they needed the exposure.

But most ordinary people never got over the arbitrariness of TV booking. One minute our show would be begging them to appear, the next minute it would "blow them off." Or, worse, people would fly to New York, to learn only when they checked into their hotel that they were not going to appear.

By four that afternoon Katz was blowing off all kinds of guests, including politicians, and he was trying to decide where in the program to place the chosen few. The politicians he had picked were Senator Pat Moynihan, a member of the Senate Intelligence Committee, and former Undersecretary of State Joseph Sisco. Then he got a call, and from the pained expression on his face, I thought perhaps we'd offended someone really important, which happened all too often. In such cases, a senior executive would usually get an angry call and have to listen to an earful from a senator's aide. But no—this call was not from Washington. It was from Kentucky—from Phyllis.

When Katz hung up, his head sank toward his desk.

"Phyllis's father-in-law died today," he said. "She won't be anchoring the broadcast tomorrow or all of next week."

Everyone stared at each other blankly. The mood was a lot different from the occasion a few weeks earlier when it was learned that Phyllis would not be on the program one day because her horse had been struck by lightning. On that occasion, everyone in the fishbowl had asked in unison: "Was she on it?" But now the "Morning News" had neither of its regular anchors for what was likely to be the busiest news day of the year.

"So, will it be Maria?" Rand Morrison asked. Then he, like everyone else in the room, remembered that Maria was on vacation. She was on some remote island somewhere with her fiancé Arnold Schwarzenegger, unreachable.

Katz stared at his half-completed lineup. All day long he had been struggling with the usual Phyllis problem, and he had been trying to work things out so that Phyllis could do the human side of the drama, while Schieffer would handle Moynihan and Sisco. Maria would have made things easier. With Maria you could be fairly sure that the word *Shiite* would be pronounced correctly. So Katz now put his head down on the desk and left it there until finally someone in the room suggested: "Terry Smith?"

Katz looked up. "Two male anchors? Two middle-aged men?" he asked.

"Nobody's tried that since Hughes Rudd and Bruce Morton," Shevlin said with a laugh.

But who else was there? Faith Daniels was by then the "Early Morning News" reader, but Katz felt she didn't have the experience to co-anchor a two-hour network broadcast. But then neither did Smith. Terry Smith had been in television only three months. He had been hired as Washington correspondent for the "Morning News" to help deal with the problem caused by Phyllis's inability to do political stories. Most of his work so far had been taped pieces or single live interviews, never a two-hour stint.

"Well, Terry will know what he's talking about at least," Pat said. "He's worked in the Middle East."

Katz looked around the room again, and was met by a gaze of hopeful faces.

"Okay, get out of here. Go on. Fuck off, all of you," he said, picking up the phone.

He made the call to Ed Joyce. Ten minutes later it was decided: Terry Smith would make his debut as an anchor.

"Terry's on his way," Katz announced, stepping into the crowded fishbowl.

There were loud cheers. Terry was well liked. As the cheers died down, Katz added, "That poor son of a bitch."

Around seven o'clock Katz made excellent use of the "Morning News" budget, ordering about $200 worth of Chinese food. Smith arrived in New York to find thirty frantic people up to their elbows in bamboo shoots and curried prawns while the phones rang incessantly and the show's lineup changed for the umpteenth time. Katz had decided that we should do a segment on the TWA pilot, John Testrake, so bookers were now calling his relatives on Long Island. The relatives wouldn't talk, but several of his friends said they would, agreeing to appear on the "Morning News" to assure viewers that Captain Testrake would be cool in a crisis. At least a half-dozen more changes would be made before the broadcast was turned over to the overnight staff.

As I was on my way out the door, Katz grabbed me by the arm.

"Hey, headline writer, print guy! Got any ideas what we should call this broadcast?"

It was nearly midnight.

"*Ordeal* is the only word that comes to mind," I said.

So it was decided: "The Ordeal of TWA Flight 847."

The next morning I made it to the control room by seven. We opened cold, with a piece of tape showing the plane still on the ground in Beirut. Several stories had broken overnight. The body of Robert Stethem was being flown to Spain. One hostage, Robert Peel, had been released for medical reasons, and from Cyprus, where he had been flown, he was able to describe the conditions aboard flight 847. That morning the "CBS Morning News" put on a first-rate broadcast. All the interviews went well. When Ajami's turn came, Katz said: "This guy better be good, McCabe, or your ass is grass." But Ajami was able to explain concisely the recent rise to power of Lebanese Shiites, and to offer reasons for their actions, no matter how misguided they might seem to Americans. Katz looked approving. It was toward the end of the program that morning that most Americans heard for the first time the name Nabih Berri, the head of the Amal militia, as the story broke that the passengers had been removed from the plane and turned over to him.

After the broadcast I talked to Terry Smith in the fishbowl. He was none the worse for his ordeal. It was only in turning to cameras and using such phrases as "we'll be right back" or "please stay with us" that he seemed a bit awkward. Terry was taking a big interest in the story; he even came to the meetings that morning, something anchors rarely did.

That Monday turned out to be easier than the frantic Sunday that had preceded it, now that the booking staff was familiar with the story's cast of characters and was armed with a new stack of phone numbers. For Tuesday morning's show, we planned another two-hour broadcast devoted entirely to the crisis, and it was agreed that we wanted the Israeli view. We booked Aharon Yariv, the former chief of Israeli intelligence. Katz also wanted a congressional panel, and a panel to tell us how the American people were responding to the crisis. We would also have five minutes of Zbigniew Brzezinski, which Roberta imposed on us, and which I opposed vehemently, to no avail. Brzezinski, in his infinite wisdom, would say that speed was of the essence in securing the release of the hostages, a point of view that turned out to be utterly wrong. All in all the program began to seem to me to be too heavy on second-guess guests, too many people unrelated to the drama offering their point of view. After I had gone over a few bookers' packets, I asked Epstein if anyone over at "Evening News" had tried to get an interview with Berri.

"There's no satellite in Beirut," he said.

"Well, how about a phoner?"

He said I should forget it, but the idea of not even trying galled me. I wandered over to the foreign desk and asked if anyone had taken a shot at getting an interview with Berri. The staffer looked at me like I was some fool ingenue who had nothing better to do than waste his time, and so around seven o'clock I went back to my over-air-conditioned cubicle, closed the door, and began making calls.

The previous week I had received a call from a reporter, Morgan Strong, who had told me he was going to Libya. He wanted to know if CBS News would be interested in using him to set up an interview with Colonel Kaddafi. CBS News ultimately was not, but in the course of checking out Morgan Strong I learned that he had great contacts throughout the Middle East. I called him now and asked if he knew any way of contacting the Amal militia. He did. He had lots of numbers in Beirut—numbers for Walid Jumblatt, numbers for the editors of the Beirut newspaper *An Nahar,* and he also had both an office and a home phone number for Nabih Berri.

It was 8:00 P.M. when I made my first call to Beirut —3:00 A.M., Beirut time. I called Berri's home. There was no answer. Then I called the office number, and a man answered. I spoke to him in French, but he did not understand me. Then to my surprise, we made contact in English.

"Nobody ees 'ere," he said.

I explained that I worked for CBS News in the United States, and that we would like to talk to Mr. Berri.

"Yes, but ees not here."

I felt like I was being asked to play the straight man in a Monty Python routine.

"Will he be there in the morning?" I asked. "Can I leave a message?"

"Yes, but I go before 'ee comes in."

"Who am I talking to?" I asked.

"I am a guard."

Shit, I thought. Does he have the American prisoners right there?

"Are you guarding the hostages?" I asked. "Can I speak with one of them?"

"No, no, no." The man chuckled softly. "I am guarding the Amal office."

Again he explained that he would go off duty before Mr. Berri came in, and I asked if I could leave a message for him to pass on to whoever took over from him, to be passed on to Mr. Berri. He said yes, he could do that. He would give the message to the guard who took over from him.

It was starting to get complicated. I asked if he could assure me that the message would be passed along to Mr. Berri, and he said: "Well, er, sometime Meester Berri get very busy."

When I hung up, the conversation seemed slightly unreal. I marveled at the simplicity of modern communications. In this freezing back office in New York, I had pressed a dozen digits and talked immediately to a man half a world away who was guarding a militia headquarters in the world's most embattled city, and for all I knew was only a few hundred feet away from a group of prisoners who were commanding the attention of both the American government and the world press. At the same time, I did not imagine that the Amal militia headquarters in Beirut bore any resemblance to a Vatican receiving room, so I figured the odds were pretty slim that Nabih Berri would get my message the day after he had taken charge of forty American hostages. My opinion was shared by the overnight producer, Bob Mayer, with whom I left the Beirut number when I walked into the fishbowl later that evening. But Mayer promised he would put through a call around six, in time to set up an interview for seven.

I went home, set the alarm for 6:15 A.M., and slept soundly.

When I walked into the control room the next morning, it was 6:59, and the place was in a flurry. I watched Schieffer and Smith clip on their microphones. Then the show opened and I heard Schieffer say: "There is news this morning from Beirut. Nabih Berri, the head of the Amal Shiites, says he is freeing three of the hostages from the hijacked TWA flight 847—today . . ."

My first thought was: this is a general announcement. Then I heard Schieffer say: " . . . and he talked about this to Terry Smith earlier this morning. . . ."

My blood jumped. The audio tape rolled.

". . . the Amal movement and myself," Berri said, his voice crackling over the line. "We move for only one thing —to save human lives—and at the same time I will consider that the American government move to save the lives of the seven hundred people in the Atlit prison. And in two hours I will release three . . . three people—Mr. Roussos, the Greek singer, and his girlfriend, and another American . . ."

In front of me, standing behind the director, Jon Katz looked like a baseball fan trying to start a wave. He leaped up and down. He let out whoops for ten minutes. He could not keep still. He got on the phone to the PR people, and told them to get their asses up to the control room immediately. Then he went over to Corvo to ask how we'd gotten the exclusive.

"Better talk to *him,*" Corvo said, with an emphatic gesture toward me.

"You! You got this!" Katz yelled. "I knew I was right to hire you, you useless fucking Brit. About time you did something right around here." Then he calmed down a bit. "So how the fuck did you do it?"

I told him, and I confess I enjoyed being a network hero for a day. And I enjoyed the papers the next morning when the story of how I'd gotten the interview ran in the *Daily News* and *USA Today.*

I was excused from the routines of the fishbowl that day.

I spent some time with Ajami, and some time on the phone with Morgan Strong, and I got more numbers in Beirut. One of these was for Colonel Akef Haidar, Berri's deputy. The next morning we opened the broadcast again with a long interview from Beirut, this time with Haidar.

I got Haidar on the phone myself at 6:30 A.M.

"Patch it through!" I yelled, and the call I had made from the special red phone in the audio room went through to the announcer's booth where Terry Smith was sitting.

No, the colonel said, in reply to Terry Smith's question, there would be no more hostage releases until the prisoners in Atlit were released. He then assured us that all the hostages were safe and well, and that they were enjoying Lebanese food and watching Lebanese TV.

I was standing in the audio room, listening over a headset. I looked at the clock, then at Terry, and I watched the audio tape roll. I knew we had several good bites, but I didn't want to start editing the interview until Terry was finished, in case Haidar dropped a bombshell. Terry finally hung up at 6:50. Then a technician and I scrambled like mad to cut a minute or two for the broadcast, trying desperately to hear the tape in the noisy control room.

Mike Whitney, who rarely got rattled, ambled toward me.

"Having fun?" he said.

It was 6:59.

"It's done," I said, marking the sound bite with a piece of white tape. "I'll cut another for seven-thirty."

I flopped back in my seat. I was sweating like crazy.

We were looking good on the story. The wires were carrying what the "CBS Morning News" was reporting, and Ajami, who had the advantage of fluent Arabic and many contacts in the Amal movement, was setting up more interviews. Around three that afternoon I went looking for him. After combing the building twice, I still couldn't find him. I asked several people if they had seen him. Nobody had.

Then on the way back from the cafeteria, I went to talk to the foreign desk, and as I walked along the corridor outside the "Evening News" newsroom, I saw him in a small room, with Anne Reingold, a producer for Special Events.

"What do you want?" she said rudely, when I stopped at the door.

"I need to talk to Fouad," I said.

"He's busy right now," she told me. "He's working for Dan."

She was literally guarding him. Fouad looked sheepish. He did not know what to say.

I was doubly offended. Not only was the "Evening News" once again automatically taking over a "Morning News" resource, it was now denying us access to our own. I asked Ajami to call me when he had a chance, and I went back to my office.

I had been working the phone for about half an hour when there was a knock on my door. A producer from the "Evening News" said that Joan Richman, head of Special Events, wanted to see me right away. I said I'd be over just as soon as I finished my phone conversation. The minute I hung up the phone, I went to see Katz.

I found him in his office and told him what was going on. He shrugged and said there was nothing he could do. "You know the story around here," he said. "You know where the throne is."

"Let me get it straight," I said. "Do I have to give them my contacts?"

"You work for CBS News," Katz said.

"That's a cop-out," I told him, and he knew it. Like everyone else in the place, I worked for the broadcast I was assigned to.

"Just remember," Katz said, "ABC's kicked the shit out of them. Remember, they're jumping out of their skins in there."

It was true. ABC's "World News Tonight" had scooped the "CBS Evening News" the previous evening, interviewing the TWA crew who were still aboard the plane.

"Handle it your own way," Katz told me, "and by the way, see if you can get an interview with a weeping hostage."

"What?" I said.

"See if you can get us a weeping hostage," Katz repeated. "Think of the impact that would make."

Suddenly I was annoyed at him. Not so much because of his line about the hostage, but because I realized he wasn't prepared to go to bat for his own broadcast. There was still speculation that his future at the "Morning News" was uncertain, and I figured he had decided to play a safe political game.

I walked back through the "Evening News" newsroom and found Joan Richman in the small Special Events control room. She was a tough, battle-seasoned CBS veteran, and when I walked in she was on the phone chewing out the Beirut correspondent, Larry Pintak, who so far had not distinguished himself. I waited while she finished her conversation, then she swung around in her chair. She told me: "You have some phone numbers. We could use them."

This time I greeted rudeness with what it deserved.

"We could use them too," I said. "You've got Fouad."

Joan Richman sat bolt upright in her chair. I could only push this battle so far. After all, I was talking to a CBS vice-president, and though she backed off a peg at first, she quickly pulled rank. I got a five-minute speech about cooperation at a time like this. Knowing I'd get no backing from Katz, I reluctantly gave her the numbers, adding that once in a while we could use a little cooperation from "Evening News." I was about to leave when Ed Joyce walked in.

He had been to the "Morning News" fishbowl to look for me and they had told him I was over here. Joyce didn't make many trips to the "Evening News" newsroom, let alone the

"Morning News," so I assumed it had to be important. We went out into the newsroom, Joyce tugging at his suspenders. I was about to tell him that I was already suffering from a normal journalistic disinclination to surrender sources, when he said:

"First, you should know this. We're having Ajami work on getting an interview with Berri for Dan."

"I know," I said.

"Nothing, and I repeat, nothing, should be allowed to jeopardize this. But since you've got good contacts, here's what I want you to do. We want Pintak to be able to take a tour of one of the houses where the hostages are held. We'd also like to get a reporter and crew on the plane."

"For which broadcast?" I said.

"We'll decide that later," Joyce said. "In the meantime let's see what you can do. But remember, whatever you do, don't jeopardize anything for Dan."

Heaven forbid, I thought.

As I walked away, Joyce called after me: "Did you give Joan the numbers?"

"If she can read, she's got 'em," I said, and I headed back to the "Morning News" fishbowl.

I had spoken to Colonel Akef Haidar only an hour ago, so I decided to wait another hour before calling him again. I went into the newsroom and read some wire copy. On my way back to my office, I ran into Katz. He was eager to find out what Joyce had said.

"They're using Fouad to get an interview with Berri," I told him. "Basically we're fucked from here on in."

"I figured," Katz said, looking a little crestfallen. "Well, see if you can get us that interview with the hostage. That's worth a lot more, and the "Evening News" people aren't going to get that."

I went back to my office and called Haidar. We were getting pretty friendly by then, and I had enjoyed several

conversations with him about the policies of various govern-
ments. I even had a long conversation with his wife about
Saks Fifth Avenue, which she seemed to know quite well. I
told him what CBS wanted. He told me a visit to the hostages was unlikely, and that he had no authority over the
plane—it was still in the hands of elements over which he
had no control.

Then I said: "Would it be possible to arrange a phone
interview between a hostage and a relative here?"

Haidar thought about this. "It may be possible," he said.
Then he added: "As for your other two requests, I should tell
you—I just received the same requests from the president
of your company."

"What?" I said. "From who? When?"

"From Mr. Joyce. A few minutes ago. I told him what I am
telling you."

I was so stunned I could hardly believe it. The president
of CBS News had gotten the phone numbers from Richman
and was using them to score brownie points with Rather.

"We are doing our best to arrange the interview with Mr.
Rather," Haidar said. "Mr. Ajami has spoken to Mr. Berri. I
think it is being arranged."

"Thank you, colonel," I said. "I'll call you tomorrow."

I sat there in a slight daze. About half an hour later Fouad
Ajami called me. I asked him if he would be in for tomorrow
morning's broadcast. He said, no, he was very tired, and that
the "Evening News" wanted him to stay until nine that
night. He then apologized for disappearing earlier in the
day. "But you know," he added, "they made it clear to me
—I have to go with the power."

"Just like in Lebanon, Fouad?" I said.

Ajami laughed softly. Within a few hours he would get
Dan Rather his interview with Nabih Berri, and the myth of
the anchor as working journalist would be advanced one
step further. Later that year, a *New York* magazine re-

porter, in a profile of Dan Rather, would write: "When ABC was scooping CBS at the scene of the TWA airline hijacking in Beirut last summer, Rather managed virtually single-handedly to keep CBS competitive merely by working the phones—most notably in securing a transcontinental interview with Nabih Berri. . . ."

I felt like sending him a note: never believe anything you learn from network PR.

For the next few weeks, I worked without Ajami's help as the TWA hostage story shifted almost daily. A fuss was made later about journalists, particularly television anchors, stepping into the role of ambassadors and negotiators. The fact was, however, that the media were only stepping into a vacuum the U.S. government itself had created. If the government's contacts with the powers in Lebanon were limited, it was inevitable that the media would try to find their own sources of information. During the three weeks of the crisis, I had many conversations with families of the hostages being held, and never once did I hear a word of complaint from them about the media's role in the affair. In fact, many of them were grateful for the coverage. They seemed to feel that if the drama was enacted in human terms, and if the personalities on both sides were known, it was less likely that any government would disclaim responsibility for the outcome, and therefore less likely that the drama would come to a violent end.

Most mornings I came in at 4:00 A.M. and worked closely with Terry Smith. He was clearly enjoying his new role. We would sit together in the small announcer's booth next to the control room and do our phone interviews from Beirut between 6:00 and 7:00 A.M. Then there would be a mad rush to cut the tapes for each newsblock. Toward the end of the first week, it became increasingly difficult to get through to

Beirut, and by then the Amal Shiites seemed to have caught on that there was a better way to secure the attention of the world press. They held their now-famous press conference with Allyn Conwell and four other hostages, at which the Beirut reporters took part in an ugly melee, while the Shiite militia struggled to restrain them.

The following Monday, the Israelis released thirty-one Shiites and the serious bargaining began. Berri was insisting that all the Atlit prisoners be released before he would free the hostages. On Tuesday he flew to Syria, where he took some heat from President Assad. He then said he was willing to transfer the hostages to a Western embassy. By then it was becoming clear that a deal was in the offing, so we sent bookers to Frankfurt, West Germany, where the hostages were to be flown, if and when they were released.

By then Phyllis had returned to the broadcast, and so Terry Smith went to Frankfurt, too. The rest of us spent another wild Sunday at the Broadcast Center, putting together another two-hour special program as the release became imminent.

At some point that day I went down to the "Evening News" area to see Ajami. He was still occupying the same small office, but he was no longer under guard, and as the hostages were being driven to Damascus, we talked about the political advantage Assad had gained.

As we talked, Rather and Stringer walked in.

"We need a graphic to show the hostages' progress," Rather was telling Stringer.

He seemed unconcerned by the presence of someone from the "Morning News," and so I said: "I used to have an old Lincoln that had a speedometer which moved like horizontal mercury."

"That's perfect," Rather said. "That's exactly what we need."

I resisted asking him if I could have Ajami back.

Later that day I watched the press conference in Damascus, at which various hostages expressed their gratitude to Assad. Allyn Conwell was especially effusive, conducting himself as if he were making the salesman-of-the-year award. I was sitting in Katz's office, watching the circus.

"And now let's have a big hand for . . ." Conwell was saying.

"Unbelievable," I said.

"This is why TV is so amazing," Katz said.

He was right.

The next morning the hostages were flown to Frankfurt. We had sent additional bookers in the meantime, including Amy Rosenblum, who had never been to Germany before.

"You're going," Katz told her. "Quit bitching. You bitched about not going to London. Okay, you're going to Germany."

Within ten minutes of arriving at Frankfurt, Amy's cab from the airport was in an accident. It did not faze her. She brought to her booking in Germany the same panache for which she was renowned at home. On the day the hostages arrived in Frankfurt, Amy made a point of offering to hold the purses of a dozen of their wives. It was a brilliant tactical move. Even in the emotional tumult of reunion, wives of released hostages do not go far without their purses, and so the wives brought their husbands to Amy, who promptly booked them. With Amy sitting on a virtual monopoly, the bookers at "Today" and "GMA" were furious. One outraged ABC booker solicited the assistance of Charles Glass, the ABC correspondent who had obtained the interview with Captain Testrake while the TWA plane sat on the Beirut runway. When Glass tried to persuade Amy to be reasonable, she told him:

"Yeah, yeah, Charles. I know who you are and I know

what you did in Beirut. But that was Beirut, this is Frankfurt."

Spoken like a true competitor. Amy did not know the
term *pool coverage,* and Glass, clearly perplexed, backed off.

And so that morning the "CBS Morning News" featured
several of the best interviews with former hostages, including a fine interview that Terry Smith did with Peter Hills,
in which Hills let loose all his pent-up anger, and then burst
into tears.

Ours was a proud little group of bookers who returned to
New York a few days later, after a weekend in Paris. The
New York Times front page had carried entire chunks of our
interviews word-for-word, with attribution.

Katz put out a memo: "Please accept my thanks for the
superb job you have all done in putting together our hostage
crisis coverage. I could never begin to tell you all the praise
coming from inside and outside the building. What we have
really demonstrated again is that this staff should have a lot
of pride in itself and optimism about the future."

He was wrong about the latter point, but nobody knew
that then.

IX.

WHEN IN DOUBT, BOOK 'EM

"We're a circus, we're a troupe of acrobats,
we're in the boredom-killing business."
     —Peter Finch as anchorman Howard
     Beale in *Network*

In the preface to *CBS News Standards,* the network's guide to journalistic ethics and practices, there is a 1976 memorandum written by Richard Salant, a former president of CBS News, which reads in part as follows:

"To the extent that radio and television are mass media of entertainment, it is entirely proper to give most of the people what most of them want most of the time. But we in broadcast journalism cannot, should not, and will not base our judgments on what we think the viewers and listeners are 'most interested' in, or hinge our news judgment and our news treatment on our guesses as to what news the people want to hear or see . . . the judgments must be professional news judgments—nothing more, nothing less."

By the summer of 1985, nine years after Dick Salant wrote his memo, those instructions had no bearing whatever on the reality of the "CBS Morning News." By then it was becoming clear that the TWA hostage crisis represented a high-water mark of sorts for the program. The TWA crisis, of course, was the news story of the year, and the "Morning News" was obliged to cover it in depth. But when it was over, and with Kurtis gone, we went back to following Joyce's mandate to restructure the broadcast around Phyllis.

It was only three months since the "Morning News" had received its complimentary notice in the *Wall Street Journal* for carrying the most news of the three morning programs. Even before the TWA crisis, however, this reputation had begun to erode. By midsummer, even the news items that made it onto the program had to be entertaining; at the same time, news events that met the criterion of being entertaining rarely escaped the program's attention. No longer was any thought given to exercising what Salant had called "professional news judgment." Each day Katz would want the show to have its share of "glitz"—celebrity interviews or features that "livened up" the program.

"Where's the glitz?" he would say at our morning meetings. "We need some major glitz here."

By then the intention was to do exactly what Salant had expressly forbidden—to serve up what the public would enjoy.

That summer, when it was less noticed because there is less news in the summer, the broadcast became as soft, and on some days even softer, than the other two morning programs. We devoted hours to the Live Aid concert, and segment after segment to the public's distaste for the new Coca-Cola. We did a segment on the threat of killer bees. Tipper Gore's stand against X-rated music videos got a lot of play, as did the phenomenon of tennis burnout. All these were certainly news stories, but they were chosen specifically for their entertainment potential. Taken as a whole, and combined with even softer features such as the standard movie reviews and consumer tips, this meant that volumes of legitimate important news were being downplayed or excluded from the program. In addition, we began to add more of the really soft stuff. That summer we devoted time to interviews with older soap opera stars, a week-long series on talk show hosts, advice on how not to spoil children, a piece on new special-effects in movies, how the summer rock tours were going, exercising when pregnant, interviews with the daytime Emmy winners, a survey of wine cooler ads, how to get rid of garden pests, and how to deal with the postvacation blues.

Katz would look at his lineup each day, and except for a lead story or two, would exclude virtually everything that had the potential to be dull or merely informative. "We need more heat, less light," he would say, and the staff was ordered to raise the temperature. A debate between two qualified people on a matter that might be of some interest to a lot of Americans wasn't enough. The debate had to feature a star, or stars, a celebrity of one sort or another, or people who would add "heat." And so we got Jerry Falwell versus Christie Hefner, Tipper Gore versus Frank Zappa, Jesse Jackson versus Ben Wattenberg—and these were the serious segments. Most of the parade of personalities had little to do with any issue.

I knew why we were doing this. We were doing it because the hostage crisis had done nothing for the ratings. The program had scored a 3.0 during those turbulent weeks. But as the switch was made to "info-tainment," the ratings declined even further, into the upper twos. It seemed to me that we were losing both ratings *and* credibility, and that it was worth retaining at least one of these.

I began to gripe at Katz.

"Jeezus Christ, McCabe!" he shot back. "You're starting to sound like one of Murrow's ghosts. Don't you think there's enough of them around here?"

During my first few weeks at the broadcast, as I sat in the control room, I had heard a lot about the ghosts of Murrow from Katz. At first his attitude struck me as odd for a newspaperman, but I soon realized that Katz thought of himself as new age rather than old style. At the papers he'd worked at, he had been a big advocate of trend pieces. Ironically, he was much more adept at dealing with hard news than he was at playing at the blurred edges of journalism. And I suspected he knew this about himself, even if he couldn't admit it, because he proceeded to dump the softer stuff into my lap.

The softer features at the "Morning News" were divided up between Pat Collins, the entertainment reviewer, Maria Shriver in Hollywood, and Phyllis. The three women were engaged in a constant turf war over who would do what, and a lot of power plays went on behind closed doors. Individual bookers, drawn to respective camps, would often book guests for a particular anchor or correspondent. Arguments ensued, especially as the program became softer, and one morning Katz called me into his office and told me that in addition to doing my regular duties, I was to straighten out the confusion.

What he wanted me to do was bring the entire mess under one umbrella, and serve as a kind of clearing house. Any entertainment interview or feature was to be cleared through me. I was to leave intact the healthy competition among the three women, but at the same time I was to delineate who would do what, and put an end to their quarreling. I knew it wouldn't be easy. Phyllis was on a major celebrity kick, and was pushing for more live interviews with big-name guests, in addition to the interviews she was doing for her "famous couples" series, which was to air in the fall. Collins not only did reviews, she incorporated bites from interviews into pieces. She also had a strong, independent team working for her, essentially a separate unit.

Shriver was biding her time; like Grant at Galena, she was waiting to be called. But she was still eager to be on the program at least twice a week with taped pieces that would present her favorably. Both Collins and Shriver had good contacts in the entertainment world—Collins by virtue of a long career in which she had managed to offend virtually no one, Maria by dint of hard work and a base in Hollywood.

I knew what Katz was getting me into.

"I'll get a job in the diplomatic corps after this," I told him.

"Well, it's your baby," he said. "I'm sick of the whining, and it needs one person to handle it."

I called all the bookers together for a meeting. From now on, I told them, live interviews were to go to Phyllis (she, after all, was the anchor), except in cases where a celebrity insisted on being interviewed by Pat Collins because of a long association. Maria was to concentrate mainly on pieces, which was fine by her, unless a particular celebrity had to be interviewed on the West Coast, in which case Maria could do it. The bookers were not to make deals with guests or with PR people over who was going to do the interview —that was the prerogative of the executive producer. And I wanted constant updates on who was pursuing what.

I faced a row of grim faces, and I knew I would encounter resistance. The next day I heard from Collins's bookers that Dustin Hoffman, who was to appear in *Death of a Salesman,* would only do an interview with Collins. That turned out not to be true. Meanwhile Phyllis took the new mandate to mean that things had been resolved in her favor, and became especially chummy. Then two days later she was in my office with a complaint.

She closed the door.

"Why is Maria doing an interview with Danielle Steel? You know she's someone I've always wanted to do."

I explained that Danielle Steel had insisted the interview be done in California, and so Maria was the obvious choice.

"But, you know I'm traveling all the time for the couples series," Phyllis said. "We're going out west next weekend."

"I know," I said. "But you're also doing interviews with Diahann Carroll and Connie Sellica. How many interviews can you do between coast-to-coast flights over a weekend?"

Phyllis dropped the subject. Not so her producer, Shirley, who came in to see me right after Phyllis left.

After arguing with me for half an hour about Danielle Steel, she said: "I just want to get it straight. Are we doing Donna Mills, or not?"

"Shirley," I said. "You are doing Donna Mills."

"Good."

Shirley marched out, and Amy who had been waiting outside came in to see me.

"I don't get it," she said, slapping down her packet for me to read. "Donna Mills would go to the opening of a mall."

The easiest of the three to deal with was Maria. She preferred to do pieces anyway rather than straight interviews, and she and her producer had plenty of original ideas. Maria had been operating independently for a long time, but she was willing to call and inform me in advance whom she intended to pursue. So the only remaining problem was the rivalry between Pat Collins and Phyllis, and by then Collins knew she was on shaky ground with Katz. I talked to her, and we resolved things, and for a week or two I brought a measure of peace to the battlefield.

Then the conflicts started up again, not between anchor and correspondents, but among the bookers. The bookers were used to invoking the names of whoever they thought would secure them the interview. To some extent I couldn't blame them. The need to get guests was hammered into the bookers, so if invoking a name helped, they would do it. They would say, "Oh, Phyllis is just dying to interview so and so," and sometimes this was the only ploy that worked because the guests the show most wanted—actors, rock musicians, comedians, television stars—were represented by PR people who were all too aware of the "Morning News" ratings.

Given its ratings handicap, it might be assumed that the "Morning News" would have done its best to cultivate PR people and to stay in their good graces. But Katz was a total bust when it came to knowing how to get the soft stuff. He had contempt for PR people, and he would regularly "blow off" a celebrity if something better came up.

One day he called me into his office wanting to know why we had not been able to get Barbra Streisand when the other two shows had her.

"Because you pissed off her PR man," I said.

"*I* did?" he exclaimed, utterly surprised.

"You pissed him off when you canceled the McGuire Sisters," I said. "They're repesented by the same person."

"Oh, bullshit! Over a little thing like that."

"It's true, Jon. That's why we don't have her."

Katz refused to believe me and he refused to adapt. And so the bookers were constantly battling the odds. In addition, NBC and ABC regularly pressured their own stars to appear first on "Today" and "Good Morning America," respectively. CBS did not. So when Stacy Keach, whose "Mike Hammer" series was returning to CBS, showed up on "Good Morning America" and not at all on the "Morning News," I suggested to Katz that since celebrities now formed a substantial part of our broadcast, maybe it was time we tried to make the competition a bit more equal.

Katz stuck his head in the sand, insisting we were still a news show. Two days later he was complaining that we had no celebrities. He wanted to know who we could get at the last minute to glitz up the program. That's the way it was. One minute he would be telling the senior staff to find ways to be different from the other two shows, then he would tell us we were getting too far from the mainstream. In the control room each morning, when stars showed up on the other shows, he would want to know why we didn't have them. The bookers threw up their hands in exasperation. They had told him the reason, but it didn't sink in. From his first day to his last as the "Morning News" executive producer, Jon Katz never recognized that the show was the butt of jokes throughout the entire PR industry.

Toward the end of the summer, with the show going nowhere and the ratings stuck in the upper twos, the bookers began to get depressed and worn out. Their day at the "Morning News" was a long one. They were expected to be at the Broadcast Center to greet every guest they booked, and they had to be in the control room while the segment in which their guest appeared was on the air. Bookers who didn't have a segment that morning—and they all usually did—would not have to be in until nine. But they rarely left before seven in the evening, and if a story was still breaking, or if they were waiting for an editor to cut tape, they often did not get home until much later. They were also regularly called at home by the overnight staff. In all, most of them put in a twelve- to fourteen-hour day, in addition to being dispatched around the country on special assignments during which they might catch a few hours' sleep over a seventy-two-hour work stint. On top of all this, if something went wrong they were the first to hear about it, even if the screwup was the fault of the anchor. Nobody yelled at anchors, but bookers made easy targets. As a result, they brought to their work a certain gallows humor, and a healthy skepticism for any well-meaning attempt to improve their lot.

One of my new duties that summer was to run the weekly bookers' meeting—a fate worse than death, a colleague warned me. The bookers were a ragtag but contentious bunch, whose paths to their present careers were as varied as they were. They were supposed to come to the meeting with ideas, and some of them did. Others came for the free meal, and some stopped coming when the meal was dropped during the budget crunch. During the meetings, I would run through the grids, establish where the guests would be, whether we needed tape for a particular segment, and how much time the segment would require. I also had to check if we needed props, if the time of a guest's appearance was fixed or flexible, and if there were any other special requirements. Then the bookers were free to offer ideas, the number of which varied in inverse proportion to the degree to which they used the meeting as a gripe session.

There was a lot of venting of spleen that summer. A third of the staff was on vacation, making for an increased work load for those who were left. Shari started the meeting one Wednesday with a gripe about a memo that had gone out from John O'Regan, advising bookers that they had to pick up their own packages in the lobby. Under the new edict, the clerks would no longer be able to run errands.

Janice chimed in: "I'm waiting for a call. So now I've got to get packages, too? While they sit around watching baseball? I don't have time to watch baseball. I wish I did."

Janice actually watched plenty of baseball. She was the show's main asset when it came to booking sports guests. (Later that year, she turned George Brett's head during the World Series. A reporter took note and wrote a column about George's infatuation. The baseball star was on the "Morning News" three or four times.)

Amy was listening as Janice complained about the clerk situation. Amy had no patience. Her perfectly polished nails were already rapping on the conference room table. She was a legend in booking, a legend that had started in Boise, Idaho, during the 1984 presidential campaign. Katz had decided that we should interview old people around the country about whether they preferred Reagan's or Mondale's policy on Social Security. On a plane to Boise, Amy had gotten up from her seat and announced to all the passengers that she was Amy Rosenblum from Long Island, she worked for the "CBS Morning News," she was doing a segment on Social Security, and did anyone have any relatives or friends in old-age homes?

"Miss, Miss," the stewardess protested, "I'm not sure you can take surveys." But Amy was already being supplied with names, and later that day she held roundtable auditions at three or four nursing homes. The resulting segments, always a risk with old people, were inspired.

"Janice, Janice," Amy was saying now, "he gets it, we all get it."

"Well, I just think there's no excuse for the clerks to be doing nothing . . ."

"Can we talk about my drunk-driving segment?"

Maggie Shumaker, whose main responsibility was booking authors, interrupted from the far end of the table.

"I need to know if we need two or three guests."

"Depends who they are," I said.

She explained, and I said two would do, if they were good.

"Of course, they'll be good!" Maggie exclaimed. "My guests are *always* good. Why don't you ever trust me?"

Maggie was always exclaiming, objecting. It was a permanent beef of hers that the show never trusted her judgment and could never make up its collective mind about which guests it wanted. Hers was one of the rougher jobs at the "Morning News." "Today" featured a lot of authors and was generally given first crack by publishers, while our coverage of new books was spotty. We went with whatever Katz felt was hot.

In the background, I could hear Shari saying, "How do Jewish girls commit suicide?"

"Pile up their sweaters and jump off!" Amy shouted across the table.

"What? What? I didn't hear that," Maggie said, having forgotten about her drunk-driving segment for the moment.

Amy repeated the joke and Maggie collapsed in laughter.

"This meeting's got about ten minutes left in it," I said to Rand, who was sitting next to me. I had brought him along for moral support.

We were saved by the appearance of Shirley, a guest appearance. Shirley Wershba was the grande dame of the "Morning News" bookers. When the *New York Times* reported that the entire human race may have been descended from one female ancestor, Bob Epstein said her name was probably Shirley. Our Shirley was less than two years from pension eligibility, and she no longer attended the bookers' meeting. Instead, she would say that her husband, Joe, a veteran "60 Minutes" producer, had asked her to lunch. Joe and Shirley had lunch together in the CBS cafeteria almost every day.

"Shirley!" everyone exclaimed in astonishment. "You came to a meeting!"

"No, I didn't," Shirley retorted. "I don't come to meetings. I came to see *him.*"

She zeroed in on Rand. Technically, he was her boss, but she overwhelmed him. Rand was a very tense, methodical person, who had a habit of playing with rubber bands. Shirley was obstinate and difficult. If she was a lot of fun for some people, she had it in for Rand, who had committed the cardinal sin of making work for her.

"Shirley, let's talk outside," Rand said. They left the room together.

"Shirley's awful mean to Rand," Shari said. "Why is she so mean to him?"

"She's mean to Katz too," Amy reminded her.

It was true. Katz was terrified of Shirley. Ever since the London trip, when she made him help her edit, he had avoided run-ins with her. Outside the door, I could now hear her going at Rand. Inside, my efforts to get the meeting going again weren't producing much. Ideas were few. Judy

Hole wanted to talk about guests for her segment on the twentieth anniversary of the Watts riots, so we talked about that. Then someone else suggested we do a segment on the new women in country music, and I said it sounded like a good idea for Forrest Sawyer, who had been sitting in as co-anchor for the vacationing Schieffer.

"How come?" Janice said.

"Because Forrest used to be a dee-jay," I told her.

There was a general murmur of approval.

"I don't really know Forrest well," Shari said. "I don't really know what he's interested in."

Neither did I.

"I'll ask him to come to the meeting next week," I said. It would be an eye-opener for him, if nothing else.

There wasn't much more. It was August, the dog days, and I soon wrapped up the meeting. Besides, I'd told Forrest I'd meet with him to talk about packets. It was becoming increasingly clear that he would be the next permanent male anchor of the "Morning News."

F orrest Sawyer had been a regular on the "Early Morning News" since July, co-hosting with Faith Daniels. (The "Early Morning News" was seen by about 1.4 million people between 6:30 and 7:00 A.M., later in some parts of the country.) He was thirty-five, not unintelligent, certainly a capable newsreader. He'd been plucked from CBS's Atlanta affiliate after his agent, Art Kaminsky, had sent Ed Joyce and Eric Ober a tape. They both liked it enough to make a deal for Sawyer to anchor the early broadcast, with the understanding that he was to have first shot as the permanent replacement on the main show once Kurtis left. He quickly established himself on the early broadcast, and was moved up to the main show when Bob Schieffer went on vacation.

Within a few days, I'd been told that the management

approved of him. I was surprised. He seemed too bland and entirely too young to sit across from Phyllis, who needed a stronger male presence as her co-anchor. But then I remembered what Kurtis had said about the choice of anchor being a fair representation of the management's commitment to the program.

Forrest looked and acted rather like one of those high school kids who always had pens sticking out of his breast pocket. Other people thought so too.

"Why the hell doesn't he buy some decent suits?" Corvo complained. Ann Morfogen, head of CBS News press, our PR department, was finally persuaded to take Forrest shopping. What he came back with was not much of an improvement; we could only hope that he would catch on with time.

But if Forrest was not much of a dresser, he impressed the CBS News management with his interviewing style. Katz, Corvo, and the management had always come down on Kurtis for what they felt was his refusal to ask provocative questions—a bizarre objection, it seemed to me, since they were intent on making the broadcast softer. Forrest, they decided, was tougher. I watched Forrest closely, and realized that he was one of the few interviewers in television who actually listened to what his guests were saying. Still, his questions didn't seem all that tough to me. In his first interview with George Shultz, he lobbed softballs at the Secretary of State, who hit them to all corners of the park. From then on, Shultz agreed to be on the "CBS Morning News" frequently, and whenever he was, he always wanted to be interviewed by Forrest.

When Sawyer first showed up and was introduced to the staff, he seemed polite and reserved. That, at least, was our first impression. Since then, however, he had anchored the "Evening News" one evening—Dan Rather had been out with a cold, Schieffer was on vacation, and absolutely nobody else was available—as a result of which he had acquired, as Epstein put it, "a head as big as Africa." Most of the bookers found him cold. But their main complaint about him was that he would not ask the questions they had written for him, and they were the ones catching the heat for the fact that his interviews, with celebrities at least, weren't going that well.

"What's with him?" Jane Kaplan asked me one morning, after a segment she had booked fell flat. "He didn't ask one question I wrote for him, and he had the nerve to complain to me about the segment."

Jane had done the pre-interview, and she knew which questions were likely to elicit the best responses. It was because of Jane's and other bookers' complaints that I was going to have a talk with Forrest about packets.

When I saw him that afternoon, he told me he was tired and said we should put off meeting until tomorrow, when we could have lunch. And so around noon the next day we were seated at the Manhattan Ocean Club. I kicked things off by asking him how he was enjoying life in New York. He said he liked it and was thinking of buying an apartment. I offered a few suggestions about buildings he might want to look into.

We had scarcely gotten beyond these preliminaries when he folded his arms, leaned forward, and said: "So, what are you going to do for me?"

The question took me aback. When I finally managed to digest its full implications, I was hard put to suppress a grin, thinking of Epstein's comment. I don't remember whether or not I responded. I can't imagine I did, at least not with anything coherent. I did tell him that the bookers were having a tough time figuring out what he was interested in.

"Hard news," he said. "Oh, I'll do the soft stuff since it's part of the game, but it's the news subjects that turn me on. I'm really a newsman, and I take a great pride in my interviewing. It's something I study and work at, and I treat it, well, almost as an art."

"Maybe you should come to the bookers' meeting next week," I said. "You'd get a chance to elaborate on your ideas to them."

"Be glad to," he replied. "Be glad to do anything I can to get this show rolling."

He then proposed that one good booker with a strong feel for news be assigned to him each morning so he could give her the benefit of his ideas directly. I told him he should probably discuss this with Katz, but that in any event the best person he could use was Jude Dratt.

"What's Shevlin like?" he said.

"Pat's good," I said, "but she's a coordinating producer." Again, I told him I thought this was something he should take up with Katz.

A couple of things about Forrest unnerved me. One was his gung-ho attitude. He behaved rather like a fresh-faced lieutenant, while most of the staff of the "Morning News" resembled veterans of a hard campaign. I knew they were not about to be impressed by a rah-rah type, especially one who didn't ask the questions they had labored over.

I decided to bring up the issue of the questions. I told him that some of the bookers were disappointed that he didn't ask what they had written for him.

"One thing you have to realize," I said, "is that the bookers are used to working for Phyllis, and working for Phyllis requires spelling out everything to the letter, including, to be honest, some of the simplest pronunciations . . ."

Before I could finish, he interrupted. "I don't know what works for Phyllis, but I know what works for me. I have to go my own route. I look for a niche, a sort of chink in the armor, then I move in. Sure, I can use every piece of information they give me, including their questions, but they can't expect me to ask the questions they write."

"You know they do pre-interviews," I said. "They're not

supposed to rehearse guests, but they do. So they have a sense of what gets a good response and what will go over like a lead balloon."

"I take your point," he said, "but it's not the way I work."

"I'm not talking about politicians now," I said. "I'm talking about the standard celebrity interview."

"I know what you're saying," he said. "But the way I work is to digest what they give me, then I go out and try to do the best job I can. Everything I have is in my head. I don't rely on notes."

He was stubborn and uncompromising, and I admired him for it. I might have admired more if his method had worked—after all, he was the anchor, the guy with the bat in his hand. But over the next few weeks his interviews produced some heavy thuds, and when I saw the skepticism in the bookers' eyes at the meeting the following week, I knew I wasn't the only one with doubts about Forrest.

As we walked back along West Fifty-seventh Street in the sweltering summer heat, Forrest told me he had found the lunch useful. Again, he said he wanted to do everything he could to get people excited about this show, and again his remark made me nervous. I left him at his office and went back to the fishbowl, where Epstein was holding the fort.

"How did the lunch go?" he asked.

"You were right about Africa," I said.

Epstein laughed uproariously. He was still laughing when Shevlin walked in.

"What's so funny?" Pat wanted to know.

"I just had lunch with Forrest," I said. "Let's just say that reserving judgment is often a matter of infinite hope."

On Thursday, August 15, Maria called to make sure I knew she was going to be in New York for two weeks. She would be substituting for Phyllis, who was going on vacation.

"Believe it or not, Maria," I said. "For once they let us know."

We talked about several pieces her producer could work on in the meantime, then she said:

"I think I can put together a funny piece on Madonna's wedding, if you need it for tomorrow. There's no way we can get to her, but we can do something funny with the cake and the dress, and all that stuff."

"I'll call you right back," I said.

I found Corvo, and told him what Maria had in mind. He liked it.

"You've got it," I told her when I called back.

"Did Katz like it?"

"I talked to David," I said. "Katz doesn't know anyone in rock 'n' roll besides Bruce Springsteen."

So that Thursday Maria went off to find out where rock star Madonna would exchange vows with actor Sean Penn. The location of the event was being kept a big secret, and this was the gist of the piece. The "Morning News'" intrepid reporter found the cake, found the dress, found several unlikely locations and shot them from a helicopter, but she couldn't find the wedding.

The piece took all day to put together, and was fed in overnight. One of the show's writers decided to try to capture its light hearted tone in his introduction, and he went a bit too far. In the control room the next morning, I listened as the long intro concluded with the words: ". . . for tomorrow . . . is the day . . . Madonna takes Penn in hand."

Corvo raised an eyebrow, nothing more.

From behind us, came an explosion: "Who the fuck wrote that?"

David Buksbaum, vice-president in charge of hard news, was throwing a fit. He had been wandering through the control room on some errand—and just happened to arrive at the moment the Penn line went over the air.

Corvo suddenly realized Buksbaum's request was serious. "I'll find out," he said. With an air of resignation, he went back to the writers' quarters.

Buksbaum sat down next to me, complaining about the standard of writing on all the shows. I was trying to listen to the rest of the piece, and I couldn't hear it because of his mutterings.

"David, calm down," I said. "If we get one phone call, I'd be surprised."

Buksbaum had a blustering manner, and was quick to anger. For a second I thought he was going to take my head off. Rank was very important at CBS News, and when vice-presidents spoke, you were expected to jump.

Buksbaum looked at me hard for a moment, then said: "Give me a cigarette." He took a couple of quick puffs, then swung off his chair as the piece ended.

"Nice piece other than that," he said, and left the control room.

Corvo returned after a few minutes and said: "Where's Buks gone?"

"He had a nicotine fit and forgot about it," I said.

Corvo shook his head. He was a solid soldier and he took a lot of heat from men less smart than he.

I told Maria the Buks story when she arrived Monday. She thought it was funny. Maria liked to have fun, and she was fun to be around, but she could also be remarkably strait-laced at times. Some of the bookers delighted in telling her stories about men, or sex, or the peccadilloes of celebrities she knew. When she professed disbelief, they would tell her she was naive. Maybe she was, but she mixed well with the staff, and she was a breath of fresh air. She was competent and willing to pitch in on stories, and some of her suggestions were good. I knew the bookers liked her.

The daughter of Sargent and Eunice Shriver, and the niece of John and Robert Kennedy, Maria had grown up among Washington society and the Kennedy social world. Her best friends were her Kennedy cousins. But despite her closeness to her family, she had wanted to do something different, something none of her famous clan had done. So she chose journalism over politics, and after graduating from Georgetown University in 1977 she worked her way up from summer intern to reporter.

Maria had been working as a reporter for "PM Magazine," a syndicated magazine show, when her agent, Art Kaminsky, heard that the "Morning News" was looking for a West Coast correspondent. Kaminsky sent Ed Joyce a tape, and Joyce liked what he saw.

"This is great," he said. "I want Van to see it."

Sauter also liked what he saw. Despite Joyce's subsequent reservations about whether Shriver was good enough to be a CBS correspondent, she got the job.

Shriver had been with the show nearly two years by the late summer of 1985, and for some time Katz had been trying to persuade her to move to New York. He wanted her to replace Pat Collins, whom he considered "too fifties" and wrong for the show. He had called Kaminsky several times, suggesting Maria as Collins's replacement. Each time Kaminsky had told him he didn't see that Maria had much to gain by taking this step. Certainly, Collins's job was not enough to persuade her to leave California, which she liked. Then one morning, late in July, Katz called Kaminsky and said: "Maybe we can skip a step. What would it take to get Maria to move to New York?"

Kaminsky told him, "The only way to get her to New York is to give her *the* job."

The afternoon before Phyllis went on vacation, I went back to her office to see her. She had just returned from a lunch with Gene Jankowski. Between several phone interruptions, while Phyllis talked to people about Kentucky crafts she had supported ever since she was the state's First Lady, we went over the status of various interviews she had taped. We also talked about a story she wanted to do on "ideal weight" —she had read something about it in a magazine that morning.

Phyllis patted her stomach, which was still feeling the impact of the lunch.

"What a time for me to be thinking about this," she said with a giggle.

She then talked freely about the lunch, and about how well it had gone, and about what a nice man Gene Jankowski was. She said he had told her that management still had full confidence in her, and that it probably had been a mistake for her to do serious subjects on the show. She said he had agreed with her—that everything was better since she had been allowed to be herself. She seemed cheerful and confident, and I wished her a great vacation.

The next morning I held my regular meeting with the entertainment bookers. They had been slipping back into invoking the names of anchors to get guests. In this case the name was Maria's, since it was Maria who was going to be substituting for Phyllis. I warned them not to do it.

"The executive producer makes those decisions," I said. They greeted the reminder as I expected they would, with silence.

Then Jane said: "You know this really makes things very difficult. People are saying they don't want to be interviewed by Phyllis."

They had told me this before, and I had discounted it. It wasn't easy to get guests in August, and I had attributed their complaints to general exhaustion from working the phones all day. But now they were insistent. They claimed that if it wasn't for Phyllis, a lot more celebrities would be willing to be on the program.

Again I started to brush their objections aside.

"They're just dying to be interviewed by Forrest?" I asked sarcastically. "We know what a great celebrity interviewer he is."

They all sat mute.

"At least Phyllis is on the same wavelength as these people," I added.

"But it's true," Jane persisted. "It's been happening all the time."

I rolled my eyes. "In the last two months Phyllis has done interviews with the Spellings, with Richard and Lili Zanuck, Helen and David Brown, Kathryn and Georgette Klinger, Donna Mills, Connie Sellica, Diahann Carroll . . . don't tell me she can't get celebrity interviews."

"But there's still lots of people who won't do interviews with her."

"Like who?" I asked.

"Dustin Hoffman."

"That's because he's an old friend of Pat Collins," I said.

Jane looked at her feet.

"No," she said, "that isn't the reason. He didn't want to be interviewed by Phyllis."

"Okay," I said, "who else?"

"Tom Hanks."

Jane had a list of at least half a dozen major names. The bookers were starting to make a believer out of me.

An hour or so later, I ran into Corvo. I suggested we go get a cup of coffee. We went downstairs to the cafeteria, and I told him what the bookers had told me. Corvo had the same initial reaction I did. He was wise to the ruses and excuses that bookers would use from time to time. I told him I hadn't believed it either at first, but now I was becoming convinced it was true. I saw him adjust, just as I had adjusted. Then I ran down the list of the names of the artists.

"The bookers are on the front line, David," I said. "They're dealing with PR people all day."

"Take a couple of PR people to lunch and check," he said. "See if it's true."

I made some lunch appointments, and several of the major PR agents admitted that their clients had balked when the name Phyllis George came up. Other clients, they said, had specifically requested not to be interviewed by her. Despite all the fallout from the Dotson–Webb interview, I was surprised. Dotson–Webb, after all, had been three months earlier, and although there had been gaffes and awkwardness since then, Phyllis did celebrity interviews better than she did anything else.

What I had not realized was it took time for the reticence of celebrities to make itself felt. The TWA hostage crisis had lasted three weeks, and during this period there were fewer celebrities than normal on the program. The bookers, who had begun to take note of the syndrome in July, saw it confirmed in August when Shriver showed up. Suddenly celebrities were willing to appear again.

"Face it," one PR agent told me as we sipped our drinks in Café des Artistes. "Your show has a major liability and her name is Phyllis George."

I told Corvo what I'd been told and he said: "Let's meet with Katz." That afternoon I laid out for Katz everything I had gone through with Corvo. Katz listened quietly. For once there was no banter. He just sat there and listened, and when I was done, he said: "Thanks for telling me this."

The following morning, when I came in for the show, I was hailed by Corvo in the corridor.

"Peter! I need that list!"

"What list?" I said.

He lowered his voice and steered me toward his office: "The list of stars who won't do the show because of Phyllis."

"How come?" I said.

"Katz needs it for Joyce," he confided, "and don't mention this to anyone."

I gave it him. It was the first hint I had that there might be a change coming.

Throughout that August Jon Katz had been hammering away at Ed Joyce. He and Ober had held several meetings with Joyce to discuss the Phyllis George situation. Ober was sympathetic to Katz's view that Phyllis was a major liability, and Joyce was being nudged. Joyce claims that it was he, and he alone, who made the decision to fire Phyllis George, but he certainly knew the mood of his troops when he did. The show by then was receiving a lot of negative mail about Phyllis, and Katz was bringing Joyce batches of these letters almost daily.

When Joyce eventually agreed that Phyllis had to go, it was a dramatic reversal of his position of only a few months earlier. In May he had ordered that the show be restructured around her. But by August, he says: "I felt it was important that we get back to being a respectable broadcast, and the only way to do this was to fire Phyllis. I also felt it was unfair to hold the executive producer accountable for the debacle that was not his fault."

But the desire to get rid of Phyllis met with opposition from above—from Sauter and Jankowski. Katz had lunch with Sauter, in an effort to bring him around to his point of view, but Sauter resisted. Phyllis, after all, was his and Jankowski's hire. In getting rid of her, Joyce and Katz would be making Sauter and Jankowski look bad. So the argument raged, with each side presenting evidence to bolster its case. Katz and Joyce were well armed—with the negative mail, and with Jane's list of the celebrities who refused to be interviewed by Phyllis.

"It was a showdown," Joyce says, "and both Sauter and Jankowski were firmly opposed at first. Until finally they acquiesced, just as I had acquiesced when they hired her. Eventually they said: 'Okay, it's up to you. Do what you like. You want to do this? Go ahead.'"

It had already been decided that Forrest Sawyer would be the next male anchor—Kaminsky had been assured of that by Joyce and Sauter. But when the CBS executives told him they wanted Maria to be Phyllis's replacement, they also said that they wanted to have Maria and Forrest on board simultaneously. They attached considerable importance to this. They wanted to coordinate the announcements, and more important they wanted to dismiss Phyllis on the Friday before Labor Day.

Early that week Ed Joyce called Phyllis's agent, Ed Hookstratten.

"I think the time has come to replace Phyllis," Joyce told Hookstratten. "How do you feel about that?"

One thing Hookstratten felt strongly about was that CBS honor the terms of Phyllis's contract. The contract said "no cut," and Hookstratten wanted to make sure that she would collect her salary for the next two years and four months.

"I was assured she would," he says, "and Joyce was quite honorable about the whole thing. Phyllis was pooped and exhausted anyway, and so it was decided."

Art Kaminsky got the call from Joyce. The Phyllis matter had been resolved. Several meetings then followed immediately because there was now tremendous pressure to get Maria's and Forrest's deals done by Friday. CBS News laid out its terms, offering Forrest more money than Maria. This was standard at the morning shows, where more importance traditionally had been attached to male anchors, who consequently had always been paid more—until Phyllis George set a new standard. But now Kaminsky was insisting on parity for the new "CBS Morning News" team.

"They had the same credentials," Kaminsky says, "and I thought they should get the same money, and finally, on the

Friday before Labor Day, I convinced CBS that they should both get the same contract."

Both anchors were to receive annual salaries of $500,000. Kaminsky thought the deal was done. Finalized. Set. He thought he had done especially well by Shriver, who until then had been making slightly less than six figures. But then, he says, another party entered the negotiations—Shriver's family.

The first call he got, he says, was from Bobby Shriver, Maria's brother.

"Shriver told me he had run into CBS chairman Tom Wyman at a party, and that Wyman had told him, 'We'll do anything to get Maria,'" Kaminsky says. "I told him I'd never heard any CBS executive say anything like that."

Kaminsky describes the next four hours as the most insane of his life. Maria, Arnold Schwarzenegger, Sargent Shriver, and Bobby Shriver, he says, all called him saying they were dissatisfied with the terms. He says they wanted to back out, and that his response was: "If you want to back out, you call Ed Joyce."

In the meantime, CBS had told Phyllis she was fired.

According to Kaminsky, Sargent Shriver wanted to know why CBS couldn't buy Maria an apartment in New York. Kaminsky says he told Shriver that nobody was going to get the kind of perks Phyllis George had gotten. Ed Joyce had made that clear.

Later that afternoon, he says, Maria called him.

"Art," she said, "we'll take the deal."

A month later she dropped him as her agent.

"It was a lousy weekend," Kaminsky says, "and when I finally called Ober and told him we were all squared away, he said: 'I feel sorry for you. You've done a great deal, and I can see you're getting no pleasure from it.' And he was right."

"**B**eware of holiday weekends," Bob Epstein warned me. "Don't assume anything. That's when they drop the bombs around here."

It was the Thursday morning before Labor Day. I had told him I planned to leave the office early on Friday afternoon.

"Don't," Epstein advised me. He explained that because newspaper circulation was down on holiday weekends, and because most of the TV press already would be away, it was a good opportunity for CBS News to muffle a big explosion.

I took Epstein at his word, and in the house of glass walls I watched for signs. By Thursday evening, August 29, I knew something was going on. Katz was still at the Broadcast Center at eight. Katz never stayed until eight, and he had been in and out of Joyce's office all day long. I trapped him in his office at one point and demanded to know what was going on. He threw up his arms and said: "Nothing!"

Corvo was more forthcoming. When I saw him in the control room Friday morning, I asked him the same question.

"I can't say," he replied, "but you already know something sure is, and I think you know what."

So it was true. It turned out I wasn't the only member of the senior staff with advance information. By eleven that morning the suspicion of imminent change pervaded the fishbowl. Throughout the corridors of the building, rumor abounded. Before Forrest and Maria left for the weekend, they had been summoned to Joyce's office. Still there were doubters.

"I don't believe it," one producer said.

"What makes you say that?" Epstein wanted to know.

"They've got three million dollars invested in this lady. You're telling me they're going to walk away from that?"

"If it's true," Roberta said, "and I think it is, the interesting thing will be to see who's going to take the fall for this. Someone's got to take the fall."

By three in the afternoon nobody could concentrate on any work. It was fortunate that Monday's Labor Day show had been booked way in advance. If there was one day of the year the show did not want to be struggling to get last-minute guests, it was the Friday before Labor Day. So we had the usual, predictable guests already lined up—labor economists, a workers' panel, a typical American working family, Merle Haggard to talk about the working man, plus a piece on tennis siblings and another on lifeguards for variety. There was no news, except in the CBS News building itself, where the swell of rumor was about to crest.

"It's happening all right!"

Amy stormed into the fishbowl, shrieking.

"I just saw Ann Morfogen in the elevator, and she had a batch of press releases under her arm, and when I tried to look at them she snatched them away."

"The intrepid reporter," Shevlin said.

"Can't anyone confirm it?" Roberta said.

Epstein got a call. He was all excited.

"It's done!" he exclaimed when he hung up. "Someone in sports just told me that Hookstratten is shopping her back to Sports, and they don't want her."

"She's toast!" Shevlin exclaimed.

It was difficult not to feel a degree of guilt, as we all sat in the fishbowl, blatantly reveling over Phyllis's demise. After all, everyone had worked closely with her, and most people liked her personally. But she had been forced upon us by management. It was management that chose the anchors, and everyone regarded it as the ultimate proof of management's incompetence that it had committed the enormous blunder of choosing Phyllis in the first place. Because of this, any feelings of sympathy for Phyllis were muted, overwhelmed by our exhilaration over the fact that the burden she represented was about to be lifted. We had struggled long enough against all odds to produce her well. We had twisted and distorted our poor show long enough in order to accommodate her. Life was about to be made easier.

Epstein took a batch of tapes off the shelf. They were Phyllis's "famous couples" interviews, scheduled to run a few weeks hence. Ceremoniously, he dumped them in the trash bin.

"You can't do that, Bob!" someone yelled.

"Can't I?" Epstein said. "You can bet your life I can. They'll never run."

Suddenly Katz appeared at the door of the fishbowl.

"Katz!" everyone yelled. "We know already."

For a minute Katz maintained the pretext that he knew nothing, then he saw there was no point.

"Everything's going to be okay," he said. "It's a new day from now on." Having offered us this assurance, he added: "I'll be back. I have to go see Ober."

I left the Broadcast Center around six and went out to dinner. Around ten that evening I drove down to Times Square and picked up a copy of the *Times* before heading out to Long Island for the weekend. The paper quoted Phyllis as saying she had resigned.

"I have come to the conclusion to rearrange my priorities," she said.

Her agent said: "I don't think she found the rigors of the early morning compatible with her family life . . ."

Ann Morfogen, the CBS spokesperson, said the decision over the departure was "absolutely mutual."

CBS News was papering over the mess. Still, by Monday it was known that Phyllis George had been pushed, but that as a result of her no-cut contract she would continue to collect $1 million a year for nearly two and a half years. Her vacation had been due to end Monday, but she did not reappear in the building. Good-byes were said over the phone.

Three weeks later I went to an opening at the Metropolitan Museum. It was in honor of Armand Hammer and his collection, the one Phyllis had called "so magnanimous you can hardly put a price on it."

Sure enough there she was, on the arm of her husband, John Y. Brown, Jr. She looked radiant and healthy and unconcerned.

I had gone to the opening with Maggie Shumaker, and we both marched over to Phyllis and greeted her. She laughed and smiled and asked us how we both were. We in turn asked her if she missed the show.

"No comment," she said with a smile, and then John Y. Brown, Jr., swept her out to dinner.

X.

DEMANDING TIMES

"If there is any one factor that has contributed to the universal reputation of CBS as the undisputed leader in broadcast journalism, it is the high level of professionalism in its truest sense —the ethical commitment to fairness, accuracy, and dignity . . ."
—from *CBS News Standards*

From its start as a network, CBS's brand of journalism was a mix of historical accident and questionable design. In 1928, when Bill Paley bought the sixteen-station radio network known as the Columbia Broadcasting System with $400,000 his father had given him, he didn't have much choice but to air lots of public affairs programming. In entertainment, the Columbia Broadcasting System was a humble second to NBC. Still, even by the mid-thirties, news accounted for only a tiny slice of the broadcast day. In those days, CBS broadcast a five-minute newscast at noon, another at 4:30 P.M., and a fifteen-minute wrap-up late in the evening. Sponsors for news were few, and there was no public demand for up-to-the-minute bulletins until war threatened Europe. Then the network hired correspondents.

After the war, things went back to the way they had been before. Though the network now had a great stable of correspondents, which enhanced its reputation, news was nonetheless shunted to the sidelines. It was a prestige vehicle, not a money-maker. Then in 1948 Bill Paley conducted his legendary raid on NBC, luring away much of the rival network's prime-time entertainment talent. Paley had recognized that entertainers such as Jack Benny, George Burns, and Lucille Ball would generate enormous profits for CBS once Madison Avenue caught on that television was an advertising medium without equal. And once Paley had a stable of entertainers who could ensure CBS's lead in the prime-time ratings, the classy flagship of the Edward R. Murrow news department became even less important to the future prosperity of CBS. This fact set the stage for the conflicts that wracked the news division in the fifties; thirty years later, the same conflict still raged—entertainment versus news.

Entertainment programming was not only profitable, it also had the added benefit of being safe and inoffensive, an important consideration for the young television industry. The political climate in the decades following the war had grown increasingly intolerant, and protection under the First Amendment was not taken for granted by those who ran the airwaves. Yet some forms of public service were deemed necessary to keep government at bay. With this consideration in mind, CBS launched the first nightly television news service in 1948. Its anchor was Douglas Edwards, who was not one of the noted group of Murrow correspondents.

Edwards, who until recently still occasionally sat in as a newsreader on the "Morning News," got the job mainly because of his background as a personality on radio programs, one of which ironically was a soap opera set in a newsroom. He had little experience in news, having worked primarily as an announcer. The Murrow group regarded him in much the same way experienced broadcast journalists today tend to regard anchors chosen for their looks or charm—as a lightweight. Murrow's group were radio personalities, too, but unlike Edwards they had earned their spurs covering the war, not introducing dance bands and reading commercials. They were men with opinions on matters of state, they were analysts and commentators, and Edwards never was, and never would be, one of their crowd.

But Edwards wasn't camera-shy. He could ad lib and he could take a script and read it without stumbling. Nor did it seem strange to anyone that the person reading the news wasn't a journalist per se. After all, radio was founded on the idea of using personalities to sell products, and nobody saw any reason why television should be any different. And, really, for the early fifteen-minute CBS nightly news program, a reader or announcer was all that was needed, for the Edwards broadcast would be virtually unrecognizable as a news program today. The program's staff consisted of a director, a couple of writers, and a few film editors who also served as cameramen. The show had no correspondents and no film crews because CBS did not hire film crews until five years later. For the most part, Edwards talked on camera, or over stills, mainly presenting ribbon-cutting ceremonies and other items typical of newsreels.

The job of livening up the program fell to the director, a young man of twenty-five named Don Hewitt, who has since come to be regarded as the wunderkind of television news. Hewitt's job as director gave him control of the technical aspects of the program, but he soon took over editorial responsibility. In his combined role, he was given a new title borrowed from Hollywood—producer. Hewitt dreamed up a variety of visual innovations that served to make Edwards something more than a talking head. He came up with many of the ideas for television graphics, and he looked for new ways to film events. People who worked with him say that in the early days he had very little interest in news itself, that his main concern was to blend whatever news there was with his own ideas, to make the program more entertaining, "to get viewers into the tent," as he liked to say. With his minimal patience for viewing a piece of film, and an attention span that was in sync with the viewers', he was ideally suited to the role of a television producer, which was one reason he survived long after most of the Murrow people had faded.

In the late forties, CBS's great radio correspondents were suspicious of television, and at first many of them doubted that television would ever become a legitimate source of breaking news. They were uncomfortable with the Hollywood-like aspects of TV—the lights, cameras, and small armies of technicians that had to accompany a correspondent on a story. But if Murrow and his group had their doubts about the new medium, they would soon recognize that it was destined to become enormously powerful and popular. By 1951, Murrow himself had made the switch to television, and within two years he was host of two television programs. One was the documentary series "See It Now," the other was an interview program called "Person to Person." The critics termed these "higher Murrow" and "lower Murrow," respectively, because much of "Person to Person" consisted of interviews with celebrities.

"See It Now" began in 1951. It was not a great ratings success, but the critics loved it, and the program was a source of considerable pride at CBS. At least it was as long as it stuck to safe, serious topics such as mine safety and the plight of returning Korean War veterans. But when Murrow took on Joe McCarthy, the program began to grate in the executive suites of CBS, and in one suite in particular. By then the network was making substantial profits, and nobody upstairs wanted to buck this trend. Keeping the fare as bland as possible was the way to ensure that revenue poured in and government stayed out.

Biographers and historians will continue to debate the merits of Murrow's case versus that of Bill Paley, the chairman concerned about his network's survival in the days when government intervention was a real threat. But when all the debates are concluded, one fact will remain: on the evening of the famous McCarthy broadcast, Paley called Murrow and said: "Ed, I'm with you today, and I'll be with you tomorrow."

Betrayals in television are often enormous, but this one set the standard by which all others can be measured. The real issue after the McCarthy broadcast was whether Paley would continue to support Murrow in the months and years ahead. Paley chose not to.

After the McCarthy broadcast, Murrow continued to report from time to time on sensitive issues—and Paley and his executives grew increasingly irate. Even if many of the "See It Now" broadcasts were not at all controversial, network greed by then had become a greater motivating force than network fear. The corporate desire was to get a more popular show into the time slot. And so in the summer of 1955, Paley decided that "See It Now" would be broadcast only eight times a year, rather than weekly. The following year he took the program out of prime time altogether, consigning it to Sunday afternoons. Finally, in the spring of 1958, he canceled it entirely, complaining that it gave him a stomach ache.

That summer, Murrow gave a speech to a gathering of news directors in Chicago about the uneasy marriage of television and journalism. "One of the basic troubles with radio and television news," he said, "is that both have grown up as an incompatible combination of show business, advertising, and news . . . The top management of the networks have been trained in advertising, research or show business . . . They also make the final and crucial decisions having to do with news and public affairs. Frequently they have neither the time nor the competence to do this."

Understandably, perhaps, Paley took this as a direct attack. Murrow's role at the network was reduced considerably. In 1961 he accepted President Kennedy's offer of a post at the United States Information Agency and left CBS.

"CBS News is an organization that struggles to resist change," Howard Stringer once told me in a moment of candor, and to a large extent he was right. The news division is an intensely tradition-conscious organization, and its concern for standards is set forth in a complex book of guidelines that cover sixty pages. Many people who work for CBS News know no other employer, and they are used to things being done a certain way. So when Sauter and Joyce took over CBS News in 1981, and without any diplomacy or stroking proceeded to hammer through a series of profound stylistic and policy changes, they were rubbing against the grain right from the start. As one producer said, "CBS News began to turn into one big unhappy family, in which all the members were becoming increasingly neurotic."

By the fall of 1985 the rift between management and the employees had been noticed by the press. CBS News was becoming a talking point in journalistic circles, as a house rife with enmity and division.

So much in television news boils down to matters of style and ego. The broadcast journalist can't pin his clippings to a bulletin board, and rarely is his reporting turned into a book. Unlike a print journalist, he can't readily point to the body of his work, and say, "See, I did this." After all, his work is contained on a reel, stored in a vault, and is quite probably the result of a collaborative effort by dozens of people. So the TV journalist struggles to be identified through a style of work. And it was style that was all-important in the rift between the CBS management and the group loosely known as the "old guard"—a group led by Walter Cronkite, Mike Wallace, and Don Hewitt.

Despite his run-ins with Paley, the legacy Ed Murrow had established at CBS was a powerful one. It represented an ideal.

"For any print journalist who wanted to work in television," one veteran CBS producer told me, "the first choice of network in the fifties was the one where Edward R. Murrow worked. In those days CBS News was really divided into two parts. There was the Douglas Edwards show and the various early incarnations of the 'Morning News,' and then there was the Edward R. Murrow news department. Working in the part of CBS News where I worked wasn't a particularly edifying experience, but working for Murrow—now that was top of the line."

And so the people who came aboard at CBS News in the late fifties and early sixties believed they were following in the footsteps of the best in broadcast journalism. They were a big part of the reason that CBS News remained the force it did in the sixties and seventies. Even if the environment turned out to be a lot less hospitable than many of them imagined it would be, they stayed at CBS News because the name meant something. CBS enjoyed the reputation, deserved or not, of being the best place a television journalist could work.

But by the early sixties, the inherent conflict that Murrow had recognized—between the corporate and the public interest—was making itself felt. Murrow was gone, as was Howard K. Smith, who had had his own run-in with Paley.

It was becoming clear that men with opinions, men who took a stand, did not have much of a future at CBS News. The news division would soon enter an era in which it behooved those who worked there to exercise diplomacy worthy of a foreign service officer rather than a foreign correspondent.

Nobody represented this style of treading cautiously better than Walter Cronkite. Cronkite had never been part of the Murrow group, even though it was Murrow who had hired him. Cronkite, like Edwards, was regarded as an announcer, and he was thought by the Murrow group to lack any interest in the analysis of events. Cronkite had been the first host of the "Morning News," then the host of a series of dramatizations of historical events, and before he took over the "CBS Evening News" anchor chair, he had learned a few important lessons. One was that objectivity and caution were safer than editorializing. Another was that you were only as good as your ratings. Cronkite had been thrown to the wolves for a few months after CBS was trounced at the 1964 Republican convention by NBC; after that, despite his phenomenal popularity a few years later, he did not ease up on himself for at least a decade. And just as his approach to news was to avoid making waves, he made it a point not to step out of line with the management. He never spoke out about the nature of television, as Murrow had. In every respect, he was the kind of journalist Bill Paley could live with, a man who knew not to step on corporate toes if he wanted to continue to draw his huge salary.

Mike Wallace's entry into broadcast journalism, like Cronkite's, was also less than distinguished. Before CBS hired him in 1963, he had been an announcer, a quiz-show emcee, and host of a local New York interview show whose theatrically aggressive style had earned him the nickname "Mike Malice." He too served his time as a "Morning News" anchor before being made a correspondent in 1968, assigned to the

Nixon presidential campaign. Two years later, he found his niche at "60 Minutes."

So none of the leaders of the old guard, not Cronkite, not Wallace, not Don Hewitt (who wound up as executive producer of "60 Minutes")—all of whom had risen to prominence at CBS News and remained there long after most of the Murrow group had departed—were in any sense purists. None of them carried any particularly heavy intellectual baggage. In their long careers in television all had made their share of compromises. All had worked in the nether regions of CBS News and had felt the snubs of men who considered themselves more highbrow. Yet in 1985, when all were at the top of the heap at CBS—Cronkite, a member of the corporation's board of directors; Hewitt, a legendary pioneer whose broadcast accounted for enormous revenues; Wallace, the top correspondent on that broadcast—all of them were extremely concerned about what was going on in the news division. More to the point, all were questioning the policies of the current management.

By September 1985, the old guard—which also included Morley Safer, Andy Rooney, Bill Moyers, and Sandy Socolow —had had nearly four years to judge the work of the Sauter–Joyce management team, and it didn't like what it saw. Not surprisingly, the management resented these criticisms, and in its off-the-record briefings to the press began to suggest that the old guard's disaffection was a classic case of innovators-turned-traditionalists finding fault with the next generation of innovators. Management began referring to the old guard as "yesterday's people," and as the lines were drawn, more and more people began to take sides.

Trouble had been brewing over stylistic changes ever since Sauter and Joyce first took over. They had not been forgiven for the changes they had brought to the "Evening

News," nor for what they did to the "Morning News" after the Kuralt broadcast was kissed off. Cronkite had let it be known that he disliked the "CBS Evening News with Dan Rather," with its emphasis on arousing viewer feeling rather than communicating facts. And Hewitt had ridiculed the new magazine show, "West 57th Street," calling it fluff and complaining that it lacked the substance of "60 Minutes." None of them had said anything publicly about the "Morning News," at least nothing that was reported in the papers, but perhaps nothing more needed to be said about the "Morning News." Everyone within the news division knew what the old guard thought of it.

Blame was being apportioned all around among the management. Tom Wyman, who had taken over as chairman of CBS Inc. in 1983, and who had overall responsibility, was being blamed for a bottom-line approach, a policy of benign neglect, and for what was construed as a failure to recognize that the news division was special. To Stringer went the blame for the Westmoreland case, for inattention to the "Morning News," and for his habit of playing Machiavellian games in the press. And Sauter and Jankowski, among the many castigations that were their due, received full credit for the "Morning News'" present condition, because it was they who had signed off on the hiring of Phyllis George.

Sauter was recognized as the force behind the overall change of direction at CBS News. It was he who had instituted the changes in the morning and evening news broadcasts, he who had been responsible for the reduction in the number of documentaries and public-affairs broadcasts. Some in the old guard claimed they had spotted Sauter as the main enemy from the beginning, but there were others who freely admitted that initially they saw Sauter as their "best hope." Sauter had worked in news, and he wasn't imposed on the division from the outside. His charm, his ideas, his tweeds and bow ties, and his habit of calling people "big guy" caused many people to see him as a friend rather than as a corporate stiff. But when his corporate ambitions became all too clear, he began to be perceived in a different light. For Sauter to have an eye on a Black Rock job was regarded as an unacceptable compromise, one that would inevitably harm the news division both in terms of its integrity and its budgets. Sauter's predecessors, Dick Salant and Bill Leonard, had viewed the presidency of CBS News as the crowning achievement of their careers, and the feeling at CBS News was that such an attitude was a prerequisite for the job. A man whose first loyalty was to his corporate superiors could not possibly act in the news division's best interests, could not possibly insulate news from corporate pressures.

But by the fall of 1985 Sauter was at Black Rock, as executive vice-president of the CBS Broadcast Group, and all the anger and frustration within the news division were coalescing around the man who had taken over from him, the man Sauter had used as a blunt instrument to effect change —Ed Joyce.

Sauter and Joyce were close friends. When they had worked together in the CBS Broadcast Center they had been inseparable. They socialized together, their wives were friends, they marched into the men's room together rather than interrupt their discussions. But if Sauter was able through charm to deflect the arrows aimed his way, Ed Joyce possessed no such ability.

Joyce had taken his first step toward alienating many of the staff in 1983 when he referred to the agents who represented CBS correspondents as "flesh peddlers." Among the "flesh peddlers" he singled out for criticism was Dan Rather's agent, Richard Leibner, whom he charged with trying to drive up salaries. For the next year, Joyce, who also had his eye on Black Rock, would continue to take a hard line in salary negotiations, and several CBS correspondents left the company as a result. But if Rather was offended by the criticism of his agent, which reportedly he was, he felt no direct impact from Joyce's cost cuts for two years. In fact, he continued to receive maximum support on every front. But in the summer of 1985, things began to change for him. When Rather complained about losing two correspondents, Jane Wallace and Meredith Vieira, to "West 57th Street," Joyce's response was blunt. He issued a memo in which he made it clear that in his opinion the "Evening News" had more than enough resources.

By most criteria Ed Joyce was right. Compared to other CBS broadcasts, the "Evening News" was a bloated walrus that ate all the oysters. Politically, however, it was a big mistake on Joyce's part to get on the wrong side of Rather. From that point on, though Rather publicly supported Joyce, he began lobbying privately to get rid of him. But for the moment Joyce wasn't going anywhere, and when the budget crunch came at the end of the summer of '85, it was Joyce who wielded the knife. Before long many CBS staffers were being made to feel that the most important issue was not how a story was covered, but how well costs were contained in covering it.

Then, in September 1985, came the layoffs. They were part of a corporate cost-cutting drive, which Wyman and Jankowski deemed necessary because revenues weren't measuring up to projections, and because CBS was saddled with debt after fighting off Ted Turner's bid to take over the company. Neither Sauter nor Joyce spoke out against the dismissals.

As usual, the layoffs were preceded by rumors. One Thursday that September I came in to work to find Epstein wearing a suit.

"What's the occasion?" I asked.

"If I'm going to be fired," he said, "I'm going out wearing a suit."

"They're not going to fire you," I said. "You're one of the main pillars of the show."

Still, Epstein looked worried. He was a natural worrier, and he worried throughout the day. He kept on worrying until it was announced that seventy-four news division employees (out of a total of 1,500) were being dismissed, and he learned he was not among them.

Throughout the building that day there was gloom and outrage. The outrage was directed at the way Joyce and Sauter had handled the dismissals. Everybody was disgusted and infuriated. Many of the people let go were people the management had grudges against, people who had opposed them. To add insult to injury, none of the normal corporate courtesies were extended to those who were leaving. Nobody was invited to talk to personnel officers. Nor did they have the benefit of an out-placement department—CBS News, a division of a Fortune 500 company, had no out-placement department. Most of those who were dismissed barely had time to clear out their desks. They were given notice on a Thursday and told to be out of the building by Friday night. Some of them had worked at CBS News more than twenty years. One woman on the "Morning News" staff, producer Phyllis Bosworth, had never held another job.

"Be out by Friday night," she was told.

Several CBS staffers whose jobs were secure went to Sauter and Joyce to protest the cuts. Rather was among them. But Rather's protest was a token effort, according to a number of CBS staffers.

"He didn't use his weight," said one. "He was Dan Rather, for heaven's sake, and he pretended to be very concerned. But his first loyalty was to Sauter."

A few weeks after the firings, Ed Joyce told an interviewer that the layoffs had been specifically designed not to inhibit the news-gathering process. When the item appeared, people in the "Morning News" fishbowl doubled over with laughter. Not only was it fatuous to suggest that losing seventy-four employees would not hurt, but in writing about the layoffs the reporter had missed the main point. By then, other cost-cutting measures besides staff reductions were having a major impact on the competitiveness and quality of CBS broadcasts.

In the course of executing the dismissals, however, Joyce made a big mistake. He made another enemy in addition to Rather. Don Hewitt had received his order to lay off "60 Minutes" staff from an intermediary, and he was outraged. Aside from the fact that Joyce had not delivered the request personally, "60 Minutes" was perennially the highest rated news show in television, generating revenues of $75 million a year. Hewitt began to call openly for Joyce's removal. Along with several other top news people—including Rather, Mike Wallace, Diane Sawyer, and Morley Safer —he put together a proposal to buy CBS News. Hewitt took the offer to Jankowski, who told him that the news division was not for sale.

When the story of the offer made its way into the papers, orders came down from Sauter. The public washing of CBS's dirty laundry had to stop. Within days, Hewitt was reported as saying nice things about "West 57th Street," a program he had been ridiculing for the previous few months. He was also reported as expressing support for Joyce; at least this was the story Joyce told to the press. And Rather told *New York* magazine that anyone's stewardship had to be seen in its full context, and that Joyce had been particularly good on a number of occasions when journalistic principles and the First Amendment had been at stake. But Rather would make no comment when asked if his relationship with Joyce had been damaged by the memo in which Joyce had told him his broadcast had enough resources. Despite the fact that Sauter was encouraging strong expressions of support for Joyce, the demise of the president of CBS News was only a matter of weeks away. As one top CBS correspondent said: "Sauter had decided to let Ed play out his string."

CBS News, of course, is a culture within a culture, a principality beholden to the larger kingdom of CBS Inc. And the cutbacks and firings at CBS News were brought about by management misjudgments that went beyond the confines of the news division. For five years, decisions had been made at the corporate headquarters, Black Rock, that were as questionable as any made at CBS News. The company's much-vaunted attempt to diversify had failed, and a number of new ventures and acquisitions had turned into big money-losers. Partly as a result, CBS became a takeover target. Many observers on Wall Street felt that even if the CBS stock was underperforming the market, the company should not have been vulnerable in the first place. "There is no question," said one Wall Street analyst, "that the management should have acted sooner to protect it."

The sharks had begun sniffing around CBS early in 1985, after North Carolina Senator Jesse Helms urged right-wingers to buy shares in CBS and thereby become Dan Rather's boss. Helms was part of an effort organized by Fairness in Media, a conservative pressure group, to buy enough stock in CBS to effect a change in what was called CBS News's liberal bias. Within a month of the Helms effort, arbitrageur Ivan Boesky and a group of investors accumulated nearly 9 percent of the company's outstanding stock, forcing CBS to take protective measures. But these maneuvers were minor compared to what would be necessary to ward off Ted Turner, the maverick Atlanta-based broadcasting entrepeneur, when Turner made a $5.4 billion offer for the company in April.

Ironically, one of the instigators behind Turner's bid for

CBS was Bob Wussler, the former president of the CBS Television Network, and the man who had done so much to advance Van Gordon Sauter's career. Since Wussler had been forced to resign from CBS, he had become Turner's right-hand man at Turner Broadcasting. And Wussler freely admits he was motivated by personal reasons in encouraging Turner to go after CBS.

"Of course I was," he says. "We're all motivated by personal reasons. And I thought we had a chance. It was a long shot, but I thought it was worth the effort, and so did Turner. Originally Turner had been interested in trying to take over ABC, but when Capital Cities moved, this caused him to rethink. We sat for hours in his office deciding how we might move. A year earlier it would have been inconceivable for us to go after CBS, but by 1985 the junk bond had become fashionable."

Like its principality, the news division, CBS Inc. was also a troubled and divided house at the time Turner made his bid. By then Bill Paley had become thoroughly disenchanted with his successor as chairman, Tom Wyman, and with good reason. Wyman's record since Paley had appointed him president of CBS in 1980 had been filled with blunders and miscalculations. But Paley could not get rid of Wyman as he had gotten rid of three previous heirs apparent. The reason was that, in 1983, the CBS board in effect had gotten rid of Paley. The founder had been pressured into finally stepping aside, and Wyman, who already had been designated chief executive officer, was given the additional post of chairman, the seat Paley had always held. Paley accepted the impressive-sounding but meaningless title of founding chairman.

In boardroom circles Wyman was considered a professional manager. He had been chief executive of the Green Giant Company until it was taken over by Pillsbury, whereupon he became vice-chairman of Pillsbury. He had no experience as a broadcaster when he signed on as president of CBS, and his critics maintained that in the interim he had gained very little. As examples of his lack of savoir faire, they cited his bottom-line approach, his failure to grasp the creative process, and his insistence on treating news as just another division. But broadcasting aside, Wyman's attempts to diversify the company were nothing to brag about, either. The acquisition of the Ideal Toy Company for $50 million was a disaster. So was Tri-Star Pictures, a joint venture with Home Box Office and Columbia Pictures. One of the final straws was the 1985 decision to pay $362.5 million for twelve Ziff-Davis magazines, an acquisition Paley vehemently opposed. Within days of announcing the deal, CBS was claiming that it had paid too much, that Ziff-Davis had misrepresented profits. Paley's judgment seemed to have been vindicated. As one Wall Street analyst said: "If that money had been spent in 1984 to repurchase stock, they would have been far better off."

But in April 1985, Tom Wyman still had the support of the majority of the CBS board, and when Turner made his offer, mostly in stock and high-risk notes, the board supported Wyman's strategy of taking on debt to defend against the bid. They also backed him in the spring of 1985, when he held the first of several conversations with Laurence Tisch, head of the Loews Corporation. Tisch had been nurturing an interest in CBS, largely because of his political opposition to the Helms maneuverings, and he suggested a number of political strategies to help Wyman stall or fend off the Turner bid.

On July 3, Wyman put up the roadblock. He announced that CBS would take on $954 million in new debt in order to buy back about 20 percent of the company's stock. CBS would pay $150 a share, $40 in cash, the rest in notes, to shareholders willing to tender their shares—up to a maximum of 20 percent of the stock outstanding. That same day

Laurence Tisch weighed in with a strategy of his own. He started buying CBS stock for himself, and in mid-July he informed Wyman that Loews owned nearly 5 percent of CBS. By the end of the month Tisch owned 7 percent.

Saddled with more than $1 billion in debt, CBS found itself forced to sell off its St. Louis TV station, KMOX —this at a time when everyone and his aunt was trying to *buy* TV stations. At the same time, profits in almost every division of the company were declining. Earnings were drained by the cost of servicing the debt, and working capital shrank. Belt tightening, it was reasoned, would soon be the order of the day. At least some belts would be tightened —others would not. Certainly appearances were being kept up in some areas of the news division, where the limousines that carried the management continued to come and go every day. And at the corporate level, prosperity was enhanced. Tom Wyman's salary that year would total $679,808 plus a bonus of $350,000. That same year the company would grant him stock appreciation rights to 62,500 shares of CBS, with CBS paying the difference between $79.50 and the market price—at the time of writing, $147.

On August 7, 1985, Ted Turner withdrew his bid, and CBS employees received a memo from their chairman. It read:

> Over the past six months our company has faced a number of unusual and difficult challenges. In rapid and surprising succession we have faced the lengthy Westmoreland trial, Senator Helms's activities with the Fairness in Media group, Ivan Boesky's greenmail effort and, most recently, Ted Turner's four-month campaign to acquire control of CBS through the proposed issuance of a variety of low-grade securities and the liquidation/sale of most of our assets.
>
> This morning Turner Broadcasting announced the withdrawal of their [sic] proposal to acquire CBS, culminating a series of dramatic defeats for them . . .

. . . This episode in our Company's history is now over. We have addressed all of these challenges with integrity and dignity—and for that we must be grateful to our shareholders, to hundreds of employees who are engaged in these matters, and to our remarkably supportive Board of Directors.

[Our recapitalization plan] is a well-balanced response to our needs and responsibilities as a company. It ensures that we are structured . . . to pursue our future vigorously, and in the best interests of our shareholders, our various publics and yourselves . . .

My sense is that as a Company we have never been closer. We have been apprehensive together, we have worked together, and we may now be forgiven for savoring our independence together. Our future is obviously bright, but the achievement of our goals will require our best efforts . . . Given the very soft conditions in several of our markets we will have to be very imaginative and rigorous to maintain and amplify our productiveness and competitiveness.

But mostly this is a time for quiet celebration and for pride —for reminding ourselves about what counts. On my list I would include quality, excellence, integrity, independence, creativity, and a belief that what we are doing is important.

Thanks to all of you for all that you have done to see us through these demanding months.

—Tom Wyman

Over the next few weeks, CBS would show what counted. And it was not quality or excellence or integrity. Within days the entire research staff of the "Morning News" was wiped out. Contributors of long standing were told that their services were no longer needed. Pat Collins, who had been the entertainment reporter for three years, was let go. So were travel reporter Dena Kaye, book critic Digby Diehl, and much-loved medical adviser Isadore Rosenfield. But this was just the start of things. Sauter and Joyce were told to collect heads, and within a few weeks seventy-four news division employees would learn how close we really were as a company.

In November, barely three months after the employees of CBS News had been urged to make time for quiet celebration and to remind themselves that quality, dignity, and integrity were what counted, another memo was received from chairman Wyman. This one sounded a slightly different note.

"In recent weeks," Wyman stated, "there has been a great deal of negative comment in the press about CBS. I think it is important to correct any misimpressions that may have resulted from this. We owe it to our shareholders, to the various publics that we serve—but most important we owe it to you, our employees."

Wyman then talked about the absolute commitment to product and service excellence—and to the thousands of people "who are CBS." Having gotten this out of the way, he then proceeded to set forth an asset-disposition program, the very thing he had said would be the result of a successful Turner bid. CBS, he said, had sold four musical-instrument companies. It also planned to sell three properties in its educational and publishing division because they did not fit into its long-term plans. Discontinued, too, were the toy, home-computer software, and theatrical film operations, including the interest in Tri-Star Pictures. Most of these had been Wyman's babies, and had represented his attempts to diversify the company. The disposition of KMOX was attributed to the fact that St. Louis was "not a very prospective market."

Wyman acknowledged that staff reductions were painful. But he added: "We do not anticipate further layoffs once the budgets are finalized at the end of this month."

And again, just as he had in August, Wyman said in closing: "I would like to take this opportunity to thank all of you for

all you have done to see us through these demanding times"
—which presumably did not include the 2 percent of the
company's employees who were no longer with us.

A few weeks later, Gene Jankowski circulated a copy of a
speech Wyman had made to corporate officers. Wyman declared:

> We have faced an unprecedented series of court martials
> in the press. But all that is history—albeit history with some
> residual scar tissue. This is the time to look *forward*.
>
> We know about the richness of CBS traditions. Our people
> have a right to very large expectations . . . We must recognize
> that some surprising failures have blurred the screen—toys,
> musical instruments, theatrical films, cultural cable. And the
> press has jumped all over them . . .
>
> A word about news—about which there has been some
> confusion. Our commitment to the responsibility to deliver
> first class broadcasts is absolute—100 percent. The idea of
> our letting the costs of CBS News become more important
> than its quality is absurd. The record of the past five years is
> clear. You may be surprised to learn that our plans for 1986
> have always foreseen spending more money on news than in
> 1985. This does not preclude the possibility and the appropri-
> ateness of working to deliver even better news broadcasts at
> lesser costs.

I was reading the memo in my office. The ceiling was
leaking, the air conditioning could not be turned down, and
I had ripped two pairs of pants on a broken file cabinet that
the company seemed unable to replace. Most of the bookers
were occupying four-by-six cubicles, and we were making
do with promoted secretaries as assistant producers. Yet
Wyman was about to set me at ease with a final reassurance:
"We realize that people are the heart of our business. Their
selection, their development, and their working environment must be our priority concerns." This time Wyman did

not thank anyone for seeing the company "through these demanding times."

By September 1985 it was clear to the staff of the "Morning News" that if we ever had been a priority concern, we were no longer. The management of CBS News was not about to spend any big bucks to bring us big-name anchors who by dint of sheer star power might give us an immediate leg up in the ratings. But given who they had foisted upon us last time, most of the staff decided this was probably a good thing. We felt the program might have a shot with two anchors who seemed to like each other and were at least competent—Forrest's celebrity interviewing notwithstanding. It would be better, we reasoned, if the anchors could at least start without the glare of publicity that had accompanied Phyllis's advent. Both were untried, and it was important that expectations not be raised too high. We need not have worried. Once the anchors passed their initiations, it was clear we were in no danger of being overpromoted.

On NBC each evening, the network usually runs three or four promo spots for "Today." Promos are those quick ten-second messages that appear just before your favorite evening program in which Bryant or Jane pops up to tell you why you should watch them tomorrow morning. We rarely got more than one promo a night. Here we were, with a beautiful Kennedy niece as anchor, the fiancée of one of the biggest box-office stars in Hollywood, and we got just one promo. It was a major source of annoyance to everyone who worked on the broadcast because if the show wasn't promoted, people didn't watch it, and if people didn't watch it, everyone felt their effort was going to waste. The network's reasoning was that the "Morning News" didn't attract a big enough audience to be worth promoting—better to devote that valuable air time to promoting a Joan Collins mini-series. The rationale was: let's see if the show starts to build; if it does, then we'll promote it. From then on, I never saw a single print ad for the broadcast, though I saw dozens for the "Evening News," exhorting us to trust Dan Rather more than we already did.

Opinion about the ability and potential of the new "Morning News" anchor team varied considerably among the senior staff. Sometimes it varied from day to day, depending upon how the show had gone. Many of the staff felt we came up short in the accepted morning-show practice of creating a facsimile family, with anchors who represented mom and dad. Our anchors were young, unmarried, childless. They lacked authority. By then Pauley–Gumbel and Hartman–Lunden were established teams, and some people felt that Shriver and Sawyer would not become as accomplished for a long time, that we would continue to labor in the shadow of the competition, playing catch-up. Maria, it was felt, had charisma, but tended to get prosecutorial in her interviews. Forrest was a decent enough interviewer of politicians, but he was a bust with celebrities, and he still looked like Mr. Bland. The bookers continued to have their problems with him.

I had continued trying to pump him for his interests, and after a few months he announced he wanted to do a series on best-selling authors. When I was shown the list of authors he proposed to interview, I realized it was all men.

"It might be a good idea to throw in a woman," I told Shirley, who was producing the series. "There are a few women who write best-selling books, you know."

"I wanted to," Shirley retorted. "I wanted Judith Krantz, but he won't do her."

I went back to Forrest's office.

"Forrest," I said, "we're doing a series on best-selling authors. We have no women. What's wrong with Judith Krantz?"

"No, I don't want to do Krantz," he said.

"So Krantz is not a stylistic giant," I replied. "We're doing Doctorow. There's no harm in balancing it."

"No. Uh-huh. Not me."

"Forrest, one good reason to do Krantz is that women watch this show, and besides she's a terrific interview."

He wouldn't budge. Normally, I would have raised the issue with Katz. And if Katz had wanted to do Judith Krantz badly enough, he might have pressured Forrest into giving in. But I was fed up arguing with Katz over celebrities, and I also knew he was having his problems with the anchors.

For all executive producers, dealing with anchors is a delicate game of negotiation. As Van Gordon Sauter once said, anchors are like Siberian tigers, who would eat their keepers in a second if they ever thought they could. Anchors are paid huge salaries, and they exercise a degree of control and power. When network news organizations are faced with disagreements between an anchor and an executive producer, the easiest solution is usually to replace the executive producer. So even though the anchors at the "Morning News" did not run the show, their inclinations and intransigencies had to be considered at every stage of the process. Katz's problem all along was that he had too many constituencies to please: the anchors, the management, the viewing public, and as he put it, "the ghosts of Murrow who haunt this damn place."

I knew Katz had argued with both Forrest and Maria.

"They both think they're Dan Rather," he said. "Maria less so."

Maria would usually do what she was asked to do, but Forrest would complain.

"He doesn't get it," Katz said. "All he's interested in is how he looks on the political stuff."

Every morning after the show Forrest would burst into the fishbowl and want to know if disclosures from any of his interviews had made the wires. He'd ask Epstein or me: "How did we do today?"

"The Teri Garr interview is all over the wires," I told him one morning. "AP, UP, Reuters, they all grabbed it."

"What? You're kidding me?"

Epstein turned away, trying hard not to laugh.

All along, I had been doing my best to steer celebrity interviews away from Forrest, but Maria was starting to object. "He has to do some," Katz told me. And so the duds came in a string. They started with starlet Jennifer Beals, who was being interviewed for her movie, *The Bride*. She was terrible on all the morning shows, ruining a lot of fantasies—she practically turned Bryant Gumbel green. But then Forrest, who still refused to ask the questions the bookers prepared for him, blew interviews with Teri Garr, Judith Ivey, Raul Julia, and Sally Field. And of course he blamed everyone but himself. Katz was hearing it from him, and I was hearing it from Katz.

"We can't hang him out to dry every day like this," Katz said.

"Jon, he hangs himself out to dry," I retorted. "He won't ask the bookers' questions. Is Maria having problems?"

"Well, make sure the celebrity can talk. And about something else besides God."

"Jon, he blew an interview with Sally Field. How could anyone blow an interview with Sally Field?"

Katz squirmed and twisted.

"Well, maybe there are more interesting ways to do the glitz stuff. Maybe we can do glitzy panels, or something. I don't know. You think about it."

"You mean like we did with Pat Collins?" I said pointedly. Katz had just fired her.

"Okay, let's get a new entertainment reporter. You find one. I've been looking for one for two years."

We were relieved of the celebrity issue for a few days by

the Mexican earthquake. Like the TWA hostage crisis, it took up the full two hours of the broadcast. There was no chance of originating live from Mexico because all communications were down, so we booked guests on the issues of disaster relief, disease, and seismology.

After the broadcast Katz sent us a congratulatory memo. ". . . First rate. Your ability to bounce back from everything from attacks in the press to budget problems is astonishing. It also convinces me more than ever before that we and the broadcast will succeed. The support from above is tremendous . . ."

"What unbelievable bullshit!" Pat Shevlin said when she read the memo.

She was right of course. As far as support from above was concerned, we had not seen anyone from the front office in the fishbowl in weeks. We had lost six producers since the firings, and by then other cost-cutting measures were having a major impact on the broadcast. Almost every day Katz and John O'Regan were summoned to the front office and told to cut, cut, cut. All these cuts flew in the face of Wyman's insistence that the commitment to deliver first-class news broadcasts was absolute. The front office, which had never fully grasped what a broadcast devoted mainly to live guests entailed, began slapping irons on us that crippled our competitiveness as well as our ability to cover breaking news. Most damaging was the order not to spend more than $8,000 a day in line charges. This meant that half the newsblock stories we'd previously covered with pictures were out. When important news was developing in South Africa, we were told we could not cover it unless something really important happened. If a story broke in Los Angeles, where line costs and studio-origination fees ran around $3,000 a pop, we were told to ignore it unless we could do a two-for-one—meaning if we could line up a celebrity interview as well, then the news story could run. Finally, to the disbelief of everyone, we were told that only guests of the stature of Marlon Brando could be flown first class.

Joan Fontaine was not considered of that stature. We had booked her, and the booker then had to tell Fontaine's agent that we would only fly her coach.

"Joan Fontaine does not fly coach, darling," the agent said. "She's Joan Fontaine."

That afternoon I stopped Joyce in the corridor and told him that such restrictions were killing us. He shrugged and said he'd talk to Katz about it. Katz then told me that the booker should fill in a travel form saying that Joan Fontaine was an invalid, and then nobody would question it. I walked away shaking my head.

CBS News, I said to myself. What a place.

On Monday, October 7, I got to work later than usual. There was a memo from Katz on my desk.

"I will be pressing in coming weeks for more Silent Scream segments," it read, "probably the single best issue treatment we have ever done. Please help me by suggesting your own ideas and bringing as much imagination, forward momentum, and intelligent presentation of information as possible."

"Silent Scream" had been Katz's big hit, his home run. The show had obtained a copy of the film the Reagan administration was using to support its position against abortion, and Katz had aired it in front of a group of leading physicians, who had pointed out the film's flaws. The initiative had received favorable treatment in the press, and was even awarded praise in a *New York Times* editorial.

But that was five months ago. Katz was no longer held in high regard in the upper echelons of CBS management. Sauter had stopped speaking to him, and Gene Jankowski had let it be known that Phyllis George had failed because of the lousy producers at the "CBS Morning News." When this comment got around, Jankowski's stock fell to a new low among the rank and file. Katz could be blamed for a lot of things, but Phyllis's failure was not one of them.

I was looking over the rest of Katz's memo when Shevlin walked in.

"Seen the *Washington Post*?" she inquired.

I told her I hadn't gotten to it yet.

"Better take a look at the Style section," she said. "It's going to affect everyone's day around here."

I opened the paper. Tom Shales had struck again.

Call me crazy, call me mad, call me incredibly forgetful, but I miss Phyllis George. She was beautiful and fresh, and just looking at her made the morning less mean. Of course you couldn't just look at her, which was where the problem developed.

Now that Phyllis has been off the "CBS Morning News" for some time, however, what was always painfully obvious has become brutally obvious: the "Morning News" is a lousy show . . . The set is cold, the weatherman is wimpy, the announcer gets on your nerves, the graphics are too busy, the music is jangly and intrusive. The program has bad manners. It keeps tugging at you and begging you not to leave. Of course if one has only six viewers [ratings are worse than they were with Phyllis], one would be inclined toward excessive solicitousness . . .

All these complaints are relatively superficial considering that the show just doesn't work . . . and just won't ever work until a new executive producer is brought in and the whole thing overhauled again.

Shales went on to dissect the broadcast for another ten paragraphs, noting that Maria and Forrest were capable anchors, but were junior varsity compared to the pros on the other networks. He concluded: "The shame of the 'CBS

Morning News' is not in being in third place. When Charles Kuralt had the show, he was in third place too, but at least it was failure with honor."

The attack was aimed at the management and at Katz. I went to the fishbowl to find Epstein and Roberta looking like the world had ended. Corvo came in and was shown the story. He studied it intently. Then, with typical understatement, he said: "Well, it isn't nice. Has Katz seen it yet?"

"He was on his way to the front office when I saw him," Shevlin said.

"Oh, then I guess he has seen it," Corvo replied.

All day long the bookers dropped by the fishbowl to read the story. *Washington Post*s that day were in short supply.

"So, who reads the *Washington Post*?" Amy asked, trying to be cheerful.

"The management does," I reminded her, "and the column's syndicated."

"Well, it's not like it's going to hurt ratings."

"No," I agreed. "Not much could."

Corvo ran the meeting that morning, and we didn't see much of Katz all day. Later that week I went to lunch with a producer on another broadcast, and he told me: "I'm hearing Katz is gone."

"It wouldn't surprise me," I said. "He's been hanging by his teeth since May. And he's told practically everyone in the division that he's burned out."

"I'm hearing that the Shales article was the final nail."

Again I was not surprised. The article had enforced the view that the broadcast, with or without Phyllis George, was a bust. I had little doubt that Shales was merely being contrary with his Phyllis stand—after all, he was among the leaders in cutting her down.

"So what do they do with Katz?" I asked my lunch partner.

"Depends how many protectors he has," he said.

I knew Katz was still close to Ober and, more importantly, to Stringer. If he did lose his job, I had little doubt that he would be "parked" or "shelved," as they say at CBS News. In any case, within a week or two, the speculation that Katz was out began to build. All the signs began to manifest themselves. Katz attended our meetings less often. The anchors began flexing their muscles.

The announcement came on October 30, accompanied by a note from Katz. "As most of you know by now, I am moving to another assignment at CBS News. [Katz's new title was Director of Planning at CBS News—we all had a good laugh about that one.] I'll never be able to express my gratitude and appreciation for the patience you have all shown in teaching me and putting up with me . . . I feel more confident than at any other time in the last three years that the 'Morning News' is going to receive the recognition, appreciation, and success it deserves . . ."

We took Katz to a farewell lunch at Shun Lee, an overpriced Chinese restaurant near Lincoln Center. Ober and Stringer were there, but not Sauter. Katz admitted he was relieved. He was no longer responsible for the unwieldy mess. He would be taking a month's vacation before he resumed his new job.

"If I can come up with a few good ideas, I'll be okay," he told me quietly. "You know this place. Nobody has ideas."

I gave him a tie with ducks on it. He would need a tie for his new job, and I didn't know if he owned any. He was being given a room in the front office—temporarily, it turned out.

Ober took the tie from him even before the lunch was over. Ober treasured ugly ties, and he decided that if Katz was allowed to walk around looking neat, it wouldn't be the same Katz.

"So, who's the next executive producer, Eric?" I said.

"I don't know," Ober said. "Ask Howard."

I looked across the table where Stringer was treating the occasion like a regular party, being expansive and open and giving nothing away.

"Ask Howard?" I said. "I'm not sure Howard would tell me the time of day."

Ober took this as a joke, but he looked a bit startled. I made a mental note that maybe something in me was starting to rebel about working at the "CBS Morning News."

XI.

THE LAST, BEST HOPE

"There is no public service if the public isn't there. In the end, that's the most important thing, and it should be."

—Gene Jankowski

The day after Jon Katz left the "Morning News," every employee of the CBS Broadcast Group received a long, rambling missive from Gene Jankowski. It contained the above admonition, and the following as well:

There has never been a time when more people were more interested in CBS, on and off the air . . . However, a lot of what has been said has more to do with changes around the borders of our business than with changes at the core, and a lot of it hasn't got much to do with anything at all. I'd like to point out some of these distinctions in this letter. It is important that we be able to see clearly what some people who report about us apparently do not.

As the senior staff of the "Morning News" read this memo in the fishbowl, most of us decided that Gene Jankowski was on shaky ground. We had been thinking that the press had been doing a pretty good job. Reporters were opening up the doors to CBS News, and despite the efforts of the management to deter them, accurate stories were being written.

Jankowski then alluded to Don Hewitt's offer to buy CBS News, which had already made the papers. He tried to suggest that Hewitt's offer was symptomatic of the current rash of media takeover bids, and had nothing to do with dissatisfaction within the news division.

> Networks find themselves in a position [he wrote] where the dollar value of their owned stations may appear to be greater than the dollar value of the company itself as measured by the stock price. This is an entirely new experience for us. It is the cause of the current rash of takeover talk . . . I will not attempt to review this complicated subject in detail here, except to say that it is behind much of the reported "turmoil" in our industry. In fact, it was this very atmosphere that gave rise to the inquiry made by some of our News personnel about there being any possibility of a sale of CBS News. However unlikely such a sale may seem, even the faintest of chances was enough for people who have given virtually all their working lives to the making of CBS News to ask whether they could present an offer, assuming any offer were to be made by an outside interest.
>
> . . . It hardly needs to be said again that CBS News is not and will not be for sale.

According to Jankowski, Don Hewitt, who admittedly was worth a few bucks, had merely been trying to get on the Turner bandwagon. Jankowski seemed to be suggesting that Hewitt was hoping to take CBS News off the company's hands by slapping down a few bundles of bills. Did Jankowski seriously expect the CBS News staff to believe this? In the fishbowl, people who read the memo shook their heads. Finally, somebody said: "Remember who signed off on the hiring of Phyllis George?" The question put everything into perspective.

As head of the CBS Broadcast Group, Gene Jankowski was ultimately responsible for prime-time programming. He had inherited a rosy situation when he first got the job, but over the course of 1985 NBC had risen from the bottom of the network pile to take the prime-time ratings lead. Critics of CBS charged complacency and arrogance. Good producers were flocking to NBC, which was being run by Grant Tinker and Brandon Tartikoff, and many of the producers who had flown the coop had once had exclusive deals with CBS.

NBC was paying Bill Paley back for his raids of thirty-eight years earlier, wresting away from CBS its image as the quality or "Tiffany" network. CBS's programming had built an audience that seemed overly rural, poor, and old compared to NBC's, which tended to be young, urban, and affluent, the audience advertisers wanted to reach. For its crowning touch, NBC's "Nightly News" featured a young, sharp anchor in Tom Brokaw, who surveys indicated was destined eventually to catch Dan Rather in the ratings.

All this was well-known in October 1985, when major developments were taking place in the stratosphere of CBS. By this time Larry Tisch had acquired nearly 12 percent of CBS's stock, leaving the CBS board little choice but to offer him a seat. Wyman walked the half block to Tisch's office to offer it to him personally, and no one was surprised when the offer was accepted. At the same time, Wyman tried to determine the full extent of Tisch's designs on CBS, but Tisch was not interested in signing any agreement setting limits on how much CBS stock he could acquire. He told Wyman so.

Larry Tisch had already met Bill Paley by the time he attended his first CBS board meeting on November 13. After the meeting, lunch was served in Paley's dining room, and the real business of CBS began to be discussed. Paley, who by then opposed Wyman in many matters, had relatively few supporters on the CBS board. One was Marietta Tree, who like Paley was a patron of the arts; another was Walter Cronkite. Wyman was still backed by the majority, the other nonbroadcasting CEO's, men of glass, engines, and computers. They included James Houghton, chairman of Corning Glass; Henry Schacht, chairman of Cummins Engine; Edson Spenser, chairman of Honeywell; and Franklin Thomas, president of the Ford Foundation. That day while everyone awaited the input of the newest and potentially most powerful CBS board member, it was Cronkite who started the ball rolling with a sweeping criticism of the state of things at CBS News.

Cronkite had been critical of the management of CBS News ever since he had vacated the anchor chair. He had no loyalty to Van Gordon Sauter, nor any patience for his "moment" theories, and he soundly lambasted the entire news division under Sauter's management, including the "Evening News," complaining that it had gone soft. Some members of the board viewed Cronkite's opinions as those of an old soldier who still harkened to the bugle's call and resented those who were on the battlefield while he was not. Nonetheless, the barrage was beautifully timed that morning to coincide with Tisch's arrival.

After Cronkite spoke, Wyman began to protest. He argued that there was nothing wrong with the way CBS News was being run. After a few minutes of listening to this, Larry Tisch stepped in. He quietly disagreed. If there was nothing wrong with CBS News, then why was it that every time he opened a paper, there was another article about the news division's problems? There had to be a reason for this. Wyman, shot down, was silent. Then Tisch suggested that maybe the problem at the news division was that there were too many layers of managers. In making this point, he was picking up on a publicized grievance of Don Hewitt's. Hewitt had complained that, whereas the president of CBS News used to report directly to the head of the Broadcast Group, now the president, Joyce, reported to Sauter, who in turn reported to Jankowski.

When the lunch was over, Wyman conferred with Jankowski. "I don't care what you have to do to fix it," Wyman said grimly, "but fix it."

The message was clear. Jankowski called Sauter. After two years of puffing his pipe at Black Rock, Van Gordon Sauter was going back to the Broadcast Center to take charge of news.

Two weeks before Larry Tisch's first CBS board meeting, there had been considerable worry at the "Morning News." The reason was Katz's impending departure. The name Susan Winston was being bandied around once again, but by then Winston was busy working on a syndicated show called "America," which turned into a ratings disaster. I sat next to Corvo in the control room one morning and asked him if he had a shot at the job.

"Are you kidding?" he said rather dejectedly. "I'm too closely identified with the old regime. That was my dumb mistake."

"But they put you in to keep an eye on Katz?" I said.

"Yeah," Corvo said. "All the more reason."

Corvo was right. Two days later, it was announced that Johnathan Rodgers would be the new executive producer of the "Morning News." Corvo, who was a good friend of Rodgers, would stay on as his deputy.

Rodgers had worked at KNXT (now KCBS) in Los Angeles, first as its news director and then as station manager.

He had since taken over as executive producer of the weekend editions of the "CBS Evening News." He was the first black to head a major CBS News broadcast, and he was reputed to be capable and diplomatic.

One of his smartest moves initially was to stipulate that he would not take the job the CBS News management was offering him, unless he was given access to the program's research.* Research had been done on the "Morning News" for some time, but management had refused to share the information with the program's executive producers. As a result, management had access to valuable information that was denied Katz and his predecessor, Ferrante. Rodgers knew better than to operate in a blind. He knew the handicap Katz had labored under, and so when Stringer took him to lunch and offered him the job, he made his demand known. Stringer agreed, and the two men went back to the Broadcast Center for further discussion with Ed Joyce.

Joyce gave Rodgers his mandate. "I want you to re-establish the credibility of this broadcast as a news program," he said.

This was what Rodgers wanted to do anyway, but then Joyce threw in a kicker.

"How would you feel about eventually having Susan Winston as a consultant to this program?" he asked.

Rodgers said there was no way he would take the job if Susan Winston was a consultant. Joyce let the matter drop. Winston's name would not come up again during Rodgers's tenure.

---

*For years, the CBS News executives had insisted they did not do audience research on their news programs, and when they were obliged to admit they did, they claimed they didn't follow it, which was patently untrue. CBS News had been pressured into conducting and following research by its affiliates, who were incensed that the news division was programming into a vacuum.

The day Johnathan Rodgers started at the "Morning News," the senior staff also received a pep talk from Howard Stringer.

"I know you've all worked extremely hard," Stringer said, "and I know how demoralizing it is not to see the ratings go up. But I think you've really got a shot now. You've got two new anchors who are starting to click, and I think with Johnathan you've got just the right person as executive producer to make a go of it. Johnathan is experienced, and I know he'll be able to work with the anchors, so, as I say, I think you've really got a shot. Good luck."

When Stringer left, everyone in the room rolled their eyes. Was this all he had to say? He had not paid a visit to the "Morning News" fishbowl in two months, and now he had come to tell us that we had a shot.

Rodgers at least had more to say.

"My first aim," he told us in his deep, rich voice, "is to restore morale here."

He then told us that he wanted to re-establish the credibility of this broadcast as a news program. Producers blinked. Could this be true? Rodgers had not said that this was an order from the management, but we could infer this.

"I'm not saying we shouldn't have celebrities," Rodgers went on, "but I want no more than two a day, one at seven-forty-five, the other in the eight-thirty half hour. And I want the contributors to be providing up to three segments a day. I intend to make this broadcast competitive with the other two, at least in the new year when we'll have a budget. For now, we have to keep our belts tightened because there is no money."

Rodgers then told us that all jobs were up for grabs. He laid out a framework of positions, and told us we could apply for whichever jobs we wanted. He would make his final decision in a few days. I opted for senior producer in charge of information, which would essentially put me in charge of all guests except those from Washington.

Two days later I had my meeting with Rodgers. He had received a copy of a memo I had sent to Joyce and Stringer. It read in part:

"I think one of the problems of the 'Morning News' is that it is bulletin-oriented, rather than inquiring. We tend to come off the news in a knee-jerk way. An acorn falls from a tree and the next day we have three dazed botanists poring over it. More often than not we ignore the stories that news camouflages. I believe we should be less of a 'newspaper,' more like a daily magazine. People want their interest piqued."

My memo continued with a list of specific ideas.

Rodgers said: "I like this. And so does Ed [which surprised me]. I think we can work together."

I got the job.

I soon discovered Rodgers to be approachable, smart, able to make decisions. He also had the ability, rare among executive producers, of being able to admit when he was wrong. And I approved of the one new person he had hired, Peter Bonventre, who had co-written Howard Cosell's book, *I Never Played the Game.* Bonventre had also been a correspondent on Cosell's ABC show, "Sports Beat," and had worked nine years as a writer at *Newsweek.*

"Well, what do you think of Johnathan so far?" Shevlin asked me at the end of his first week.

"I like him," I said. "He's direct, no bullshit, capable. How about you?"

"I wish he hadn't told us to wear jeans on Fridays," Shevlin said. "I don't look good in jeans."

"I like this new guy he's hired, too," I said. "It's a change to have someone around here I can go have a drink with, and not have to worry that what I say will wind up as a knife in my back."

"Thanks a lot," Pat said.

She knew I didn't mean her. I had beaten her out for the job I'd been given, and the next morning she had marched in, stuck out her hand and said, "Congratulations, you deserve it." I thought she had a lot of class.

During Rodgers's first week I argued strongly with him about his decision to devote three entire two-hour shows to the upcoming Geneva summit.

"It promises to be one of the dullest events in history," I said. "How much can anyone stand of it? How much can you stand?"

"Like I said, I need to re-establish credibility," Rodgers replied.

"Johnathan," I argued. "I'm sympathetic. You know how I feel. But people will be tired of it."

But he was adamant. Besides, Missie had drawn up all kinds of plans for elaborate segments, and she was supported by Corvo, who almost always backed what she did. So we had three days of unrelieved boredom, with Forrest doing his best to be Dan Rather, even interviewing Rather at the end of each broadcast. These interviews were made to seem spontaneous, but Rather had already told Forrest what questions to ask.

The second day, I sat in the control room falling asleep.

On the monitors Johnathan watched the other two morning programs break away from the summit shortly after eight.

"Okay, okay, if the ratings go down this week, I'll admit you were right," he said.

"Here's an idea," I said. "Tomorrow, let's try and book Chevy Chase to do a 'Weekend Update' on the summit."

Rodgers looked shocked.

"Chevy Chase on the summit," I repeated. "Why not?"

"What! You mean he'll do a weekend update and at the

end of it he'll fall off his chair, and say: 'And I'm Chevy Chase, and you're not'?"

"Precisely," I said.

"No way," Rodgers said, his mop of Afro hair shaking wildly. "No way."

The ratings took a dive, and we were trounced one day in the press for one of Missie's ideas. She'd decided that Terry Smith and a Soviet expert should hold up Reagan-Gorbachev summit scorecards. The following week Rodgers admitted he was wrong, though I made it clear to him that I understood his point about credibility.

We received a memo from Stringer on the summit:

"Your broadcast's surge towards journalistic supremacy in the morning continues unabated. The coverage of the Geneva summit was superb. Congratulations to all."

With fewer celebrities on the program, Forrest was becoming less difficult. He was also making strides. He did one full half-hour interview with the country's four leading authorities on AIDS, and he handled it brilliantly. Not only did he and Maria seem to get along, but Maria's periodic giggle attacks, as well as her weekly exchanges with sportscaster Warner Wolf, added warmth to the show.

Maria was first-rate with celebrities, but sometimes she didn't grasp an issue or would see it only from the peculiar perspective of a privileged Catholic woman, born to one of America's leading families. Every morning after the show, she and her mother Eunice would talk on the phone, and at times it seemed to me we were getting an input we didn't need. And occasionally both our anchors would act as if they were more important than they really were.

"Forrest who?" Corvo would remark, when told Forrest didn't want to do something.

But Rodgers seemed to work well with both of them, and toward the end of the year, even without any extra money being spent, the ratings began to show a blip. Up. I was in Stringer's office the day he got the news, and so I first heard the ratings advance from Stringer himself.

"Guess what? You've got a 3.4." Stringer was clearly pleased.

"That's encouraging," I said.

"I know it is," he went on. "A 3.4 is only one point away from the upper threes, and then you've really got something going. I think what you have to do now is figure out how to sell these anchors. I mean you've got the content, now you need to present them in a light that makes them more visible."

A few promo spots wouldn't hurt, I thought.

I'd actually had several ideas to make Forrest more visible, but he'd turned them all down. He told me he liked auto racing, and I suggested he take a lap around Daytona the week before the 500. He said no. It was the kind of thing Kurtis would have jumped at. Walking through rubble, flying in the cockpit of a B-17—it didn't matter to Kurtis, he loved being out in the field as a reporter. But Forrest considered himself an anchor, and anchors were supposed to be dignified and immobile. When David Letterman began making cracks about the name Forrest Sawyer, I urged him to go on Letterman's show, and if necessary take a chain saw to Letterman's desk. Forrest thought I was joking.

If Stringer was talking about enhancing visibility, he wasn't talking about doing it in any way that required spending money. Even with the ratings up, we were being constantly pressured to hold down costs. It was hard even to build a bank of taped pieces for the show. We were now forbidden to do post-tapings after the broadcast, and all the constraints that had been slapped on us two months ago remained in force. We were still trying to persuade major celebrities to fly coach, and I had not been allowed to replace two bookers who had recently quit. The rest were objecting again to the workload despite the fact that they liked Rodgers and had rallied to support him. I told him about the problem, but he said there was nothing he could do. His hands were tied.

I went off to impart this news to Pete Bonventre, who was in a general state of disbelief. Having come to CBS from ABC, he was suffering culture shock. Bonventre had been trying to scrounge up a booker to work on a series for the new year on the baby-boom generation turning forty. I was on my way to see him when I ran into him in the corridor. He had news.

"Hey," he said. "Guess what? Joyce is out. Sauter's coming back to news."

"You're kidding me?"

"No, it's true. Come on, walk down the front hall with me. You can't believe it. The place is buzzing."

I knew, even before we reached the front hall. There was something in the air, the same extraordinary buzz of rumor that Katz had detected on the day I had first walked along the "Evening News" corridor with him. He had said, "Something's going down, I can feel it, I can smell it." Now my antennae were similarly attuned.

Tisch's suggestion to Wyman was being carried out. One layer of the CBS News management was being eliminated. Sauter was cashing in his old friend, Ed Joyce, who was being parked, shelved, moved to senior vice-president of CBS Worldwide Enterprises, whatever that meant. Sauter, who had had an eye on Jankowski's job, was being made to stick with what he had started.

The news traveled fast to the "Morning News" fishbowl.

"Well, we can do sports again," was Epstein's reaction to the news. "Oh, and the dress code around here goes way down."

Among the old guard there was a sense of victory, but rejoicing was muted. As Bill Moyers had told friends, reinstating Van Gordon Sauter as president of CBS News was like reinstating Richard Nixon as President of the United States.

That winter I began the process of fence-mending with PR people. Rodgers understood the need for this, and promised he would go out of his way not to cancel guests unless there was a news emergency. He also suggested we give a party in Los Angeles for PR people.

And so in mid-January I got a break from the CBS News building and the New York winter. Jane Kaplan and I flew out to Los Angeles (tourist class). Corvo and Rodgers took a later flight. Jane had been at CBS News eight years, and in the course of a five-hour flight I had a lot of time to hear about her career. She predated George Merlis at the "Morning News," and she had seen a lot of regimes come and go. Shortly before we landed in Los Angeles, I asked her if she still liked her job. She said she did, even though the hours were brutal and the place was nuts. She liked producing.

"How about you?" she said.

I said I had mixed feelings. I liked Johnathan, I told her, and most of the other people I worked with, but the the novelty of television had worn off.

"I'll guess I'll take it day by day," I said. "Right now I have a sense the ship is under control, but if it ever starts spinning again, I'll jump."

"To where?"

"Back to print probably."

"You shouldn't think all television is like the 'Morning News,'" Jane said.

I grinned.

"How could it be?" I said. "But my suspicion is that certain things about it are endemic."

"Like what?"

"Oh, lies, bullshit, hypocrisy, star worship, treachery as a measure of the Zeitgeist, you know."

"Don't be cynical," Jane said.

We landed in a yellow haze, rented a smart car, and drove to the Beverly Wilshire.

The day before the party, Forrest, Maria, and Johnathan held a press conference for the TV writers. All acquitted themselves credibly. The press in general was taking note of the team's improvement. There were no longer free-swinging attacks in the papers—Shales had been silent for three months—and although we still fell short of the other broadcasts in terms of anchor experience, the program had reached a higher standard in terms of content.

I sat by the pool of the Beverly Wilshire, trying to soak up what sun I could in two days. Jane had gone off with Forrest to produce an interview with Joan Collins, who was to appear in a CBS mini-series called "Sins." Johnathan had said he thought the chemistry would be better if Forrest did it rather than Maria. I warned him.

Around noon Jane came back to the pool. From the look on her face I guessed how it had gone.

"So?"

"Well, he was very polite," she began, "but he hated her. And she's such a bitch. She had this assistant fussing around her, and she asked Forrest: 'How long will it take? Ten minutes?' "

"Love at first sight," I said.

"The worst thing," Jane confided, "was in the hotel corridor. Some guy went by and called out, 'That's Joan Collins,' and his wife said: 'Who's that with her?' "

"Mr. Bland," I said.

"Forrest who?" Jane replied with a giggle.

"So, is it airable?"

"Oh, sure," Jane said, "but nobody's going to think they're having an affair."

Around four o'clock we went to get ready for the party. I had told Jane to get Forrest to mingle, since this was the purpose of the event. But when we went downstairs to the room where the party was being held, and the PR people began to arrive, he stayed in a corner talking to some old friends from Atlanta. He had been there half an hour when Johnathan came up to me.

"Can't you get Forrest up?" he pleaded. "I've tried."

"So has Jane," I said. "I'll give it another shot."

I went over to Jane and told her to use her charm to get Forrest circulating. Jane breathed hard.

"Everyone only wants to meet Maria anyway," she said.

"We're under orders from Johnathan," I said. "He's desperate, and besides, it's rude."

I finally found an ally in actress Lisa Hartman's mother, who ran a PR company in Hollywood. Her daughter had been on the broadcast a few weeks earlier because she had been featured in a swimsuit on the cover of one of the sports magazines. Forrest had asked her a half dozen questions about her TV series, "Knott's Landing," but declined to mention the magazine or hold up the cover because it showed a peek of breast.

"Where is that young man, Forrest Sawyer?" Mrs. Hartman wanted to know. "I want to meet him."

I rounded up Jane, and said, "Mrs. Hartman wants to meet Forrest, let's go."

We marched across the room. Faced with no alternative, Forrest got up.

"I'm Lisa's mother," Mrs. Hartman said. "What a real pleasure it is to meet you."

She was a charming woman who spoke with a faintly southern accent.

"I thought you did a wonderful interview with my daughter," she said, "but why didn't you ask her about the magazine cover?"

Jane and I started to sidle away.

"He's not going to forgive us for this," I said when we were at a safe distance. Jane was laughing too hard to answer.

When Jane stopped laughing, we met up with Corvo. We all agreed the party had been a big success. It might even have done us some good. The biggest hit of the evening was Arnold Schwarzenegger. He was wearing a black leather jacket, and Maria, in a stunning flaired scarlet dress, was clinging to his sleeve.

"Now there's an anchor couple," Jane said.

Corvo laughed.

"At least there wouldn't be any arguments," he said.

We had to go make the rounds again. Toward the end of the evening Johnathan asked me for feedback from the PR people.

"They're appeased somewhat," I said. "They still can't believe we're not flying people first class."

"It is kind of embarrassing," Johnathan admitted.

He told me he was not flying back to New York. He planned to go straight to Miami, where we were going to set up shop for a week of shows.

"Take Jane out somewhere nice," he said. "She's earned it."

I said I would. And I did.

We'd had producers in Florida for three weeks, booking guests for the late January shows that were to originate from Miami. Rodgers had told us to start coming up with story ideas in December, and by January we'd put together all the predictable segments on guns, drugs, and immigration, plus lighter features on seafood restaurants, Palm Beach, and the usual mix of celebrities who spent time or lived in the Sunshine State. It had been eight months since the "Morning

News" had done its London broadcasts, and since then "Today" and "GMA" had been on the road more often than Charles Kuralt. Budget crunch or not, the "Morning News" had to do something merely to stay in the ballpark. So Miami was chosen, and for two reasons: one, it is an interesting city; two, the management wanted to make the local affiliate happy. Which of the two was more important, I have no idea.

When I arrived back in New York, the only senior people in the fishbowl were Shevlin and Epstein. By then Epstein was in charge of the "Early Morning News" and the news-blocks for the main show. The poor guy had virtually given up on ever going on an extended remote; once again he was being rewarded for his competence by being stuck in New York. It looked like we were in for another easy week, a repeat of London. And that's the way it was, at least through Monday.

We sat up in the control room, relaxing. I had time to catch up on paper work, and time to meet with people. On Tuesday morning I met with Norman Glubok, a former piece producer who had opted to take early retirement during the cutbacks of the previous October.

"Norman, you look so healthy, it's disgusting," I said. "How is life in the real world?"

"It's just fine," Glubok said. "I don't miss the work, but I do miss the people—some of the people."

He told me he had been doing some PR work since he had left, and had a few story ideas he wanted to suggest on behalf of clients. He had just gotten started when Maggie Shumaker came by. She was an old friend of Norman's and was delighted to see him, and the two sat in my office and talked.

The TV was between them, tuned to CNN, and suddenly the clean white trail on my monitor went blurry.

"Move back a bit, Norman," I said. "And could you turn up the sound a bit . . ."

". . . There appears to be something wrong . . ."

I made a dash for the fishbowl.

"I know," I told Shevlin as I ran in. "I saw it."

Within a few minutes the extent of the space shuttle Challenger tragedy was apparent. During those few minutes, I sounded like a paging service. "Peggy, it's Peter. Come down to the fishbowl . . . Jane, could you come to fishbowl immediately . . . Amy, we need you in the fishbowl, the space shuttle just blew up."

"How many bookers do you think should go to New Hampshire?" Shevlin asked. (New Hampshire was the home of Christa McAuliffe, the civilian grade-school teacher who perished aboard the shuttle.)

"Two," I said.

We sent Jane and Amy.

"Just go," we told them. "Call us when you get there."

Part of the bookers' job was to be prepared for such eventualities. They didn't bother to pack. They would buy clothes on the way. They went downstairs to the cashier, got cash advances of several hundred dollars, and departed into the cold January day.

We sent another two bookers to Houston. Meanwhile other bookers were already calling former astronauts—John Glenn, Frank Borman, Harrison Schmidt, Jim Lovell. We also booked Leo Krupp, the space expert who had sat at Cronkite's side all those years during the early launches.

"What about Cape Kennedy?" Shevlin said.

"We've got six bookers in Florida already," I said. "I presume they know about this in Miami."

There is in all news people some part of them that blocks moments of horror or tragedy, and makes them think solely in terms of how to cover the event. In the few minutes that had elapsed since the shuttle blew up, I'd already begun to examine some of the implications of the tragedy in terms of what it would mean for the rest of the week's broadcasts from Florida. So had Rodgers.

"Johnathan on 47," said a page, sticking his head into the fishbowl.

Epstein, Shevlin, and I all grabbed it.

Johnathan was cool.

"Okay," he said with sigh, "tell me where we stand."

We told him, and he said: "Okay, okay, let me think . . . If we all decide to come back to New York today, can we book shows for Thursday and Friday?

"Sure we can," I said.

"But your bookers will be scattered," he said. "New Hampshire, Houston . . ."

"Yeah, but there'll still be news from the shuttle. Are you thinking of canceling Miami altogether?"

"I don't know yet. I have to talk to the front office."

"Or do you stay in Florida," Epstein said, "and come out of Cape Kennedy?"

Across the desk Shevlin was saying to me: "They should come from where the news is."

For the next three hours Rodgers talked to the front office about where we should originate from.

"Jeezus," I kept saying, "when are we going to get an answer?" We had half the former astronauts in America on hold, not knowing whether they should fly to New York, Miami, or the nearest affiliate.

Finally it was decided. Tomorrow's show would come out of Cape Kennedy. Then we would return to Miami for the remaining two days of the week. But most of the booking that day was done in New York. In fact by five o'clock we had done it all.

"It's going to be weird," Epstein said later that evening as he put on his coat. "Two cheery shows from Miami—after this!"

"I know," I said. "But if there's any advantage for us in

this, it will be tomorrow. At least we'll be on the scene, and I'm sure the others won't."

The next day's "Morning News" was excellent. Against a backdrop of the Kennedy Space Center and the Florida coast, the broadcast was something to be proud of. But, essentially, the week in Florida was blown. The broadcast went back to Miami on Thursday, but it continued to carry the story of the Challenger disaster. The whole thing was incongruous: the Miami segments didn't blend with the nation's mood.

Things were equally incongruous in the fishbowl on Friday. On the day of the disaster, most of the staff had had time to absorb some of the impact of what had happened, but Epstein, Shevlin, and I had been working flat out. On Friday, as we listened to Reagan's tribute to the astronauts, and the camera panned to the pained expressions of their grieving families, the three of us openly began crying.

"Close the door," Pat said, wiping away tears, "I don't want any of the bookers in here."

Bob got up and went to his office, and on his way out closed the door. A few minute later he came back.

"I feel like a total fool," he said.

It was one of the most endearing things that I remember in my time at the "Morning News."

In February the show carried a lot of news: the Philippines, South Africa, Haiti, Halley's comet. Ratings were steady and occasionally improving. Midway through the month, a memo from Gene Jankowski landed on my desk: Ed Joyce had left the company.

In the first week of March I took my first vacation since coming to the "Morning News." I went to the Caribbean and lay in the sun for a week. The day I got back I ran into Vicki Gordon as I came into the Broadcast Center lobby. She was the most conscientious of bookers, so driven that you constantly had to order her home or she would never leave the building. This morning she was all excited.

"Guess what?" she bubbled. "Guess who I got a three-part interview with?"

"Charles and Diana?"

"No—silly."

"Is this going to cost me a lunch?" I said.

I had a standing offer of big lunches for really major hits.

"Katharine Hepburn!"

"Nice going," I said. "How the hell did you manage that?"

She told me how she had pulled it off. Forrest had done the interview, and this time it had gone really well. The only thing was that Hepburn had asked him to lunch, and he had declined.

"Do you believe that?" Vicki shrieked. "He turned down a lunch invitation from Katharine Hepburn!"

A few nights later, Corvo asked a group of us to dinner at a restaurant on the East Side. Forrest was among those invited. Unrecognized in the crowded restaurant, he talked on and on about his Hepburn interview.

"Well, what I want to know, Forrest," Bonventre began, "was did she do it with him or not?" Bonventre had taken up needling Forrest since I had let up on him.

"Did she do what?"

"Did Katharine Hepburn do it with Spencer Tracy? I mean that's what everyone really wants to know."

"Are you seriously suggesting I should have asked her that?"

"Well, Forrest. I mean, how much time did you spend with her?"

"That's about the dumbest thing I've ever heard! I mean Katharine Hepburn's probably the greatest American actress, and you want me to ask . . . ."

"Yeah, but we know all that." Bonventre, who was with

his fiancée, had packed away a few drinks. "What I want to know is did she, or didn't she?"

"Who cares if she did or didn't?" Forrest exploded. "That's got nothing to do with any kind of journalism I care about!"

Slowly, ever so slowly, it began to dawn on Forrest that he was being needled. But by then Bonventre had returned his attentions to his fiancée.

That March I came to the Broadcast Center one morning, and realized that I didn't mind being there. It was a feeling that wasn't destined to last.

On Wednesday, March 16, an item appeared in the *New York Times* written by Peter Boyer, our former media critic. It marked the start of yet another upheaval at the "Morning News." The item said that a group of CBS executives—Neil Derrough, head of stations; Neal Pilson, vice-president of the Broadcast Group, and Sauter—had met the day before with Jesse Jackson to discuss the policies of CBS's Chicago station, WBBM, regarding minorities. The executives assured Jackson, who was representing the interests of a group called People United to Serve Humanity (PUSH for short, and known around CBS as SHOVE), that a number of issues, including the hiring of minority on-camera and management-level employees, would soon be addressed by WBBM.

For the previous six months PUSH had been urging viewers to boycott WBBM. The boycott had begun when WBBM's black anchor man, Harry Porterfield, was demoted to make way for the returning Bill Kurtis. (As Epstein reminded us, you could thus blame the troubles at WBBM on the hiring of Phyllis George, because it was Phyllis who caused Kurtis to go back to Chicago.) In any case, PUSH was claiming that its boycott had been responsible for a ratings decline at WBBM. It was hard to substantiate such a case. As

Chicago Sun Times columnist Tom Fitzpatrick noted: "If WBBM's ratings are dropping, it's because people suddenly have decided they don't like Kurtis's shirts . . . or they want a new weatherman. More to the point, they're probably tired of Dan Rather."

PUSH was demanding that CBS donate $11 million to designated black causes as a price for ending its boycott. It didn't matter that Porterfield wasn't exactly out on the street cadging quarters. He was earning a six-figure salary as anchor of WLS, the rival ABC station. Moreover, as the *Sun Times* editorialized: "[WBBM's] personnel record establishes that the station has not been among the laggards in minority hiring and career advancement."

But CBS management felt threatened, especially after PUSH said it intended to spread the boycott to other CBS-owned stations. A week earlier WBBM had fired its vice-president and general manager, Gary Cummings, who was white, and now it was about to adopt what columnist Fitzpatrick called "a fairly craven public stance" and commit "a public act of self-humiliation."

That Wednesday I ran into Johnathan in the corridor. I had seen the *Times* item already, and had noted that the job of general manager at WBBM reportedly had been offered to an unnamed black, who had turned it down.

"Was it you?" I asked.

Johnathan wouldn't say. But he was wearing a very smart suit, and immediately after the broadcast he disappeared to go to Black Rock. Later that day he told me that Pilson had offered him the job as general manager. He had gone to Sauter, who advised him to take it. "It's the fastest track for your career," Sauter said.

So Johnathan was going to Chicago. He was taking a plane the next day.

"It was a cost decision, among other things," Rodgers says. "The CBS television stations bring in huge profits to the company, and the 'Morning News' loses $10 million a year."

I still found it hard to believe. I knew that CBS News would have had to look long and hard within its ranks to find another executive—no less a black one—with Rodgers's experience and ability, but there was no question that the company had yielded to a threat of extortion that may have had little substance. As Fitzpatrick said: "My bet would be that they [PUSH] haven't changed the ratings at Channel 2 by a dozen viewers."

Still, CBS had caved in. Management had urged Rodgers to make the move; in the process it hammered yet another nail into the coffin it was building for the "Morning News."

With Rodgers gone, a note from Sauter said that David Corvo would now be responsible for the "Morning News," but nobody thought he would get the top job. Corvo was a trouper, and he was competent, but he never displayed, to Sauter and Stringer at least, whatever qualities they felt a "Morning News" executive producer should have. Even though he had held Katz in check, and even though he was highly regarded by Rodgers, they regarded him as a number-two man, someone else's deputy. He was depressed, naturally, and he turned down management's offer to go to Paris as bureau chief, waiting to see if they would offer him anything else. They didn't. What they had in mind was that he should be the transition man, while Sauter and Stringer went about consummating the courtship they had begun a year before, with the former executive producer of "Good Morning America"—Susan Winston.

A week or so after Rodgers left, I sent a memo to Sauter and Stringer, arguing for something I had been discussing with Rodgers. My idea was that the "Morning News" should try to have one segment every day that would set people talking. In my memo I made a comparison to magazines:

"If, like a good magazine, you give the reader one hefty, memorable thing to read . . . he or she will go looking for your next issue, with the expectation of re-experiencing the good feeling they felt when they last read you. My point is: one great segment a day can build more loyalty than any amount of topical mundanity, because you've given the audience something special, something they can go to the office and talk about."

At the time I sent the memo, renovation work was finally proceeding in the booking area. The main effect of this work on my quarters was to raise the temperature from 45 degrees to 90. While the work was going on, several of us whose offices were affected were moved upstairs temporarily to offices overlooking the new "Evening News" studio, which was being built at a cost of several million dollars, even though Rather wasn't sure he liked it. I was near Sauter's grand suite, and one morning, after sending me a note complimenting me on the memo, he dropped by to see me. I hadn't many direct dealings with him—just a few during the TWA crisis—because until three months ago he had been based at Black Rock.

"This," he said, waving the memo, "is one hell of a good idea."

We talked about the memo, and off and on over the next few days we talked about the broadcast. I was struck by his willingness to receive ideas, and by his obvious recognition that television in general lacked initiative. I was also pleased, of course, that he agreed with me. In the end, however, nothing came of my suggestions. When I told this to a veteran CBS correspondent, he laughed. "Don't you understand. Van has never had stick-with-it-ness. He's talented, but the real test is to carry things through, and that's where he's lacking."

From the vantage point of my office, I watched Sauter and Rather daily, as they examined the new, nearly completed studio. Some days half a dozen executives—Sauter, Ober, Stringer, Mark Harrington, (Stringer's deputy), Buksbaum —would trail along after Rather, like a procession behind a royal train, hands clasped behind their backs, saying "why —ye-es," with very grave, hesitant faces. I felt like jumping up and yelling "Alms for the poor!" as I watched all this high-priced executive time being spent once again on the "Evening News," while the "Morning News" continued to languish in the gutter.

Bonventre appeared in my office.

"Look at those clowns," he said. "What the hell do they do all day?"

He had picked up my familiar refrain: "CBS News. What a place!"

Five weeks went by before any announcement was made about a new executive producer. The management wasn't going to make Corvo a better offer. His depression lifted only slowly. To make matters worse, he wasn't able to make any substantial future plans for the broadcast. Why bother when a new executive producer would likely throw them all out—new executive producers tended to be that way. The Winston rumors continued to circulate, and after a while Corvo seemed to resign himself to whatever would be. His dry humor returned.

"Did I tell you my idea for a segment on Alzheimer's disease?" Rand Morrison asked him at a meeting one morning.

"Maybe you did," Corvo said, "but I've forgotten."

By far the most exciting thing going on the "Morning News" were the preparations for Maria's upcoming wedding to Arnold Schwarzenegger. We had a lot of ideas on how to capitalize on it, including having Arnold carry her off the set the Friday before. "Maybe we'll get Madonna to cover it," I suggested to her one morning, knowing by then that it was going to be a major event. When Maria had first announced her marriage plans, she had told her mother she wanted a small wedding. Eunice Shriver had replied: "Fine, dear, the lawn at Hyannis only holds a thousand."

Then one Monday evening in April, around six-thirty, I was walking from the fishbowl to my office when I ran into "Evening News" correspondent Harold Dow.

"Staying around?" Dow said.

"Not if I can help it," I told him. "Any quiet night around here, and I split."

"But it looks like they're about to bomb Libya any minute," Dow said.

I went through the fishbowl area to Corvo's office and told him what Dow had said. As I finished telling him, I saw Epstein dashing through the newsroom.

"That goddamn foreign desk!" he exclaimed. "They've fucked us again!"

It was typical. Once again the "Evening News" had kept a little secret from us. Unfortunately, this time they kept it even from their own people, and they were soundly licked by both ABC and NBC. We spent another crazed late evening, with the whole show being torn up at six, and bookers called back from home. Six hours and a few hundred dollars' worth of Chinese food later, we turned a more-than-respectable broadcast over to the overnight shift.

In the morning I came in and watched the broadcast, and afterwards I went downstairs with Bonventre for coffee.

"You know what Corvo just told me?" he said. "Not once, yesterday or today, did anyone from the front office call to ask about the show. For all they cared, we could have been airing reruns of Donald Duck."

Bonventre had another story to tell me. He was still close to Howard Cosell, whose book he had co-written. Cosell, it seemed, had run into Gene Jankowski at a dinner one night. Bonventre did wonderful impersonations of Cosell, and he did a perfect one of the line Howard had shot Jankowski: "So if it isn't Gene Jankowski. Well, Gene, is it true that the much-vaunted CBS News is going to hire Susan Winston and Frank Gifford?"

Jankowski had demurred, but he hadn't denied it. And it was well known around CBS News by then that Winston and Gifford were close. They were close enough that Bonventre felt he would have no choice but to resign if Winston came in as executive producer and brought Gifford in as anchor. Through Howard's mouth, he had said a lot of less-than-kind things about Gifford in his book.

So rumor built upon rumor, and for the next few days speculation increasingly centered on a new executive producer and new anchors, which didn't help either Sawyer's or Shriver's spirits any. Finally, one afternoon later that month, Corvo called us to his office and gave us the news.

It was Winston.

XII.

GOOD-BYE TO ALL THAT

"The history of the 'CBS Morning News' is a history in microcosm of everything that has happened in broadcasting."
—Dick Salant, former president of CBS News

Susan Winston turned out to be an attractive, fashionably dressed woman of thirty-four with large brown eyes and a tense, set mouth. It was well known by April 1986 that Sauter had initiated the love affair. He was her biggest admirer; indeed, many people suspected that he had been more than happy to let Johnathan Rodgers go to Chicago in order to bring Susan Winston on board. In the meantime he had enlisted Stringer to the Winston cause, and it was Stringer, as the executive with hands-on responsibility for the program, who brought her by the newsroom the day after her hiring was announced to introduce her to the assembled staff. Winston would not be starting for another two weeks because she still had business commitments in California.

"As some of you know," Stringer said, "I've been trying for a year to get Susan Winston to come to this program, and

I'm very pleased to be able to announce that at last I have succeeded. One of the problems for other executive producers of the 'Morning News' has been that the pressures of the job have never allowed them time for planning, and so for the next two months Susan will be executive director in charge of planning, and she will be developing a new program for the 'Morning News.' Susan has worked in morning news shows, she understands them—as I'm sure you know, she was the executive producer of 'Good Morning America.' So I have great confidence that her new program will finally bring us the results we have all hoped for, and for which you have all worked so hard. When Susan submits her plan to us, we will make the change, and it will be unveiled to our affiliates."

He turned to her. "Susan."

Our new boss rose to speak.

"Well, I'm not as bad as many of you might have heard," she said, by way of breaking the ice.

The staff laughed nervously. Winston then made a brief speech about the importance of coming up with a new formula. When she finished, she asked for questions. Nobody had any.

After an awkward silence, Stringer turned to Corvo.

"David, why don't you take Susan around to meet the staff individually," he said.

Corvo slid off a desk. For a second I thought he might tell Stringer to introduce her himself. I knew he was mad. Earlier that day Mark Harrington had asked him to find suitable office space for Winston. Corvo had told him: "I'm not going to look for office space for her. You guys hired her. You find her office space." But now he did as he was bidden. He escorted her slowly through the crowded newsroom, and eventually into the fishbowl, where she was introduced to each of us in turn. Corvo gave her a job description of what each of us did.

After she left, there was considerable discussion in the fishbowl. Winston brought with her an aura of show business and a reputation for being tough. There was speculation that she would make wholesale changes, not only to the program but to the people running it. Several "Morning News" producers, including Amy Rosenblum and Ann Northrop, had worked for Winston at "Good Morning America," and their opinions were sought.

"No, I would never call her nice," Northrop said. "Tough, determined, capable, and humorless, yes. But not nice."

Bonventre had a story, too. When Winston was at "GMA," he said, she had read that Howard Cosell was disparaging her program. She sent Cosell a note, suggesting that he stop taking shots at "GMA" because they were all part of the same ABC team. As a result, Cosell had called Bonventre into his office.

"Read this infantile shit," he groused. "She can't even spell my name right. My God, they've handed this network over to children."

A few days later, Cosell ran into Winston in the corridors of ABC. He told her: "Listen, sweetie, I'm Howard Cosell. I say what I like, and I don't need to receive any more little notes from you."

Bonventre had already decided to quit the program once Winston took over, but he was going to stick around until she did. He wasn't about to miss this moment for anything. In the meantime he seemed to have the best intelligence of anybody at the "Morning News," and that afternoon he told us that Winston's search for new anchors, which he assured us was already underway, wasn't going well.

"Who's she going to get?" he asked rhetorically. "Who would want to come to this program?"

We had moved downstairs to the cafeteria by this time, and his audience of several bookers suggested various names.

"Connie Chung," Vicki Gordon suggested.

Chung's name was being bandied about as someone the management of CBS already had talked to.

Bonventre shook his head.

"As for Gifford," Bonventre said, "I can't see how even *they* can buy into that."

"Just remember *they* hired Phyllis," someone reminded him.

I went back up to the fishbowl in time to catch Sauter on the monitor. He was in the new "Evening News" studio taping his presentation for the upcoming affiliates' convention, and we were receiving it on the in-house feed. Epstein was in the fishbowl alone and he was laughing as I walked in.

"You should stick around for this," he said. "He's already blown it twice."

Sauter did not look pleased. When the director gave him his next cue, he began talking about the success of the various CBS News programs, until he finally reached the bleak spot in the schedule—the morning.

"It is in the morning that we continue to have problems," Sauter admitted, "and it is here that we need your continued support." Sauter then went on to say that the management had gone some way toward addressing the "Morning News' " problems by hiring Susan Winston as executive director of planning. "Our research has demonstrated that the morning audience falls into two categories," Sauter explained, "the light viewer and the heavy viewer. The 'Morning News' is competitive with the other two shows when it comes to getting light viewers, the viewer who watches about twenty minutes of morning TV, but it is the heavy viewer who continues to elude us, the one who watches virtually the whole two hours." Then, as if he himself couldn't quite swallow this oversimplified explanation for the "Morning News' " lack of success, Sauter tripped over his words yet again, and unaware or unconcerned that he was being watched by half the building, he exclaimed: "Oh, fuck!"

Epstein broke up.

"He was never very good at this," Epstein said. "That's why he didn't make it when he put himself on the air at WBBM."

When I had watched enough of Sauter, I went upstairs to get some notes. On the way I ran into Maria. She had just been to see Stringer, to find out where she stood amid all these rumors. Stringer had told her everything was fine, that no discussions had even been held about getting new anchors.

When we reached her office, she said, "Come in, sit down. I want to ask you something."

She did not look too happy for someone who was going to be married in two weeks.

"Tell me the truth," she said. "Are we that bad? Do you think the anchors are the problem with this show?"

It was a surprising revelation on Maria's part. She was usually so confident.

"You've both improved tremendously," I said. "The real problem around here is the constant need for a quick fix."

"So you don't think it's us?"

"Look," I said. "You know I could strangle Forrest sometimes when it comes to celebrity interviews, and you know your own weaknesses. The point is, however, that it takes time to build a morning program."

"I guess I needed to hear that," she said. "So what are you going to do?"

"Punt," I said. "I'll see if I get along with Winston. And if not, it will be a nice vacation. I won't have to get up at six A.M."

I went back to the fishbowl to write the teases for the next day's show. In the newsroom a small group of bookers were still discussing Susan Winston. She was all anyone seemed able to talk about.

When my taxi pulled up in front of the CBS Broadcast Center on Monday, May 5, 1986, the usual line of limousines was disgorging guests. I went in past the photos of WCBS-TV's friendly local anchor team whose prominent display in the lobby always struck me as a fair barometer of the current state of affairs at CBS News. When I got to the control room, Forrest was winding up an interview with George Shultz. Shultz was smiling. I could guarantee that in two hours Forrest would be down in the fishbowl wanting to know if he had made the wires. But this morning I was less interested in Forrest than I was in the attitude of the woman in the checked dress and broad belt who was occupying the executive producer's chair for the first time. She was watching the show, scribbling notes to herself, and making periodic comments to Corvo, who seemed ill at ease. I took the chair next to him, and he said, "You've met Susan, right," knowing of course I had. I said hello, and Winston handed me a copy of the *New York Times Book Review*. It was open to the bestseller list, and there were circles drawn around the names of inspirational authors Leo Buscaglia and Harold Kushner.

"I want you to book these people," she said.

Corvo gave me an odd look. He went back to listening to Winston's critique of the show he had put together, and I went downstairs to see Maggie Shumaker, who booked authors.

"Here's your first assignment under the new regime," I said.

Maggie looked at the circled names, and exclaimed: "Are you kidding? She wants these people?"

"You go argue if you want to," I said. "My impression was there wasn't much room for argument."

I went back to my office to get ready for the regular morning meeting.

It was to be held in Corvo's office. We had been told that Corvo was still running the program while Winston drew up her new plans. But as soon as the meeting started, it was clear who was calling the shots. Corvo deferred to Winston. He ran through the lineup, and she said "yes" or "no" or "why are we bothering?" Then Vicki Gordon stuck her head in the room to say that singer Gladys Knight had canceled.

"Get her back," Winston snapped. "Call her PR agent, and tell her I said she's to do the show. Just tell her that."

The room was silent. When Vicki left, Winston turned to Rand. "So what do you have for us, Mr. Contributor Man?"

At 10:30 that morning, once the lineup meeting was over, the senior staff of the "CBS Morning News" filed into the fourth-floor conference room to hear from its new executive director what was wrong with their broadcast. Winston had brought with her a batch of manila folders, on top of which was a yellow pad with the notes she had taken from that morning's show. She wasted no time with formalities.

"Understand this," she said. "I've been brought in here to get ratings, and I'll do anything, *anything* to get ratings. I know how hard everyone works on these shows, and don't think I haven't asked myself 'Why would I want to get into this grind again?' But I've been hired to do a job, and I'm going to do it. I've done it before at 'GMA,' and when I left 'GMA' it was the top-rated morning show, and it was top because everyone pulled together, and realized it could be done. So if anyone here feels they are burned out, if anyone here feels they don't want to make the effort, let me know right now, and I'll be happy to accept their resignation."

The room was hushed. People stared at their yellow notepads. The moment for offering resignations passed, and Winston proceeded to find fault with nearly every aspect of the morning's broadcast. Corvo stared at his cuffs. The show was perhaps the best broadcast the "Morning News" had aired in a while because the staff had worked hard, knowing it marked Winston's debut.

"Let's talk about content," she began. "This show's a clone. It's boring, flat, and predictable, and I'm going to change it. First, why did we even bother having Eli Wallach on the show? He's not the kind of celebrity I want. And the Terry Smith piece was dreadful. And almost every intro to the segments was too long. People don't want to listen to a lot of words."

When she was done, she told us she wanted to meet with each of us individually, and that we should call Elizabeth Citrin to schedule appointments.

"I need to know who reports to each of you," she said, "and I want a list of pluses and minuses about this show, as you see them."

"Can you give us some idea what you want the new program to be?" I asked. "Amount of news content, that sort of thing."

"Everything is news to me," she said. "George Shultz is news, Reggie Jackson's news. There's a whole new audience out there, and they're interested in the things you and I are interested in."

"What are you interested in, Susan?" Bonventre asked boldly.

"Money. We're all interested in money. Working women are interested in money and in business. I want a lot more of those kind of segments. Also consumer segments."

"While we're on the subject of money," I said. "We've been operating here under a very tight budget . . ."

"Ignore the budget," Winston interrupted. "The budget isn't a consideration. It's the show that's important."

Give it a week, I thought. She'll know a lot more about budgets by then.

When the meeting broke up, I went back to my office to find that Bonventre had gotten there ahead of me.

"So where's all the killer ideas?" he said. "What's she doing? Waiting to spring them on us?" He got up shaking his head. He had to go to Boston to produce an interview with Reggie Jackson. "When I get back," he said. "I'll tell her I'm quitting."

That afternoon Winston had a suggestion for the next day's program. We had been running with the Chernobyl story for a week, a story Stringer had described as "our kind of story—a world event and we can't spend money covering it." Winston's idea was that we should examine one of the schoolchildren who had just returned from Kiev for evidence of radioactivity. We had booked one of the kids for the next day's show.

"I want Faith to run a geiger counter over him," she told Corvo.

"But Faith reads the newsblocks," Corvo said.

"I know. It's not a whole segment. Faith will ask him a few questions, then she'll pass the geiger counter over him, and we'll see what the thing registers."

"In the middle of the newsblocks?"

"Sure, why not. It's good television."

Pat Shevlin called one of the bookers and told her what was wanted. A few minutes later, the booker called back. The teenager we had booked had been contaminated, but only slightly. The radiation had been on his clothes, which had long since been destroyed, and he himself would not set off the machine.

"I can't believe that," Winston said. "Those things are highly calibrated."

The booker was insistent. The geiger counter would not respond.

"See if you can find another kid," Winston said.

That Wednesday afternoon I had my meeting with Winston. By then I had come to believe it was unlikely that I could ever work with her. Editorially we were at odds, and I didn't like her style. Our meeting turned out to be the clincher.

I had given her a copy of the memo I'd sent Sauter, and we talked about it briefly. I told her about the morale problem on the show.

"There's been a vacuum since Rodgers left," I said. "And a lot of people are trying to second-guess you. The sooner you can clear the air of uncertainty, the more productive people will be."

"Let's talk about the bookers," she said. "Who's good? Who's bad?"

I gave her a breakdown of the people who worked for me. When I was done, she said: "What you're telling me is that some people aren't pulling their weight. Okay, I look to you to motivate them. If you can't, I'll get rid of them."

It seemed to me she had missed the point.

"You can't blame the bookers," I said. "They've worked endless hours for four or five executive producers and seen little in the way of results."

"So their attitude is bad. Who's fault is that? From what you're saying, it sounds like you're pretty burned out yourself."

I wasn't sure what to make of this charge.

"What makes you say that?" I said.

"Well, you haven't exactly been bubbling over with ideas these past two days."

"Most of my ideas are on the grid," I said. "Unlike a few other people on the staff, I haven't been saving them up to impress you."

"Well, I don't know that. I can only go by what I see."

We talked about ideas and about news. I told her that under Rodgers I felt we had re-established the broadcast's credibility as a news program. I said I felt it was important that this not be allowed to slip away. She said she was interested in news too, but we were talking at cross-purposes. Having Henry Winkler and Donna Mills do interviews for the program didn't quite fit into my idea of news, no matter how far that rubric was extended.

Her intercom buzzed. She said she had to go to a meeting with Stringer. I left her office and went downstairs to the fishbowl. Missie was scrambling about, trying to decide if a taped piece about Andy Summers was good or bad. Half a dozen bookers were on hold because Missie wouldn't make a decision. Corvo's door was closed, and the bookers stood around in the newsroom wearing their collective look of exasperation.

"So how did your meeting go?" Shevlin asked.

"It went," I said. Using some pretext or other, I left the building early.

As I walked home, I recalled the mental note I'd made to myself at the beginning—if it ever got too crazy, I'd get out. I realized I had grown rather fond of this poor show—despite its many faults it still had the capacity to be a decent news program. But I could see it wasn't going to be one under Winston, and with the political gamesmanship that was going on, I could also see how I might begin to like the people I worked with less and less. Then I remembered what Jane Kaplan had said about not judging all of television by life on the "Morning News," and I thought: "Maybe she has a point."

When I got home, I typed a note to Stringer requesting a transfer to another broadcast. I knew it would not please him. On the day it was announced that Winston was coming, he had told me he expected her to be a "keg of dynamite" for the "Morning News."

The next morning I left my letter with Stringer's secretary and went to my office to find Bonventre sitting there with his feet on the desk. He had given two weeks' notice the day before. On the monitor he was watching an exclusive interview with a team of explorers who had just returned from an overland trip to the North Pole. They were the first team to make the trip since Admiral Peary.

"This was your idea, wasn't it?" he said.

"It's my last," I said. "I just requested transfer to another broadcast."

"Holy shit!" Bonventre said.

I didn't see Winston that day. She was making a quick trip to Los Angeles. Nor did I see Stringer. The following morning I called his secretary to remind her that I wanted an appointment. She told me Stringer was aware that I did, but that it might be difficult that day. I soon found out why. Tom Brokaw had tied Dan Rather in the evening news ratings, and panic had set in. A sacrifice had to be made. Lane Venardos, the "CBS Evening News" executive producer, was about to be replaced. He was being moved to Special Events, one of several burying grounds for former executive producers. His replacement was Tom Bettag.

Later that afternoon a memo was distributed from Sauter and Stringer. It stated:

"We believe that under Tom's leadership the 'CBS Evening News' will meet its challenges with originality and imagination, giving Dan Rather and the organization the support needed to report the news and tackle the great issues of our times. Tom's vision will help maintain the dominance of the 'CBS Evening News with Dan Rather.' "

Venardos was quoted in next day's *New York Times.*

"Sometimes," he said, "this can be a very sudden business."

With Stringer pouring oil on the troubled waters of the "Evening News," I did not get to see him until Monday. By then I had received a call from Kevin Goldman of *Variety*, asking me if there was truth to the rumors he was hearing that I had been fired from the "Morning News." I told Goldman the rumor was not true, but I had a feeling that one of Stringer's land mines had just gone off. His secretary had set the meeting for three-thirty, and Corvo came by to see me shortly before this to find out what was going on. I said I had asked for a transfer to another broadcast.

"Good luck," Corvo said.

He added that he thought it was unlikely I would get my wish, given the way things were right then at CBS News.

I said: "David, I frankly don't give a shit." Then I went to see Stringer.

He waved my letter as I was shown into his office.

"What can I do?" he exclaimed. "I'm being told to collect heads around here. There's nowhere I can assign you to. 'West 57th Street' is under review. 'Nightwatch' is in trouble."

We faced each other over a long silence.

"Work it out with her," Stringer said finally. "I'll talk to her. I'm sure it can be worked out."

"Howard," I said. "Who are we kidding?"

I got up and left his office and went to search out Bonventre. I needed a drink.

In the morning, Susan Winston called me from the control room.

"I can't operate like this," she said. "Let's meet."

"Whenever you like," I said. "I'm in my office."

I read the papers and watched the show. This morning it seemed to be devoted entirely to "Hands Across America." As soon as it ended, Winston marched in. She was shooting from the hip, and the encounter was brief.

"I see no point in prolonging this," she said. "Are you resigning from this broadcast or not?"

"I haven't resigned," I said.

"Then you're fired," she told me. "I don't think we have anything more to talk about."

"Fine," I said. "Put it in writing."

Suddenly I was on the outside looking in, as part of one always is in moments of crisis.

"I want you out of here by close of business today," she said.

I laughed. "Susan, there is no such thing as close of business at the 'Morning News.' It's a twenty-four-hour-a-day game."

She was already gone. A few minutes later, a rather startled Pete Bonventre appeared at my door.

"Hi," I said. "I just got fired."

"You okay?"

"Sure," I said. "It isn't every day one gets fired from the most benighted show in television."

"Come on," he said, "let's go down to the cafeteria. You've no idea how much you're going to miss the CBS coffee."

For the rest of the day, I was to discover that CBS News couldn't even fire anybody correctly. I called the contracts attorney—he didn't know about it. I called Harrington, but his secretary said she was sure he wasn't aware of it. I didn't feel like calling Stringer, so eventually I reached the business affairs vice-president, Vincent Loncto, and told him I'd been fired and would appreciate a few basic instructions on procedures.

Three hours later he called back and told me I'd been "unilaterally terminated."

"This makes me realize what a shitty business this is," he said.

"Thanks, Vince," I said.

I pulled my personal stuff together—Rolodex, kid's photos, files. A group of bookers, Janice, Amy, Jane, were congregating outside my office. I told them to come in and we closed the door. The phone rang and I started to answer it.

"You don't have to do that," Amy said, "let it ring."

"It may be from personnel," I said.

It wasn't. It was a standard PR pitch.

"We think Dr. Diet would make a wonderful guest on your program . . ." an enthusiastic voice said.

"Tell her to go suck a big one," Amy suggested.

The other bookers dissolved in giggles. The PR woman rambled on and on, until finally I interrupted her pitch.

"Let me see if I've got this right," I said. "You want five minutes of free publicity on the 'Morning News.' You want to expose Dr. Diet to Maria Shriver, with the hope that five minutes of his unscientific ramblings will sell a few books. Is that right?"

" 'scuse me?" said the PR woman, astonished.

"You're hoping that the Kennedy glamour will mean the difference between Dr. Diet's book sales and all the other idiotic tomes on how to lose weight. Isn't that correct?"

"Is this the 'CBS Morning News'?" the woman asked.

"It sure is," I said. "Can the doctor do cartwheels or stand on his head? I bet he can't set off a geiger counter."

"I'll tell you what," I continued. "Let me put you through to Susan Winston. She's just the person for this segment. And if you can't reach her, try Howard Stringer."

I transferred the call and hung up. The senior staff came by to offer me condolences, and I did my best to look sad. I went to lunch with Bonventre and when I came back I finished packing my things. Then, as I was making a final check of my office I heard the irritating little sound that had plagued me for the past year. The gray contraption attached to my belt—the little gray beeper which over the past year had gone off in movies, on Saturday mornings, in cabs, on the beach, on the nightstand at three A.M.—sounded its familiar beep, beep, beep.

I took it off my belt and laid it on my desk. Then I borrowed a shoe from one of the bookers, and with one blow I sent the thing to beeper heaven.

XIII.

THE BEST REVENGE

"When the twelfth-largest company in the world controls the most awesome propaganda force, who knows what shit will be peddled for truth on this network."
— Peter Finch as anchorman Howard Beale in *Network*

Whenever anyone left the "Morning News," they were told by their colleagues: "Sleeping late is the best revenge." For the next week, I tried to sleep late, but my body clock refused to adjust. For more than a year it had been conditioned to waking up at six, and it wasn't about to reset itself on the spur of the moment. I continued to wake up early, and of course I watched the show.

Each day it seemed to me to be becoming more and more like "Life-styles of the Rich and Famous" or "Entertainment Tonight." So many segments seemed to have celebrity pegs. I wasn't the only one who thought so. One morning I opened *Newsday* and came across a commentary on the "Morning News": "I have a modest proposal for Susan Winston and

'CBS Morning News,' " it said. "Why don't they pick up several of the world's great newspapers, and take a good close look at the way the news is presented . . . How intelligent we can be when given the story neat and straight . . . How about it, CBS? Just do the news the way it deserves to be done."

The following week I received a letter from Gene Jankowski. It was dated two days after my firing. It informed me that I was "special."

"We are part of something special," the letter read, "endowed with a history and a spirit. We are part of CBS . . . we are today writing broadcast history. '60 Minutes' is writing this history. 'Dallas' is writing it. All of us, at this time, in this place, are CBS . . ."

I dropped Jankowski a note, thanking him for thinking of me as special, but reminding him that I was no longer a part of CBS.

That same week Susan Winston went to the affiliates' convention in California. She told the affiliates that she would unveil her news plans for the "Morning News" later in the summer, and that she expected to demonstrate progress by the fall. Her announcement was met with rapturous applause. Winston would not say what her plans were, but she assured the affiliates that she was considering "some really radical changes" and that a rethinking of the anchor formula would be the least of it. I used her trip to California as a propitious time to go to the Broadcast Center to turn in my company ID and credit cards.

When I walked into the building, I was met by a group of bookers returning from lunch.

"So how's life on the show?" I asked them.

"Terrible," they assured me.

"How come?" I inquired.

"We've all been assigned copies of out-of-town newspapers to read," one booker said. "We don't want to miss any fascinating human interest stories. I'm stuck with the *Albuquerque Journal*—you'd be surprised how little happens in Albuquerque."

"I got told to book Whitney Houston," another booker complained, referring to the pop singer. "And guess what Susan told me?"

"What?"

"It's your career."

I let a week go by before I watched the show again. Then one morning I checked in. Forrest had gotten himself a game-show host haircut, and Maria was smiling less. I watched an interview with two men who had invented Zinka, the creamy stuff people were wearing on their noses at the beach to protect them from the sun. It was followed by an interview with the wife of Greek Prime Minister, Papandreou, who was supposed to talk about the help she was offering Peggy Say, whose brother was being held hostage in Lebanon.

Prime Minister Papandreou had recently met with Syria's President Assad, and his wife had become involved on behalf of the hostages' families. All well and good, except that Mrs. Papandreou seemed unaware of the time constraints of morning television. She began by talking at length about her background. She told us she was American-educated, and that she had two children who were born here. By then, three of the five minutes allocated to the interview had elapsed. Maria was turning white. Finally she jumped in, asking Mrs. Papandreou if President Assad of Syria had given her husband some idea of the hostages' condition. At this point, the satellite went down.

I, of course, enjoyed the segment immensely. But by then I was watching almost as a normal viewer, seeing the incident as a guffaw, a triviality, a moment lost like a phosphorescent burst at a disco. If I had been in the "Morning News" control room, it would have been a different story. I knew that some poor booker was already feeling the accumulated torque of a lot of boots.

When the satellite went down, the "Morning News" dumped out into a commercial for plastic surgery. When it came back, we were introduced to three male soap opera stars. The caption on the screen read "Hunks." There was no way the "hunks" could amuse me as much as Mrs. Papandreou, and so I dispensed with the "Morning News" in favor of the *Times.* I did not watch the show again until the week before July 4, when the broadcast was doing its salute to the Statue of Liberty. I tuned in one day, and watched for five minutes before turning it off. I didn't much care what America meant to Linda Gray and Priscilla Presley, and from the way the ratings were going, it seemed most other viewers didn't either.

Susan Winston had opened her latest round of discussions with the CBS News management in March 1986. She admits now that she saw an opportunity for herself that went beyond the role of executive producer of the "Morning News." Management wanted a design concept for the show, but Sauter had also told her he had big plans to expand news programming, plans to tie in news with other genres. Winston's deal with CBS was based on a two-tier contract. First, she was to come up with a concept for a new "Morning News"; then in October, if management liked her plans, the second part of her contract would go into effect.

At one of Winston's first meetings with Sauter and Stringer, the executives held up two photographs. One was a picture of an old Appalachian man with no teeth. The other was of a migrant worker and his extended family. They told her: "This is your current audience, the people who only get one channel."

Winston told the executives that her idea was to come up

with something different, something that would appeal to a new, younger audience that currently did not watch morning TV. Sauter and Stringer agreed this was the way to go, and Winston says they promised her the financial support to make the program competitive. Though other CBS executives insist money was never discussed, Winston says she was told she would be able to hire the personnel to implement her plans, and that when the time came, she would get promotion for her new program. But within days she ran into a problem. Stringer and Sauter began counting heads. Wyman and Jankowski had ordered cutbacks, as a result of which Winston was not allowed to hire people for the positions that were open. There was another ominous sign. Sauter asked her for a hypothetical idea for a quick fix. If they wanted a quick fix, he said, who would she suggest they hire as anchors? Winston says she gave them two names: Connie Chung, whose contract with NBC was about to run out; and Frank Gifford, who was feuding with ABC, which had demoted him.

Winston says that CBS News opened negotiations with Gifford, but soon decided against him. When the discussions began, ABC News and Sports president Roone Arledge had been telling his colleagues that he had "no idea" what Gifford's plans were. Within a few weeks, however, Gifford was back in ABC's clutches. He had re-signed.

On the female anchor front, Winston says, the problem with Connie Chung was that someone at CBS Inc. decided they didn't want her. Winston doubts that it was Sauter —Sauter had often said that letting Connie Chung slip away from CBS to NBC was the biggest mistake he ever made. According to one high-level insider, the decision not to hire Chung involved Jankowski, but another insider says that CBS News Management was simply paralyzed with indecision. One thing is certain: when Sauter, Stringer, and Dan Rather ran into Chung's agent, Alfred Geller, on West Fifty-seventh Street one day, they stood around in a group attracting a great deal of attention from passersby as Geller tried to explain to the CBS executives that they had better make up their minds soon or they would lose their shot at his client.

The CBS executives didn't make up their minds. A few days later Chung re-signed with NBC. Winston was back to square one.

"In any event," she says, "[Gifford and Chung] were the two names I gave them. I'm not saying they were the ideal people, but the research showed that [viewer] response to Chung was unbelievably good."

Her statement directly contradicts what CBS spokesperson Ann Morfogen told me. "CBS News does not do research on anchors," Morfogen said.

Nonetheless, it was research, Winston says—research that tells television executives how audiences react to their "talent," and which CBS News denies it uses—that already had decided the fates of Forrest Sawyer and Maria Shriver. The research had been done twice on Forrest and Maria, and it had led the CBS News executives to decide that both would have to go. Forrest's agent, Art Kaminsky, who at one time had also represented Maria, said: "We just assumed it was the end of the game once Winston was there. It was a case of anybody but Forrest and Maria."

Winston says, however, that she had no hand in the decision to get rid of Forrest and Maria. "When I got there, the decision was already sealed in cement," she insists.

Though discussions about replacing Sawyer and Shriver had begun in March, that did not stop Stringer from attending Shriver's wedding. (Sauter declined the invitation.) Shortly after the wedding, Shriver and Winston went to lunch at the Russian Tea Room, where Shriver asked Winston point-blank if she planned to replace her.

"Be straight with me," Maria said. "That's all I'm asking.

If you're going to get rid of me, that's okay. But just be straight with me."

Winston said there had been no such discussions. "I haven't even talked to other anchors," she said.

"Then why were you meeting with Sandy Hill in Howard Stringer's office?" Maria asked coolly. (Sandy Hill was a former co-host on "GMA.")

"Oh, that was just social," Winston said.

Once Maria had established she was on to them, the game got rougher. CBS News management resorted to one of its favorite tricks, a rabbit punch in the form of a leak to the press. An item was planted in Clarence Fanto's column in the *New York Post*. It read: "Newlywed Maria Shriver, co-anchor of the 'CBS Morning News,' is expected to leave that job in several months 'for personal reasons,' according to top sources at the network . . .

"She is eager to shed the grueling grind at CBS and move back to the West Coast to be with her husband full time. She has been spending alternate weekends with him in Los Angeles, where Schwarzenegger is making another movie.

"Insiders report CBS News management did not try to argue her out of the move.

"The two people who talked to me," continued Fanto, "were both high-level management sources, and both of them had to have talked to Sauter shortly before they talked to me."

When Shriver read Fanto's story she hit the roof. She stormed in to see Sauter and Stringer.

"Who's saying this?" she demanded. "Was it you? Was it Susan? Look, if you guys want to get rid of me, you're going to have to fire me. But I'm not leaving to be with Arnold, or to have babies, or for any other reason."

The CBS executives assured Shriver it wasn't them. They had not planted any leaks like this. Oh, no, they insisted, they were innocent.

Shriver and Sawyer continued to anchor the "Morning News," both knowing their days were numbered. Both had careers ahead of them at other programs or at other networks, and both were determined to be troupers to the end. "They won a lot of respect from the staff those last few months," recalls one senior producer. "It was not easy for them and they both showed a lot of professionalism in a tough situation."

Throughout May and June, Susan Winston continued to work on her plans for a new morning program. Between running the show as it was and drawing up her new plans, she was putting in a lot of hours. She told one producer she could hear the blood pumping through her veins. She got little input from the management. Like George Merlis four years earlier, she says she gave management her ideas, and it accepted them. She did not consider the CBS executives a creative group, but she was pleased at least that what she submitted was greeted with enthusiasm, first by Harrington, then by Stringer, then by Sauter, and even by Jankowski.

"They all loved my ideas," she says, "and they all understood that the new show would cost more money. But the final bill was not going to be more than the budgets for either of the other two network morning programs."

Winston says she did not want her new show to be what she called "another Ken and Barbie routine." She claims she wanted an "intelligent, human, and gritty broadcast," without the "vanilla people." But if the management liked what she presented, there was less enthusiasm among the people who actually put on the program. They were already suffering from celebrity overload, and some of Winston's ideas, such as having senators' wives interview other senators on matters of government, seemed crackpot to them.

The staff, after all, was mainly concerned with the content of the program, the news content, whereas Winston was more interested in the presentation. She says she did a lot to loosen Forrest up, "but he is what he is, and on camera he looked scared of Maria. Nobody had worked with either of them on performance, and the body language between them was terrible. Performance is important—Dan Rather pays attention to his performance."

The long-expected announcement came on July 1, 1986. The network would not be renewing the contracts of Maria Shriver and Forrest Sawyer as co-anchors of the "Morning News." And in the fall CBS would introduce a new type of program, tentatively titled "Across America." The new show would feature a regional format, with multiple hosts in Los Angeles, Chicago, and New York, and possibly Dallas as well. News would be woven in throughout the program. Celebrity interviewers would be used, and New York–Washington stories de-emphasized.

Charles Osgood, the CBS correspondent who anchored the network's "Sunday Night News," and whose genial commentaries had made him the hottest property on CBS Radio, was the leading candidate for one of the New York anchor slots—if he could be freed from his radio contract. Another top candidate was Linda Ellerbee, whose whimsical style had earned her a cult following as co-host of NBC's short-lived "Overnight" and whose memoir, *And So It Goes,* had just burst onto the best-seller lists. Shriver had been offered the Los Angeles position, but she hadn't accepted it yet. Sawyer had not been offered anything, and was reported to be seeking another assignment within CBS.

By this time, the CBS News executives had turned down several of Winston's anchor suggestions—specifically, Chung and Gifford. They had also turned down her idea of Geraldo Rivera—after all, there were limits. But Winston was confident she could sign Linda Ellerbee, and when the big meeting was arranged for her to present her plans to CBS chairman Tom Wyman, Winston had no doubt that

Ellerbee was as good as locked up. By then it also seemed certain that Osgood could be released from his radio contract.

One high-level insider at CBS says that when the meeting took place, Wyman was "fascinated" with Winston. He was impressed with her anchor choices, too. He considered Osgood an excellent idea, and he liked Ellerbee. And Winston's presentation for the show itself reportedly was convincing. It was detailed, and she delivered it in her high-powered style. Sauter, Stringer, and Harrington all sat quietly as she went through it. When she finished, a clearly impressed Wyman had one question.

"How much is this going to cost?" he asked.

"Forty-two million dollars," she told him. That was $8 million more than the "Morning News' " $34 million budget.

"That's a lot of money," Wyman said.

"It's not a lot of money," Winston retorted. "You're way under budget now. All I want is to be competitive with the other morning shows."

Wyman gave no definite answer. But in a rare interview with the *New York Times* that week, he talked about a new, more expensive morning program that would be something drastically different for CBS. He added that his hopes for the new show were "not necessarily finishing first, but being something more than a distant third." It looked as if Wyman was prepared to sign off on Winston's plans.

Things began to unravel a few days later. First came the news that Linda Ellerbee had signed with ABC. Winston had been supremely confident of getting Ellerbee, at least partly because Ellerbee's agent, Ralph Mann, was her agent, too. She now claims that the CBS News executives were "unbelievably slow and dragged their feet, and didn't appreciate that Ellerbee had become a hot property since her book hit the best-seller list." But whatever the reason for the delay, Winston had blundered. She had misrepresented things to Wyman, and according to one CBS source, "when the chairman of CBS heard that Linda Ellerbee was not locked up with CBS, but with ABC, he was pissed."

That same day Maria Shriver turned down the offer of the position in Los Angeles. Winston and the CBS News executives were suddenly scrambling. Jane Wallace, whom Sauter had turned down as "Morning News" anchor a few years earlier in favor of Phyllis George, abruptly became the leading contender for the job. But her availability depended on whether "West 57th Street" would be renewed; if it was, Wallace presumably would not be available.

The situation left the CBS executives with no choice but to put off making their much-heralded unveiling of the new show to the affiliates. The anchors were not in place. With the announcement postponed for two weeks, Susan Winston flew to London to supervise the following week's "Morning News" coverage of the wedding of Prince Andrew to Sarah Ferguson. She left New York on Thursday, July 17. By then certain events had been proceeding for a month—"events which," as one CBS News executive noted, "Susan Winston chose to ignore."

At my first meeting with Susan Winston, when I was still at the "Morning News," she had told me to ignore the budget and to concentrate on the show. I had read into that remark a certain naiveté on her part. After all, I had been working at CBS for more than a year by then. I knew the management better than she did. I knew that Sauter's policy was to go along with what his bosses mandated, and I knew that in the meantime Sauter had aligned himself with Wyman. And Wyman and Jankowski were demanding more cuts.

There were other signs of trouble, too, signs obvious to anyone who read the newspapers. The company's financial picture was showing no signs of improving. Broadcast revenues were down, as were revenues from other divisions. The "CBS Evening News" had been unable to regain its lead in the ratings. In fact, one week the "Evening News" had come in third behind NBC and ABC. When a reporter asked Stringer how Dan Rather felt about the challenge, Stringer insisted that Dan was the "soul of relaxation." That didn't jibe with what a source was telling me. He said Rather was going to a drama coach and dyeing his hair.

But another remark in the paper around the same time intrigued me even more. It was a quote from Sauter about the new "Morning News." "One can say, 'Aha, we're going to create an entirely new form in the morning.' That's a marvelous idea, but it's an excruciating gamble and if you fail, you can never come back to the table. I don't know if a gamble of that dire necessity is in front of us."

I puzzled over this remark. Was this a hint? Or was it an offhand comment, something Sauter might not have wished to be quoted? On the one hand, it seemed, CBS News management was telling the affiliates that its hopes were pinned on Susan Winston and her plans; on the other hand, Sauter seemed to be saying that the news division might not be prepared to go out on a limb. What was going on?

Whatever management's intentions, it was clear there was a budget crunch coming. Sure enough, Bob Epstein's warning about being wary of holiday weekends applied again. Despite Wyman's assurances of the previous year that there would be no more layoffs, it was announced on July 2, 1986, that 700 people in the Broadcast Group (out of a total work force of 8,000) would be let go—ninety in the news division alone. Once again Jankowski insisted in a memo to the staff that "the quality and competitive nature of our on-air product will in no way be diminished by these actions."

The people who were to be dismissed were to learn their

fate in two weeks. Only two programs at CBS News would not be affected—"60 Minutes" and the "Evening News." Employees of the other broadcasts spent an anxious fortnight, and this time, when the individual names were finally announced, there was even more outrage and gnashing of teeth than the previous year. A number of veteran correspondents got the ax, but the dismissal of two in particular —George Herman and Don Webster—threw the news division into an uproar.

George Herman was sixty-six years old. He had begun work at CBS News in 1944, during the Murrow era. He'd been a war correspondent in Korea and a White House correspondent during the Eisenhower Administration. He had been working recently for Kuralt's "Sunday Morning."

"I'm fired, laid off, not renewed, call it what you will," he told reporters.

Don Webster had been CBS's Middle East bureau chief. He was fifty-two and had been at CBS News for twenty-five years. In 1977, in the course of his work for the network, he had been thrown in jail in Angola. How he got there was interesting. A call had been made to CBS's Paris bureau chief, asking him to go to Angola when the troubles broke out. But the bureau chief begged off because the cameraman who was to accompany him didn't want to go.

"Send Webster," the bureau chief said, and so Webster went.

The Paris bureau chief was Van Gordon Sauter.

Plans for the "Morning News'" coverage of the royal wedding had been underway even before I had left the program. This time Bob Epstein was lucky; he got to go to London. So he was pleased, as were the bookers who got to go with him. But by the time Susan Winston departed for England on July 17, to take charge of the three broadcasts that were to originate from London, she was far from pleased. In fact she was feeling generally disenchanted with the management of CBS News.

Many of her suggestions had not been acted upon, and she felt she had lost Linda Ellerbee because of management's incompetence. But she was still working hard toward her goal, and before she left for London she called Howard Stringer and told him that somebody from the organization should assure Charles Osgood that everything would turn out fine.

Nobody from the management called Osgood, but this was not accidental. Unbeknownst to Winston, the executives of CBS News were planning to hold a series of meetings the next day at the Ritz-Carlton Hotel, where they intended to discuss the entire matter of the perennial money-loser known as the "CBS Morning News."

The meetings were attended by Sauter, Stringer, and Harrington, as well as another CBS News executive, David Fuchs, a veteran of Black Rock who had been appointed vice-president of news the previous year. The group examined all the reasons for the failure of the "Morning News." For some reason, the research was showing that the name "CBS News" turned viewers off.

Never mind the fact that the "CBS Morning News," anchored by Bill Kurtis and Diane Sawyer, had once scored a 4.2 rating and had briefly overtaken "Today." Never mind the fact that when Diane Sawyer quit, the CBS executives dallied and delayed over a replacement while ratings eroded. Never mind the fact that they then selected Phyllis George, and in doing so alienated their male anchor, while the ratings eroded further. Never mind the fact that they then selected two young anchors, paired them with a smart executive producer, and just when he was coming to grips with the program and the ratings were starting to rise, dispatched him to Chicago in response to an extortion threat they should have had the courage to face down. All these facts were considered incidental. As far as the executives were concerned, viewers simply didn't want to watch a morning program produced by CBS News.

Convinced that the old ghosts of Murrow and Cronkite had been thoroughly discredited, Sauter, Stringer, Harrington, and Fuchs decided they had two options. They could go back to a hard-news format and risk losing affiliates, or they could run with Winston's proposal—assuming they could get it by Wyman and Jankowski. There were plenty of reasons to think they might not. Wyman was already upset by the fact the Ellerbee had gone to ABC, and his resistance to spending another $8 million a year on the "Morning News" was obvious, even if he had not definitely said no. Besides, the news executives were already hammering at Jankowski, trying to get him to agree to renew "West 57th Street," on which they all had a lot riding.

And so they began to back away from their plan of three months earlier, the plan to turn the "Morning News" over to Susan Winston. They began to admit that her ideas were expensive, and that success could not be guaranteed. After all, it seemed there were no high-profile news people available. Who did they have besides Charlie Osgood? And even if they lined up someone terrific, what if the show failed? As Sauter had said—they might not be able to go back to the table again. The conversation had reached a decisive point.

In an interview later with the *New York Times*, Sauter said: "We reached the conclusion we were looking at a broadcast when we should have been looking at a time period."

Those innocent-sounding words masked what was really going on. The men in the Ritz-Carlton were about to betray a principle that went back thirty years at CBS News, the principle of protecting the news division's turf against the corporate bosses. Sauter and Co. knew their bosses would be pleased with their new pattern of thinking, and they began to ask each other what would happen if they simply killed the thing. This was an even more decisive turn. It was inspired. It was the ultimate solution.

The *Times* article made it seem as if their act was sacrificial, a decision made solely by CBS News for the benefit of CBS News. That was not quite true. Not by any means. Because one thing the *Times* article neglected to point out was that Gene Jankowski, who represented the interests of CBS Inc., attended the Ritz-Carlton meetings and played an active role in the deliberations.

And so the decision was made. According to one management insider at CBS News, "it was a cost decision on the Broadcast Group's part. Jankowski nudged it through." According to another source, Jankowski had begun to think less and less of Winston's ideas—"he didn't want an expensive hit, he wanted an inexpensive hit." And so they decided that in the "Morning News" time slot there would be a different broadcast entirely, one not produced by the news division, but by a special unit that would report to Sauter. It would be an entertainment program.

On Tuesday of the following week, Van Gordon Sauter took the Concorde to London to talk to Susan Winston. He checked into the Hyde Park Hotel and called her. When she came over to see him, he gave her the news.

CBS management, he said, had looked at the entire issue of a new "Morning News" program from a business standpoint and had decided that it did not wish to spend any more money. Certainly not $8 million more. In fact, Sauter said, they wanted to spend less than they were spending on the current program. What they had in mind was a new program that would be produced by a new division, possibly a program with a studio audience. Sauter wanted Winston to be the new program's executive producer because he liked what she had submitted so far.

Winston was stunned. And the reception Sauter got was not what he expected.

She told him: "Not only do I think this is a terrible idea, but it's insulting to me and to CBS. How much more of a morale breaker do you need?"

Sauter said he didn't see it this way. He saw it as an opportunity to create a whole new genre.

"Who cares what kind of division puts out this program?" Winston said. "The viewing public doesn't care. And why do you want to turn this into a big announcement?"

She told Sauter she didn't want to take charge of his new program. She told him she thought he was digging a grave.

Sauter continued to discuss the matter with her, but Winston, who had gotten very little sleep the past few days while working on the London broadcasts, was exhausted and angry. She felt the CBS News executives had no idea what they wanted. She told Sauter she had come to CBS for a very specific reason. She wanted CBS News on her résumé. She wanted to obtain a great news credential. She told Sauter maybe he should rethink the decision. She told him that in any event she would appreciate it if he sat on the decision until she got back to New York on Monday.

Sauter said he couldn't wait that long. CBS planned to announce a decision on "West 57th Street" on Friday, and he wanted to tie the two announcements together. The implication was that "West 57th Street" and a new program in place of the "Morning News" would represent a trade-off. Would Winston take charge of the new program?

She said she at least wanted the night to think about it. Sauter agreed. He then called his bosses in New York and explained that Susan Winston was less than thrilled with his idea. Then he took the plane back to New York.

On Friday, July 25, the overnight staff of the "Morning News" was going about its regular tasks of preparing for the next morning's program. The time sheets had been written, the tapes transferred. The limo drivers were on their way to pick up guests. The overnight staff had reached the stage in the nightly proceedings when they could relax a little and have some coffee. Then the early edition of the *New York Times* arrived.

For all the staff except for Winston, that edition of the *Times* contained the first hint of the show's demise. The vehicle was an article by Peter Boyer. His story did not say that the "CBS Morning News" was being replaced by an entertainment program. It simply said that, according to CBS officials, Susan Winston was leaving the network.

When Winston heard about the article over the phone from New York, she was stunned. She was also distraught. This was not what she had expected. She had been told she would be meeting with Jankowski when she returned on Monday. She called the control room in New York and talked freely to one senior staffer about her meeting with Sauter, and about his new proposals.

"Who do they think they're going to get for a studio audience at seven A.M.?" she said. "They couldn't even get winos if they offered free doughnuts and coffee."

At ten that morning, Sauter called the "Morning News" staff to a meeting in the newsroom. "He gave a truly strange speech," one senior producer recalls.

First Sauter said there was a definite possibility the time period could go elsewhere. Then he said no final decision had been made. He told the staff there was reason to be concerned, but not despondent. He said that the problem with the show was that it had never been able to come up with a successful formula. He added a remark that caused everyone to gape.

"Even Phyllis George could not get us ratings," he said.

Was Sauter still a believer?

That afternoon the "Morning News" staff received a memo saying that the show would be canceled at the end of the year. At the same time it was announced that "West 57th Street" was being renewed.

Down the halls and the corridors of the Broadcast Center, groups of producers drifted aimlessly. Shell-shocked. Stunned. Confused. Some hysterical. Some left the building. Some went straight to their typewriters to update résumés. Some cried. In one of the back offices, Vicki Gordon was on the phone making bookings for the following week. Amy tapped her on the back, and Vicki waved her off while she finished her call. Amy leaned closer.

"Vicki," Amy said. "I've got something to tell you."

"Wait a minute, I'm on the phone," Vicki said, irritated. "I'll be off in a minute."

Amy spun her around in her chair.

"Vicki, read my lips," she said. "There is no show."

Among CBS veterans there was shock and outrage. In the *New York Times* the following morning, Fred Friendly, Murrow's producer and a former president of CBS News, described the decision as "so tragic it takes your breath away." This was a ratification, he said, of what had happened a few years back when they took Charles Kuralt off the air.

On Tuesday the staff listened to what one producer called Winston's "Joan of Arc speech." Many of the staff said they were not sorry to see her go. They didn't care for her propensity for giving so many segments a celebrity peg, and they didn't like it that she made a big fuss of wanting to arrange a special send-off for Forrest and Maria, whose demise many still felt she had caused. Others on the staff said they had liked her. They said they found her spirited and energetic, and she gave them answers.

That morning she told her staff that she would be staying until her contract was up in October, but the CBS management had other plans. Later that day a memo went out saying that Winston would be leaving at the end of the week. This was the day Forrest and Maria were scheduled to leave, and when Friday came they said their polite words of good-bye on the air, then made their good-bye speeches to the staff in the newsroom.

So the show died. As Robert Arnot, the show's medical correspondent said: "They had shot it in the head." With substitutes Faith Daniels and Charlie Rose filling in, the ratings collapsed—within two weeks they sank to 2.5. But something else would not die, and for the next few days it began to boil. The anger that was spreading throughout the news division could not be contained.

According to one source, Dan Rather was in a state of shock. Even if the vast diversion of resources to the "Evening News" had been one of the contributing causes to the failure of the "Morning News," Rather was livid when he found out about Sauter's decision to cancel the program outright. He had supported Sauter for years out of a sense of loyalty, feeling he owed Sauter for his help in restoring the "Evening News" ratings in 1982. But there were no stirring speeches from Dan Rather in defense of Van Gordon Sauter this time. Instead, Rather criticized Sauter in a letter to the *New York Times.*

"The professionals at CBS News who are directly involved in news gathering, editing, and broadcasting," Rather wrote, "do not believe that having the name 'CBS News' on a broadcast drives audiences away. We believe the opposite is true . . .

"We refuse to allow any editorial decisions to be dictated by . . . public opinion sampling. We base editorial decisions on journalistic experience and ethics and not on what polls and entertainment consultants say."

Poor Rather, I thought, as I read his missive. Maybe he should have dropped into a "Morning News" editorial meeting some time, or sat in Sauter's or Stringer's office when they were going over the research, trying to come up with a new program idea or deciding to get rid of Forrest and Maria. He was either defending CBS News despite the weight of overwhelming evidence that it was not what he was suggesting it was, or he was blind to what it had become.

But if Rather's public reaction was relatively restrained, the reaction of other CBS newsmen wasn't. Early in August, less than two weeks after the "Morning News" was killed, Andy Rooney wrote a syndicated column taking CBS management to task for its decision to drop the program.

Rooney had once been a writer for "Calendar," the "Morning News'" predecessor, and he was deeply offended by the decision to cancel. He said he wrote the column because "I love CBS" and "I am trying to do the best thing for the company."

"CBS, which used to stand for the Columbia Broadcasting System," Rooney wrote, "no longer stands for anything. They're just corporate initials now.

"If it was money the company wanted to save," Rooney went on, "firing a couple of $150,000-a-year V.P.'s would have saved more than firing a lot of $50,000-a-year people . . . The people running network news operations would like to see their news standards maintained, but they are company men first, and newsmen second. Unlike some of their predecessors, they are not willing to die professionally for journalistic principles. For them, news is a business enterprise first and a moral enterprise second."

Rooney's column ran in more than 300 newspapers. He said the "Morning News" had provided air-time for important news stories that otherwise might not have been broadcast by CBS, and he told an interviewer that its cancellation was "a sad day for the country." He had stirred the emotions of many of his colleagues. They called and congratulated him on having the courage to speak out.

CBS News management was furious. There were reports that they discussed firing Rooney, reports which they denied. But one insider maintains: "It wasn't because they didn't want to; they just thought it would be unwise."

Two days after the column appeared, another outspoken CBS newsman announced that he would be leaving the network in November. Bill Moyers had been battling the CBS News executives on matters of policy for nearly a year, and he was fed up. But Moyers was to save his main blast for four weeks later, timing it to coincide with an event that by then everyone involved was looking toward—the next meeting of the CBS board of directors, which was to take place September 10.

Van Gordon Sauter was proud of the speech he made before the CBS News bureau managers' meeting at Park City, Utah, on August 24. He had worked on it for ten days and had told several colleagues how satisfied he was with it. They included one executive who still strongly supported him. "You have to realize" he told me, "how hard it was for Van to go back to the news division after he had been exposed to, and come to understand, the realities of Black Rock."

I spoke to Sauter shortly after he gave the speech. He re-emphasized everything contained in it, adding that as far as the "Morning News" was concerned, "the ultimate test of what it did was what it did on the air. If it had worked, fine, but it didn't, and that's life. I don't have the stomach to go over it all again."

In his speech to the bureau managers Sauter talked again about the problem of the elusive "Morning News" viewer, particularly the one who watched for a long period. This viewer, he said, "seeks entertaining information and consistently found us too businesslike, too serious, too interested in conventional news stories." As for his decision to kill the show, Sauter said "it will conclude the awkwardness we have all felt about a CBS News broadcast becoming something more than a news broadcast."

I had not noticed that Sauter felt any awkwardness when he foisted Phyllis George upon us.

Sauter continued:

> The "Morning News" decision had the adverse impact we anticipated. The layoffs of this year and last, combined with the "Morning News" decision, formed a powerful storm cloud which looms above us. And the disillusionment, lack of confidence, and anger resulting from this has focused on me, which is fine. I've spent eighteen years at CBS, and seventeen of them have been glorious. This past year has been very difficult.
>
> I'm more than constitutionally capable of dealing with negative attitudes about me, with unflattering publicity, with dissatisfaction about how I run the news division and my continued employment at CBS. I've been a manager of one sort or another here since 1968, and enjoyed a front row seat at some compelling dramas here. It has led me to a very simple realization about my compact with CBS. If it likes my work, it will take care of me. If it doesn't like my work, I'll be gone. It's fair and simple and comfortable to live with.
>
> I'm also convinced that the steps I've taken over the past years, the steps that many here find so distressing, are protective of CBS News. And no matter who was sitting in my chair,

the same steps would have been necessary. You can change the players, but let me assure you, you don't change the rules.

... There are some who feel I should have thrown my body in front of budget cuts or layoffs or the "Morning News" decision. There is a feeling I did not adequately represent the news division at Black Rock. I increasingly feel I did not adequately represent the forces of the outside world to the news division.

... Our organization is spending far too much energy on gossip and speculation. Some of that is inevitable, but we stand the risk of losing sight of our purpose ... which is to do the best broadcast journalism in the world and to serve the needs of our public. As we all know, the anger, the anxiety, and the apprehension have also hatched an unbecoming strain of petulance and self-righteousness in our organization.

... I thus urge you to urge those who work for you to tighten the focus of their work.

I had been told that Sauter's speech had been distributed around the news division. After I read it, I called a former colleague and asked him how people were reacting to it.

"I have never seen people so enraged by any single document in all the time I've worked here," he said. "How the man has the nerve to walk the corridors of this building, I don't know."

Many of the CBS old guard felt the same way. And by the first week of September the battle lines were being drawn. Don Hewitt and Bill Paley were chewing things over in their summer houses in the Hamptons. With the CBS board meeting less than a week away, Larry Tisch, who by then had increased his stake in the company to just under 25 percent, was cementing the social relations he had established with a number of top CBS News people, including Cronkite, Wallace and Hewitt. Tisch knew how they felt. What he did not know was that Tom Wyman, who suspected that Tisch might try to seize control, was quietly shopping

CBS all over town. Sauter meanwhile was having lunch with his old friend, Bob Wussler. According to Wussler, "Van was planning to hang tough. He hoped to ride out the storm."

On the air, things were getting downright weird. The week after Labor Day, Dan Rather began signing off the "Evening News" each night with the single word "Courage." Then on Monday, September 8, *Newsweek* hit the stands with a cover story titled "Civil War at CBS." The story reported Wyman's shopping expedition, which was subsequently denied by network officials. It also contained an interview with Bill Moyers. Compared to what Moyers said, Rooney's column of the previous month had been positively mild.

"The line between entertainment and news [at CBS] was steadily blurred," Moyers told *Newsweek*. "Our center of gravity shifted from the standards and practices of the news business to show business. In meeting after meeting 'Entertainment Tonight' was touted as the model—breezy, entertaining, undemanding. In meeting after meeting the discussion was about 'moments'—visual images containing a high emotional quotient that are passed on to the viewer unfiltered and unexamined . . . Pretty soon tax policy had to compete with three-legged sheep, and the three-legged sheep won. There were periods when I thought the British royal family had signed on as correspondents, so frequent were their appearances. And now we're trapped . . . Once you get it into your head that your viewers are consumers instead of citizens you drive them away. That's because viewers tune in to sitcoms to be amused and news to be informed . . . When you don't respect their intelligence you lose them—not the mass audience, but the critical audience that makes the difference in a tight competitive race. That's why we lost our big lead in the 'Evening News.' Over the long run, the better journalistic outfit tends to win. That's what CBS used to believe."

By the time the CBS board meeting began at 9 A.M. on Wednesday, September 10, an hour earlier than usual, a great deal of discussion has already taken place. For a month Bill Paley had been rebuilding his old alliances on the board in the hope of unseating Wyman. But as late as the evening prior to the meeting, nothing had been decided. A dinner for all fourteen CBS directors had been scheduled for that evening at the Ritz-Carlton, but at the last minute Wyman canceled it. Several directors met anyway, and there was debate about Wyman's continued role at CBS, but again nothing was decided.

Camera crews surrounded Black Rock the next morning when the board convened. They remained in place all day as the meeting continued for nine and a half hours. Wyman started by presenting a plan for the future of CBS. He had called his loyalists on the board a week before, hoping to find an advocate to present his case for him. Nobody was willing to do so. As he talked, the other board members stared at him. His presentation seemed unfocused and dispirited. The room grew restless. Then Wyman dropped a bombshell. He told the board he had been trying to sell CBS to the Coca-Cola Company. The directors were flabbergasted. The loss of confidence was clear already, but this was the straw that broke the camel's back.

Wyman's plan for the future of CBS was rejected unanimously, and Paley and Tisch demanded his resignation. They left the room, leaving it to the other board members to make the decision. After several hours of discussion, the board concluded that it was not willing to put the company up for sale. Wyman resigned, and the rest of the meeting was devoted to arranging to hand over temporary control to the new team of Tisch and Paley.

It was decided that Tisch would become acting chief executive and chairman of a new management committee. Bill Paley was named acting chairman. A new executive search committee was to be formed. Around seven o'clock the CBS board went downstairs, where it was met by a mob of reporters and cameramen. True to form, Cronkite took most of the spotlight.

"It was a calm and thoughtful meeting," Cronkite told the press. "They took their time. It was serious and non-acrimonious."

The news was flashed to Rather, who announced the decision on the air at the end of the "Evening News," and the rejoicing around the Broadcast Center began. As it happened, a party was being held that evening at a Park Avenue apartment to celebrate Mike Wallace's new marriage. The event turned into something quite unexpected as Cronkite and Tisch turned up to congratulate Wallace and share the stunning news with him and a group of CBS colleagues that included Hewitt, Diane Sawyer, Morley Safer, and Andy Rooney.

Paley sent his best wishes to the couple, but despite pleas from Mike Wallace, he declined to come.

Van Gordon Sauter had not been invited.

The following morning, Tisch met with Gene Jankowski. He assured Jankowski that his job was secure, but Van Gordon Sauter's was not. Later that afternoon Jankowski met with Sauter and asked for his resignation. Sauter obliged, then departed to Wyoming on a fishing trip. Howard Stringer, it was announced, would run the daily operations of CBS News—for the time being.

XIV.
THE
AFTERMATH

They say the opera ain't over until the fat lady sings. Within a matter of days after Sauter resigned, it was clear that the fat lady had already sung for the "CBS Morning News." Despite the change in management, there were no plans to reinstate the show. After the "Early Morning News," CBS planned to offer a half hour of hard news, from 7:00 to 7:30 A.M., then it would carry something else entirely. The "Morning News," as it had existed, would cease to exist.

I generally hate morals, and I found few in the "Morning News" story, other than that it had taken at least two of its persecutors down with it. But the program did seem, as Dick Salant said, to be a microcosm for much of what has happened in broadcasting. Or perhaps it was just the latest installment in the conflict Murrow had identified thirty-odd years earlier, the conflict between news and entertainment.

For nearly four decades news programs have had to compete against entertainment programs for television time, and apart from a few exceptions, such as "60 Minutes," broadcast journalists have consistently run second to entertainment producers in terms of supplying the product television executives like to deliver most—a sizable audience.

Size of audience is what counts. It is what television delivers to its most important customer, the advertiser. The content of a program is almost incidental. If people want to watch it, then the network wants to show it. In this sense, television is a department store window, in which the product displayed most prominently is whatever sells best.

In the aftermath of the CBS summer of '86, I sought a number of perspectives on the "Morning News" and CBS News in general. One senior producer at the "Morning News," who asked not to be named, said: "Face it. They were never willing to spend the money on the show, even to bring it up to par with the competition. And they never had any patience, ever, with any of the anchors. What they really did was waste five years.

"What surprises me is how little blame Jankowski has taken for all this. He, as much as Sauter, is the culprit. He represents the financial mentality. He doesn't know programming, he knows sales. Blame him for Phyllis George, too. He passed on Connie Chung when she wanted to come back, and he said 'yes' to Winston, and then 'no' to the money. He had to be hammered to put 'West 57th Street' back on the air, when if they'd left it on the air all along, it probably would have been more successful. So blame Jankowski. He's a business guy trying to be a broadcaster."

Gene Jankowski declined to be interviewed for this book. He told the *New York Times,* however: "The other networks are treated like networks. We're always treated like a value system."

I called Bill Leonard, the former CBS News president, and we talked about the recent events. Leonard said: "I always thought of CBS News as an institution, and when I left I always hoped it would continue to be one."

"Do you think it still is?" I asked him.

Leonard chuckled: "That's for you to figure out."

He wouldn't say more, so I went to see someone who would—Steve Friedman, the executive producer of "Today." It was my first time in the "Today" show's third-floor offices at Rockefeller Plaza. They were neat and tastefully decorated, totally lacking the gritty feel of a newsroom.

Friedman's office overlooked the Rockefeller Center skating rink. When I arrived he was showing three tourists around the floor. "Three people just somehow wandered up here," he said. "How they got past the guard, I don't know, but they're fans of the show." On his wall was a list of quotes he had given to newspapers and magazines over the past few years. One read: "CBS? You could write a book about what they've done on how to destroy a morning program." Another read: "If CBS were a brain, it'd be dead."

We talked about the CBS News management and the "Morning News."

"They went looking for saviors," Friedman said, "and in this business there are no saviors. They were in constant turmoil, but in the morning the worst thing you can do is to give people turmoil. In the morning, people have their routines; you don't want to disrupt them. And even if you have only a 3 rating, if you change things, you disrupt the millions of viewers you have. But still they didn't get it.

"When Bryant Gumbel came here, they told me: 'We'll look at this show in two years,' and when you've got two years to do something, you do it differently than if someone is looking at it every three months. No anchor on these broadcasts is good right away. It takes time, and you have to establish the anchor with the viewer."

We paused to watch a newsbreak on the monitor in his office.

"You know, all they really needed was an 18 or 19 share,"

Friedman said. "It's not really a big leap from a 15 or 16. With an 18 or 19 share, they'd have made money. Excuse me a moment."

Two producers had come in to discuss the next day's show.

"Eyewitnesses at 7:09," Friedman said. "Terrorism think-tank people at 7:16. Have Bryant do the witnesses, she can do the think-tank people."

I thought of the hours and hours spent in Katz's or Corvo's offices, vacillating over the lineup. I thought of the endless scrambles, the exasperated bookers standing around in the newsroom, waiting for their assignments to be changed for the umpteenth time.

"But you know something else?" Friedman said. "And I mean this. I really do. In all the time I worked here, competing with them, I never once expected them to throw in the towel."

I wished Friedman well.

I walked back along the neat corridors humming with quiet efficiency and took the elevator down to the lobby. Then I walked several blocks in the steady autumn rain.

EPILOGUE

Three months after the decision was made to kill the "CBS Morning News" . . .

Maria Shriver was working for NBC—at a vastly reduced salary—as a correspondent on the news magazine show, "1986."

Forrest Sawyer was still at CBS, with the title of "Morning News" correspondent.

Dan Rather continued to anchor the "CBS Evening News," which remained locked in a tight three-way race with NBC's "Nightly News" and ABC's "World News Tonight." (As of this writing, CBS and Rather were second in the ratings, a tenth of a point behind NBC's Tom Brokaw.)

Bill Kurtis was enjoying himself back at WBBM in Chicago, where he felt he was once again anchoring a solid news show.

Phyllis George was spending most of her time down in Kentucky, where she continued to draw her huge salary from CBS and continued to turn down requests for interviews.

Susan Winston was working for Lorimar Telepictures in California as an executive producer in charge of developing various television projects.

Jon Katz was still working as director of news planning for CBS News. "I feel I have found my niche in life," he said. Katz also wrote a documentary about Atlantic City, which the network broadcast in the fall of 1986—and which was produced by former "Morning News" producer Jude Dratt.

David Corvo, who remained in charge of the "CBS Morning News" into the fall of 1986, agreed to take over as executive producer of the truncated show that was scheduled to begin airing in January 1987. He would also be in charge of the "Early Morning News," the half-hour newscast that would precede it. (Bob Shanks, a former vice-president of ABC Entertainment, was hired to run the new entertainment program that CBS planned to start broadcasting from seven-thirty to nine in the morning, and actress Mariette Hartley and former local anchor Rolland Smith were signed as its anchors.)

Pete Bonventre surprised his friends by returning to CBS —as Shanks's No. 2 on the new morning show.

Gene Jankowski was still comfortably ensconced as president of the CBS Broadcast Group—according to insiders, still enjoying the confidence of Laurence Tisch.

Tisch continued to cement relations with the news division's top people. Among other places, he paid a visit to the "Morning News" control room, where he urged David Corvo to "call me Larry."

Van Gordon Sauter was living on Park Avenue, still unemployed.

Howard Stringer, who had taken charge of the news division when Sauter resigned, was officially named president of CBS News on October 29, 1986.

Ed Joyce was living in Connecticut and writing a book about his career at CBS. Jankowski had taken him to lunch in an effort to talk him out of doing the book, but Joyce insisted he was going ahead with it.